ROUND MR HORNE

~~~~y Johnston appeared with the vocal group Design on over fifty
~~~~vision shows in the 1970s. He presented the breakfast show on
~~~~A-AM in California and has broadcast on BBC local radio and
Radio 5. He now runs BarryMour Productions and has produced
more than sixty audiobooks.

He is the author of *Johnners: The Life of Brian*, a biography of his
f~~~~r, Brian Johnston, and has edited several books, including
L~~~~rs Home 1926-1945 and *A Delicious Slice of Johnners*.

Round Mr Horne

The Life of
KENNETH HORNE

BARRY JOHNSTON

Aurum

First published 2006 by
Aurum Press Limited
25 Bedford Avenue
London WC1B 3AT
www.aurumpress.co.uk

This paperback edition published 2007

A catalogue record for this book is available
from the British Library.

ISBN 978 1 84513 232 3

10 9 8 7 6 5 4 3 2 1
2011 2010 2009 2008 2007

Text design by Roger Hammond

Typeset in Minion by SX Composing DTP,
Rayleigh, Essex

Printed and bound in Great Britain by
Bookmarque, Croydon, Surrey

For Fiona and Charles, Julian and Sandy,
Rambling Syd, Daphne and Seamus,

and for Susan, with thanks

Contents

Acknowledgements

This book would not have been possible without the assistance of many important people. I would like to express my sincere thanks to Kenneth Horne's step-daughter Susan Montague for sharing her invaluable memories of Kenneth's personal life, and for her generous support and encouragement. For help with Kenneth's family background I am most grateful to David Horne, John Horne, Margaret Horne and Richard Bull. Thanks also to David Hayes, Editor of *Camden History Review*, for allowing me to quote from his excellent research into the life of Reverend Charles Silvester Horne.

For information about Kenneth's schooldays and for answering all my questions so willingly, I am indebted to Alan Groves at Kingsland Grange School, Shrewsbury; Pam Weatherly, the Archivist at St George's, Harpenden; Dr R. Hyam, LittD, the College Archivist at Magdalene College, Cambridge, and Dr Chris Thorne at the Cambridge University Athletics Club.

Many thanks to Nancy Barker at Information, Management & Storage for her research into the history of Triplex Safety Glass and also to Hugh Barty-King for the facts and figures contained in his manuscript 'The Triplex Story 1912–1976'. For details of Kenneth's RAF career I must thank Mrs P. Williams at the Personnel Management Agency, RAF Innsworth and Guy Revell, Assistant Curator at the RAF Museum, Hendon.

For their help with Kenneth's broadcasting career and personal life after the war I would like to thank Brian Cooke, Tony and Belinda Innes, Andy Merriman, Jean Merriman, Eileen Miller, Mollie Millest, Tim Murdoch, Bill Pertwee, Jonathan Rigby and Lyn Took.

My grateful thanks to Erin O'Neill, Archives Researcher at the BBC Written Archives Centre, Caversham, for her invaluable assistance and for permission to quote extensively from BBC correspondence and programme files. I must also thank Rod Hamilton and the helpful staff of the National Sound Archives at the British Library, as well as the British Newspaper Library at Colindale and the Westminster Reference Library.

I owe a special debt of thanks to the late Norman Hackforth, who interviewed many of Kenneth's former friends and colleagues for his book *Solo For Horne* in 1976. Most of them have since died, including Lady Mary Pelham-Clinton-Hope, Joan Burgess and Joyce Davis, and his interviews were a vital source of information. Ron Moody was featured on the radio programme *Horne of Plenty*, presented by Jonathan James-Moore and broadcast on BBC7 in 2004.

Additional thanks to Belinda Innes for allowing me to use the unpublished war memoirs of her father Richard Murdoch, and to Susan Montague for permission to quote from Kenneth Horne's letters; also to Mollie Millest for allowing me to use extracts from her scripts, articles and correspondence with Kenneth and Marjorie Horne.

Excerpts from *The Kenneth Williams Diaries* (copyright the Estate of Kenneth Williams) are reproduced by permission of PFD (www.pfd.co.uk) on behalf of the Estate of Kenneth Williams.

The excerpt from *In My Mind's Eye* by Michael Redgrave is reproduced by kind permission of Weidenfeld & Nicolson, an imprint of the Orion Publishing Group; the excerpts from *The Life of Charles Silvester Horne* by W.B. Selbie are by kind permission of Hodder & Stoughton Ltd.

Extracts from the scripts of *Much-Binding-in-the-Marsh* and other radio and television programmes written by Richard Murdoch and Kenneth Horne are reproduced by kind permission of Belinda Innes and Susan Montague; extracts from the scripts of *Variety Playhouse* and *Beyond Our Ken* written by Eric Merriman are by kind permission of Andy and Jean Merriman; extracts from the scripts of *Round the Horne* written by Barry Took and Marty Feldman are by kind permission of Lyn Took and Lauretta Feldman;

the 'Judy Coolibah' sketch from *Round the Horne* written by Brian Cooke and Johnnie Mortimer is by kind permission of Brian Cooke.

Amongst other books consulted, particular use was made of: T.C. Barker: *The Glassmakers – Pilkington: 1826–1976*; Asa Briggs: *Sound & Vision*; Mat Coward, *Classic Radio Comedy*; Russell Davies, ed.: *The Kenneth Williams Diaries*; Jonathan Dimbleby: *Richard Dimbleby*; Paul Donovan: *The Radio Companion*; Andy Foster and Steve Furst: *Radio Comedy 1938–68*; Denis Gifford: *The Golden Age of Radio*; Norman Hackforth: *And the Next Object . . .*; *Solo For Horne*; Kenneth Horne and John Ellison: *Quizzically Yours*; Roy Hudd: *Roy Hudd's Book of Music-Hall, Variety and Showbiz Anecdotes*; Barry Johnston: *Johnners: The Life of Brian*; Mark Lewisohn: *The Radio Times Guide to Television Comedy*; Andy Merriman: *A Minor Adjustment*; David Nathan: *The Laughtermakers*; George Nobbs: *The Wireless Stars*; Derek Parker: *Radio: The Great Years*; Bill Pertwee: *A Funny Way to Make a Living!*; Michael Redgrave: *In My Mind's Eye*; Wallace Reyburn: *Gilbert Harding*; Barry Took: *A Point of View*; *Laughter in the Air*; *Round the Horne, The Complete And Utter History*; Barry Took with Mat Coward: *The Best Of Round the Horne*; Barry Took and Marty Feldman: *Round the Horne*; W.B. Selbie, ed.: *The Life of Charles Silvester Horne*.

My grateful thanks to Piers Burnett and all at Aurum Press for believing in this book and for their friendly help and advice, and to my copy-editor Bernard Dod for his excellent work correcting the manuscript.

Finally I would like to express my continuing love and thanks to my wife Fiona and our two children Olivia and Sam, with a special mention to Button the dog, without whom this book would have been finished considerably earlier.

Introduction

IN JANUARY 2004 I went to see a performance of a show called *Round the Horne . . . Revisited* at The Venue theatre, off Leicester Square in London. For the next ninety minutes I rocked with laughter, along with the packed audience, as I was transported back to the golden age of radio comedy in the 1960s. When I was growing up I made a point, like millions of others, of tuning into the old BBC Light Programme every Sunday lunchtime to hear *Round the Horne*, with its magical, irreplaceable cast of Kenneth Williams, Hugh Paddick, Betty Marsden, Bill Pertwee, Douglas Smith and, of course, Kenneth Horne. Now, thirty-five years later, here were five talented actors recreating the radio series on stage, impersonating those unforgettable voices and using the original scripts, and the comedy sounded as fresh and as hilarious as ever.

Although Kenneth Williams, played with an extravagant verve by Robin Sebastian, was the most prominent member of the cast, the heart of the show – as in the original series – was undoubtedly Kenneth Horne, played by the delightfully urbane Jonathan Rigby. After the show I found myself thinking about Kenneth Horne – that tall, jovial character with the warm, dark brown voice and the brilliant comic timing, who seemed to be more like a successful businessman than a comedian. As the scriptwriter Barry Took once put it, Kenneth sounded 'like the managing director of a firm which had just made an enormous profit'. Even though I had listened to Kenneth Horne for years, I realised that I knew very little about him. I decided it was time to find out more.

Kenneth Horne is a unique figure in the history of British comedy. In a broadcasting career spanning more than twenty-five years, he starred in three of the most popular radio comedy series of all time, *Much-Binding-in-the-Marsh*, *Beyond Our Ken* and *Round the Horne*. At a time of great cultural change in the 1950s and 1960s, he was one of the few personalities to bridge the generation gap and, while remaining essentially the same, he managed to make the extraordinary transition from the gentle, reassuring humour of the war years to the harder-edged, more anti-establishment comedy of the Swinging Sixties.

I had recently completed writing a biography of my father, the late broadcaster and BBC cricket commentator Brian Johnston, and the more I learned about Kenneth Horne, the more I was struck by the parallels in their lives. They were both born before the First World War, and were youngest sons who lost their fathers at an early age, Brian when he was ten and Kenneth at seven. They both went away to boarding schools and then on to university, Brian to Oxford and Kenneth to Cambridge, where they played sports instead of studying. After leaving university with no qualifications, Brian joined the family coffee business in the City and Kenneth went into the family glass business in Birmingham. During the Second World War they both served as officers, in the Army and the RAF, compered variety shows for the troops, and went on to have highly successful careers in broadcasting after the war.

But that is where the similarities end. While my father was married for forty-five years and enjoyed a happy and healthy life until he died at the age of eighty-one, Kenneth had three disastrous marriages, was only really happy when he was working, and suffered a decade of ill-health before he died at the early age of sixty-one.

And yet, nearly forty years later, his legacy of laughter lives on. The BBC cassettes and CDs of the radio series *Round The Horne* have now sold more than half a million copies and continue to be among the best-sellers every year, as each new generation discovers his timeless comedy. The original radio shows are repeated constantly on the digital radio channel BBC7 and the theatre production of *Round the Horne . . . Revisited* ran for more than a year in London's West End before embarking on a sell-out national tour.

So who *was* Kenneth Horne? On 27 February 2007 it will be the centenary of his birth. He was the youngest of seven children of the Reverend Silvester Horne, a celebrated Congregational preacher and Liberal MP who died in 1914. Sadly, and not surprisingly, most of Kenneth's contemporaries are now also dead, including his six brothers and sisters, his three wives, and all of the cast of *Round the Horne* except for Bill Pertwee.

At first it was difficult to establish the precise details of Kenneth's personal history. His widow, Marjorie, destroyed all of his archives after he died, leaving only a handful of photographs. Sometimes the only clues were to be found in a previous biography, *Solo For Horne* by Norman Hackforth, which was published in 1976. Once I started doing my research, however, I discovered that many of the facts and dates given by Hackforth were totally unreliable, often being years out. For instance he claimed that Kenneth went to Cambridge in 1925, when he was only eighteen, instead of a year later in 1926. According to Hackforth, Kenneth made his broadcasting debut on *Ack-Ack Beer-Beer* in late 1939, when the series did not even start until July 1940. Later he described Kenneth making his first appearance on the radio series *Twenty Questions* in 1958, when he had already been chairman for two years from 1949 to 1951.

Small details, but important when trying to piece together Kenneth's life and career. The only solution was to go back to the original sources. I had long conversations with Kenneth's step-daughter Susan Montague, who provided invaluable information, and several of his nephews and nieces. I trawled through old school magazines and files at his co-educational boarding school, St George's, Harpenden, and also at Magdalene College, Cambridge; I spent many days at the BBC Written Archives Centre in Caversham, near Reading, recreating his broadcasting career from his BBC personnel files. I also listened to hours of his radio shows at the British Library, sitting in a small soundproof cubicle, wearing headphones and trying not to laugh too loudly, while learned scholars sat nearby poring over esoteric texts.

One of the joys of researching this biography was discovering just how funny Kenneth Horne was from the very beginning of his career. He first became a household name after the Second World War when he co-wrote and co-starred in the hugely successful radio series *Much-Binding-in-the-Marsh* with Richard Murdoch. It was the most popular show of its day and it is still as entertaining as ever. Kenneth played a dim-witted, senior RAF officer, although his slow, bumbling character could not have been further from the truth. For as well as being a broadcaster, Kenneth was also a successful businessman, the Sales Director of Triplex Safety Glass Limited, and was in reality well organized, always on time and totally efficient.

For a dozen years after the war he managed to combine both careers, appearing on hundreds of radio and television programmes such as *Twenty Questions* and *What's My Line?*, until he was felled by a stroke in February 1958. After making a valiant recovery, he was forced by his doctors to choose between his two careers, and decided to concentrate on broadcasting. Within a few months he was starring in the hilarious radio series *Beyond Our Ken,* which would run for six memorable years and was succeeded by *Round the Horne*, which has been described as 'the funniest comedy series in radio history'.

I could not find a single person who had a bad word to say about Kenneth. He was kind, loyal and generous, always giving presents to the cast and the production staff at the end of a series. He was almost the only person whom Kenneth Williams actually admired, and Barry Took once described him as 'the most ungreedy man' he knew. It would seem that everybody whom Kenneth met was enchanted by his charm and his genial, larger-than-life personality; everyone, that is, except his wives. He married three times but each marriage ended in failure. His first marriage was annulled, the second marriage ended in divorce, and the third only survived for twenty-three years because his wife threatened to kill herself if he left her.

He found refuge and solace in his broadcasting career, travelling the length and breadth of the country to appear on dozens of different radio and television programmes. He used to claim proudly that he worked a minimum of sixty hours a week. It made him popular and successful, although he was never wealthy, but it could not make him happy. In the end, he ignored his doctors' advice and worked himself to death.

According to *The Times*, Kenneth liked people to think he was 'a friendly, good-natured old buffer, who was simply doing his best, apparently lost in wonder at the glossier, more spectacular talents of those among whom he found himself'. Jonathan Rigby, who portrayed Kenneth so perfectly on stage, thinks this is a popular misconception. 'Kenneth Horne is often thought of as the straight man in *Round the Horne*,' says Rigby, 'the establishment figure who did not understand what was happening around him. But he knew exactly what was going on. Kenneth was really a stand-up comic with a posh accent. He was obviously a very warm and charming man and part of his genius as a comedian was that he was able to be himself.'

It was a clever trick which made millions of radio listeners laugh at him and with him for more than a quarter of a century. Thanks to the recordings and the theatre shows, they are still laughing now. After Kenneth Horne died of a heart attack on 14 February 1969, at the early age of sixty-one, the *Sunday Mirror* paid him a warm and fitting tribute when it described him as 'perhaps the last of the truly great radio comics'.

Barry Johnston
February 2006

Here are, the answers to last week's questions. The answer to question one: complete the first lines of the following songs – 'If I Were a Blackbird I'd . . .' The answer is I'd Whistle and Sing, and I positively will not accept any other suggestion. The second song was 'There's a Rainbow Round My . . .' Now we got an amazing number of replies to this. We haven't had so many since we asked you to complete 'Over My Shoulder Goes . . .' Really, it makes it very difficult for us to keep up the high reputation for sophisticated comedy we've never had.

Round the Horne
13 March 1966

Son of a Preacher-Man

KENNETH HORNE USED to enjoy telling journalists, 'You wouldn't think anybody could be born in Tottenham Court Road, but I was.' In fact he was born about half a mile away in Ampthill Square, on 27 February 1907, the seventh and youngest child of the Reverend Charles Silvester Horne.

In an age of great preachers, Silvester Horne was said to be one of the greatest. When Kenneth once described Winston Churchill to an old friend as a great orator, his friend looked at him and said, 'Yes, but then you never heard your father speak, did you?'

Silvester had also been the youngest son of a clergyman and his father Charles was a Congregational minister in the village of Cuckfield, in the middle of the Sussex Weald, when Silvester was born on 15 April 1865. Later Charles Horne's health gave way 'owing to the nervous strain of the pastorate', and he resigned from the ministry, moving with his family to Newport in Shropshire, where he became the editor of the local newspaper, *The Newport and Market Drayton Advertiser*.

Silvester went to the local Haberdashers' Grammar School in Newport where, just as his youngest son would be, he was regarded as something of an idler but excelled at sport, ending up as head boy.

While still at school, Silvester became involved with the local Congregational church and preached his first sermon at the age of sixteen. He gained a bursary to Glasgow University where he obtained an M.A. degree and then won a scholarship to read theology, as one of the six original students at the newly founded Mansfield College, Oxford.

His reputation as a preacher was already so great that in 1887, while still at Oxford, Silvester was invited to become minister at the Congregational chapel in Allen Street, Kensington. It was one of the principal Free Churches and one of the wealthiest in London. They were even prepared to wait eighteen months for him to complete his course.

He took up the appointment at the age of twenty-four and on his arrival in Kensington, his preaching is said to have galvanized the Allen Street congregation. A Children's Guild at the chapel was run by Katharine Maria Cozens-Hardy, the elder daughter of Sir Herbert Hardy, QC and MP for North Norfolk. In August 1892 Katharine and Silvester were married at Allen Street and, probably with some financial assistance from her father, they set up home in Campden Hill Gardens in Holland Park.

Silvester's health was never robust and the strain of his London pastorate soon began to take its toll. As early as 1895 he suffered the first of three nervous breakdowns. He was absent from the pulpit for a year but life in the open air gradually restored him to health. His doctors warned him that he had to slow down but he chose to ignore them and on 15 April 1897 he wrote in his diary:

> Today I am thirty-two years old, and the last two years have been somewhat painful ones, despite the sunshine that has come into them from the love of friends. It is far from easy to acquiesce in a medical verdict which would impose upon one that very hardest of duties, the duty of half-a-life. It is curious how hard such a duty seems . . . However, it is open to me to disbelieve the doctors.

It is sobering to realize that Kenneth would utter almost the same words as his father nearly seventy years later.

Silvester returned to work and his reputation as a 'silver-tongued orator' continued to grow. After more than a decade in Kensington, he was approached by several important churches around London but he turned down all offers until the death of his father in March 1903. The following day he announced that he was going to accept a 'bold challenge' and take on a debt-ridden, enormous red-brick chapel in Tottenham Court Road called Whitefield's Church.

Silvester had ambitious plans for the church. He wanted to transform it into a Congregational 'Central Mission' with an adult school, a library, clubrooms, a lounge, a canteen, cooking and sewing classes, choirs and bands. The new Whitefield Central Mission opened in September 1903. A large banner was hung across the chapel's façade, depicting a medieval knight ascending to shining towers, burdened by a broken comrade. The mission's motto was 'No quest, no conquest'. At night arc-lamps lit up the front of the building, drawing attention away from the two pubs opposite. When one of the pubs eventually went out of business, Silvester took over the building as part of the church.

People came from all over London to hear him preach. The church could hold about a thousand people but still they had to place camp-stools down the aisles in order to accommodate all those who wanted to be there. On Sunday there were three services. The morning service was relatively conventional. The afternoon service was for men only and had more of a political complexion, often featuring guest speakers such as Cabinet ministers and writers, including George Bernard Shaw and Jerome K. Jerome. The most popular service was the evening service at 7 p.m. which attracted 'prodigious crowds', and the 'FULL' sign would often go up an hour before it was due to begin.

In March 1903, when Silvester was thirty-seven, the *British Monthly* wrote:

In Edinburgh, Glasgow, Manchester and Leicester he conquered vast audiences by the magic of his oratory. He understands better than any speaker of his years, with the possible exception of Mr Lloyd George, how to quicken slow blood, kindle light in dull eyes, and bring the flood-tide of enthusiasm sweeping into all creeks and inlets of the spirit. His youthful appearance, grace and winsomeness of gesture, attractive delivery, and clear, well-modulated voice delight every company that hears him.

He also had a very good sense of humour and Kenneth believed that it was one of the reasons why his father packed his church three times every Sunday: 'He wanted his congregation to have a good laugh and sing some good songs, and then tell them what they had come to hear.'

Silvester moved his family into a small house in Ampthill Square, behind Euston Station, ten minutes' walk from the church. It was far removed from the leafy, privileged streets of Holland Park. It was not really a square, more of a crescent with a private central garden, and it was bisected by the London & North Western Railway, so the steam engines must have layered the houses and gardens with soot as they made their way in and out of Euston. The Horne family lived at Number 20, a detached villa on the corner of Houghton Place, with a large L-shaped back garden where the children could play.

Kenneth described it as 'a very humble house'. It was certainly a very crowded house, with Silvester and Katharine and their five children, not to mention their long-serving nursemaid, Nanny May. A year later their sixth child, Ruth, was born and then on 27 February 1907 they had their seventh child, Charles Kenneth Horne. He was given the first name Charles in honour of his father and grandfather, but he was always known as Kenneth.

The seven children all had nicknames, the origins of which are long forgotten. Dorothy was 'Doge', Oliver 'Hoax', Bridget 'Boge', Joan 'Jarkis', Ronald 'Plackus', Ruth 'Puth' and Kenneth 'Sparg'. The three youngest also developed their own special language and could carry on a conversation without being understood by anyone else.

Silvester was often absent from home, travelling around the country on speaking tours and later constituency and Union business. He would frequently leave Kings Cross on Sunday at 9 p.m. after his evening service and speak, preach or lecture every weekday, arriving back in London at 7.30 a.m. on Saturday. Whenever he was away he and Katharine wrote to each other every day. He also wrote letters to the children, full of fun and often illustrated. In a typical letter to his sister Joan, Silvester once wrote:

It still fogs. Indeed I may say it fogs worse than ever. Woman's suffrage is in a 'fog' at this moment. I do not wonder that the great poet exclaimed:

O pea-soup fog! O pea-soup fog!
For thee I do not care a jog!
(It should have been 'jot' but it had to rhyme)
Yet I do love thy grease and grime
Because it smears me o'er with slime,
It plugs me up with hideous ooze
Till I can neither breathe nor snooze
(It should be sneeze, but that wouldn't rhyme either)
Therefore I lie like any log
And yell 'I love thee pea-soup fog!'

The children always looked forward to Sundays because Silvester's preaching commitments at Whitefield's meant that he would usually be at home. Every Sunday Katharine would take all the seven children and Nanny May to the morning service and they would sit in their own pew at the back.

One of Kenneth's earliest memories was going to watch his father in church. Being the smallest, Kenneth was allowed to stand on the pew so that he could see better, and for fun he would sometimes try to sing the hymns faster than the others so that he could beat them to the end. Years later, Katharine confessed to her daughter Ruth that while her head was bowed in prayer she used to occupy herself by biting her initials K.M.H. in the top of the pew in front – although she did admit that she found the K. rather difficult.

The pew in front was usually occupied by her father, now entitled the first Baron Cozens-Hardy of Letheringsett, after he was appointed Master of the Rolls in 1907, making Katharine the Honourable Mrs Silvester Horne. Lord Cozens-Hardy would travel every Sunday from his home in Ladbroke Grove to hear his son-in-law preach. He was devoted to his grandchildren and once promised to give them a sixpence for every baby tooth that fell out, an extremely generous offer as the going rate for pocket money was then about two pence a week. Kenneth and his sister Ruth used to work on any loose tooth all week so that they could put it in a matchbox on Sunday and pass it forward to their grandfather during the prayers. The matchbox always came back containing a sixpence.

The seven children were raised to uphold the principles of Congregationalism but it was by no means an austere household. Silvester was a benevolent father as his eldest daughter, Dorothy, revealed in the biography *The Life of Charles Silvester Horne*, edited by W.B. Selbie, which was published in 1920:

When his key sounded in the front door, there was always a stampede in the nursery, and we almost fell downstairs in our excitement to be first to give him a welcoming hug. I think the reason why children adored him so whole-heartedly was his entire absence of superiority and aloofness. Although he could be stern when there was any question of wrong-doing, he naturally met us children as a friend and an equal. We were never in the least afraid of him, but our love for him made us terribly afraid of doing anything which would make him sorry. It would be difficult to imagine a happier childhood than ours. Religious teaching, if teaching it could be called, was a thing of joy.

Kenneth agreed. In an interview towards the end of his life he recalled: 'There's nothing like being a member of a large family. We spent our time laughing and having a jolly good time.' At Christmas, each child was allowed to buy a present for his brothers and sisters, and according to their age they were limited to spending one penny, sixpence or a shilling per present. For weeks beforehand Kenneth used to drop hints that, at the nearby shop, you could buy a quarter-pound of sweets for a penny.

His father once told him quite a good joke, which Kenneth always remembered: 'A missionary in Africa was teaching some little black boys to speak English. One method he found quite useful was to translate a hymn into their language and then get them to translate it back into English. One day he gave them the popular hymn "Rock of ages, cleft for me" and one of the little boys came up with the answer, "Very old stone, smashed for my benefit"!'

As befits an orator, Silvester loved the use of words, an enthusiasm which he passed on to his youngest son, and every year he would write a play for his children to perform on Christmas Eve. A typical cast of characters included Queen Elizabeth, Lord Nelson, a suffragette and Father Christmas, who was always portrayed by Silvester himself.

Somehow, despite the constant demands on his time, Silvester managed to find time to relax; he was a keen golfer, although apparently not very successful. During the summer he would take the whole family on week-long cycling holidays and he also built a small holiday home, which he named The Bluff, at Sheringham on the Norfolk coast.

Meanwhile the improvements at Whitefields all had to be paid for and, to raise funds, Silvester was forced to travel far and wide on intensive lecture and preaching tours, including several trips to the Continent and two visits to North America. His concern for the rights of 'the poor' led him to become increasingly political in his speeches. He was a dedicated supporter of the Liberal Party and during election campaigns he would speak in support of as many parliamentary candidates as possible. Finally he decided to stand for Parliament himself and on 17 January 1910 he was elected as the Liberal MP for Ipswich.

The day he took his seat in the House of Commons, Silvester wrote to his mother: 'I felt I must write a line to you from this historic house, just to assure you that I actually am here. A few minutes ago I made an affirmation of everlasting loyalty to the King and Constitution. I sincerely hope that means loyalty to the people and especially to the poor. There is no other reason why I should be here that I can see . . .'

His new political career did not go down well with his superiors in the Congregational Church but Silvester was convinced of his ability to carry out both jobs. He wrote: 'Nothing will induce me to give up Whitefields. But I do not believe that the House of Commons need unmake one spiritually, nor Whitefields unfit one for things secular.' His maiden speech in the Commons was on Home Rule for Ireland and over the next four years he would speak out strongly on behalf of the poor and destitute, both at home and abroad.

The tremendous pressure of his ministry and his parliamentary work began to take its toll. In 1913 Silvester noted in his diary: 'The last doctor's report is that I have one permanently damaged kidney. It does no work, the ne'er-do-well! But that is not the worst of it. Such is the solidarity of the body corporate that the whole suffers, and must suffer, for its neglect. It is a very pretty parable, and would sound more admirable in a sermon than it does out of one.'

The holiday home in Norfolk had become too small for his growing family, so Silvester built a much larger house on the edge of Church Stretton, in his home county of Shropshire. During the summer of 1913 the family left Ampthill Square and moved into the White House, a large country house with nine bedrooms, a large hall, library and drawing room, and a long veranda looking out over the large garden, which had two grass tennis courts.

By now Silvester's mesmerizing voice had grown hoarse and his confrontational style of politics had also begun to concern the deacons at Whitefields. Reluctantly, he decided to resign his pastorate and on 30 January 1914 *The Times* reported:

> Acting upon imperative medical orders, the Rev. C.S. Horne after ten years work at Whitefields Tabernacle, has resigned. It is his intention at a later date, if health permits, to take up the work of the ministry again in some other less exhausting sphere. It is understood that Mr Horne finds himself unable to carry on the work of the mission and at the same time to pursue an active political career.

Despite his failing health, Silvester accepted an invitation from Yale University to deliver a series of lectures on 'The History of Preaching'. It would be his third visit to North America. His doctors warned him against over-exertion, but allowed him to make the journey, in the belief that a relaxing sea voyage might do him some good. In March 1914 Silvester and Katharine set sail for the United States, leaving their seven children in the care of Nanny May.

The lectures at Yale were hailed as a great success. From there the Hornes travelled by train to Niagara, where they spent a day looking at the Falls. On 2 May they boarded a ship at Lewiston to take them across Lake Ontario to Toronto, where Silvester was due to address a large meeting. As the steamer entered Toronto harbour, Silvester was walking on deck with Katharine when he suddenly collapsed. She cradled him in her arms but before any help could reach him, he was dead. He was just forty-nine years old.

They had been due to stay at the house of N.W. Rowell, KC but now his body was taken there instead. The planned meeting of the Toronto Brotherhood became instead the first of many memorial services for Silvester. After a few days' Katharine brought his coffin back to England and Silvester was buried in the peaceful 'additional burial ground' at Church Stretton. Forty-four years later, in 1958, Katharine would be buried alongside him.

In a warm tribute to his friend, Sir William Robertson Nicoll declared: 'In private life he was dearly loved but his full powers were apparent only when he was thrilling a great multitude with the expression of his passionate conviction.'

At his memorial service, it was reported: 'Within was a gathering of many sorrowing men. At least they had come with sorrow in their faces, but the strange thing was that very soon there was none sorrowing in the entire building. It was not mere poetry when Ramsay MacDonald MP said they heard the voice of the dead Pastor as we feel the fragrance of flowers that have been removed from a room.'

Silvester had described the Free Churches as 'an unconquerable spirit dedicated to the service of an indestructible ideal'. As Kenneth once pointed out, his father would have been perfectly justified if he had said the same thing about himself.

After Silvester's death, the family were united in their grief. Although they had known he was in ill health, the suddenness of his death had been totally unexpected and had left no time for goodbyes. At seven years old, Kenneth was probably too young to take in the enormity of his loss but his eldest sister Dorothy, then aged twenty-one, wrote: 'The shock of his death came on us like a thunderbolt from a clear sky. We could only find comfort in the knowledge that our relations with him had been perfect, and that his presence would continue to fill our home, as it always had done.'

As he grew older and learned more about his father, Kenneth became increasingly proud of his reputation and his achievements. They were very similar in character – charismatic personalities and eloquent public speakers, blessed with compelling, distinctive voices and a wonderful sense of humour, but also driven workaholics, who pursued two careers simultaneously until their health was destroyed. There would be many times in his life when Kenneth would miss the wise counsel and paternal authority of his father, and his life might have turned out very differently if Silvester had not died so tragically young.

For the next few years the family continued to live at the White House. After war was declared in August 1914, Kenneth's eldest brother Oliver, who was then nineteen, volunteered for the Royal Army Medical Corps. His son David thinks that Oliver refused a commission in the Army because he did not want to kill anyone. Dorothy joined the Ministry of Labour as an inspector of working conditions in clothing factories. The younger Horne children, apart from Kenneth, were being educated at boarding schools and in 1916, when he was nine, Kenneth was also sent away to Kingsland Grange School in Shrewsbury, an independent preparatory school for boys. The school was founded in 1899 and it is still going strong. During the First World War there were about forty-five day boys and forty-five boarders at the school between the ages of seven and thirteen. No school records survive from that time, but judging by the distance of about twelve miles from Church Stretton to Shrewsbury, and the limited means of transport at the time, it is probable that Kenneth was a boarder at Kingsland Grange.

During the summer holidays the family played tennis on their two grass courts and it was here that Kenneth started to develop his future skill at the game. Sometimes he would make up a foursome with his older siblings Joan, Ronald and Ruth. They even organized an annual Church Stretton tennis tournament, a three-day affair which was taken quite seriously and was played on their own and their neighbours' courts.

The local countryside was their playground. They used to bicycle for miles and would camp out under the stars in the local valleys. At other times the children would play their own version of golf over the hills, with one club each but only one ball.

In the days before radio and television the children had to make their own entertainment, and according to Kenneth they 'used to stand round the piano and sing our hearts out almost every night'. Their particular favourites were the songs of Gilbert and Sullivan, a passion which stayed with Kenneth for the rest of his life. In the winter they carried on their father's tradition of staging a special play every Christmas Eve, always written and produced by members of the family.

They were elaborate affairs, with titles such as 'The Hermit of Helmeth' and 'Caravanserai'. Scenery would have to be painted and costumes designed, making good use of Katharine's store of dressing-up clothes. All of the Horne children were encouraged to write verses, scripts and songs, a skill which Kenneth would later find invaluable in his broadcasting career. They would write funny lyrics to popular songs of the day, many of them by Gilbert and Sullivan. The scripts would be carefully typed and would contain a large number of in-jokes about friends and neighbours, as well as comic references to topical subjects such as crossword puzzles, which had made their first appearance in 1921 in England.

Kenneth became quite adept at putting new lyrics to well-known tunes, but he always claimed that his brother Ronald was much better. One of Kenneth's favourite stories was of an occasion when they were all sitting around the piano singing 'The Honeysuckle and the Bee'. It occurred to Kenneth that the words 'Mount Popocatepetl' fitted the rhythm of the music exactly. He bet Ronald that he could not write new words to the melody, starting with the line 'I am Mount Popocatepetl' and making it rhyme perfectly. Ronald took up the challenge and less than five minutes later he returned and stood triumphantly by the piano. His sister Ruth played the tune while he sang:

I am Mount Popocatepetl,
You will agree
When I erupt I scatter metal
Over land and sea.
Don't let your molten matter settle
On my vertebrae!
It's safer far to pat a nettle
Than to sit on me.

In a postscript to Kenneth's childhood, Whitefield's Tabernacle was destroyed on Palm Sunday, 25 March 1945, when the last but one V-2 rocket to land on London scored a direct hit over the chapel organ. At the time, this was the largest instrument in the capital but not one fragment of the organ was ever found. A smaller replacement chapel, the neo-Georgian style Whitefield Memorial Church, was finally opened in 1958. The building now serves as the interdenominational American Church in London. Ampthill Square also no longer exists. It was controversially demolished in the late 1960s to make way for council housing in what is now known as the Ampthill Estate.

In 1917 the Silvester Horne Institute was officially opened in the main street of Church Stretton, opposite the local Congregational church and it is still in use as a focus of village community and cultural life. The White House eventually became a nursing home and in recent years has been under threat of demolition.

Aim Higher

IN SEPTEMBER 1918, when he was aged eleven, Kenneth and his sixteen-year-old brother Ronald were sent to St George's School at Harpenden, in Hertfordshire. The school had been founded in Keswick, in the Lake District, by the Reverend Cecil Grant and had moved to Harpenden in 1907. It was said to be the first purpose-established coeducational boarding school in England and carved in stone above the main entrance are the words: AIM HIGHER.

The intention was for children to 'live in an atmosphere closely related to family life, based on sound Christian principles'. Whole families were encouraged to join the school and ages spanned from ten to nineteen years old. This obviously appealed to Silvester and Katharine Horne who believed that families should be kept together as much as possible throughout the early part of life. All seven of the Horne children were educated there – a record for any one family. At that time there were 215 pupils at St George's, and Kenneth and Ronald joined their fourteen-year-old sister Ruth, who had entered the school in the previous term. For the next two years, until his brother left St George's, Kenneth would be known as Horne II. He entered the school in the Lower IV Latin class, but his first term would be severely disrupted.

The Great War was drawing to a close. Many Old Georgians had enlisted in the forces and nineteen out of the sixty-four boys who volunteered had been killed, including a former Head Boy who had left the school only in 1916. On 11 November at 11 a.m. Germany surrendered and signed the Armistice. News of the signing reached St George's quickly, thanks to a local builder called Mr Jarvis, who had a telephone. Bells at the school rang out joyously and pupils ran outside to see what was happening. On 15 November the country celebrated Victory Day and the school had a whole day's holiday 'spent in the most exhilarating and approved fashion'. But soon after the Armistice rejoicings were over, a devastating outbreak of influenza hit the school.

An epidemic of Spanish flu had caused millions of deaths around the world, especially in China and India. More US servicemen had died of the disease than from wounds suffered in battle, and scientists had been unable to develop a vaccine. In September 1918 the influenza reached Britain, possibly brought home by returning British servicemen. By October many schools across the country had closed and in London more than two thousand deaths from the disease were being reported each week.

In mid-November it reached St George's. According to the school magazine *The Georgian*: 'Then in quick succession, school, staff, maids and nurses, all fell victim. Service that will never be forgotten was rendered by those who remained well enough to help, and on Wednesday 8 December, we returned thanks in chapel that God had spared us all who make up the community of School House'. Not all were spared, however, and a twelve-year-old girl pupil, Lillian Dunhill, died from the influenza. Her parents donated an annual Lillian Dunhill Prize to the school in her memory and it is still awarded today. It was all too much for the Headmaster, the Reverend Cecil Grant, who was forced to be absent from the school during most of 1919 'suffering badly from over-strain'. His wife, Mrs Grant, 'also suffered heavy strain' that year.

It is probably fair to say that Kenneth was never much of an academic at school but he quickly developed into a remarkable athlete. R.S. Postgate, one of his contemporaries at St George's, recalled: 'He was moderately successful in work, he was very successful in all games and one of the notable personalities of his school generation.'

Now that the war was over, masters who had been serving in the forces returned to the school and life began to get back to normal. Sporting activities were resumed and in his first summer term at the school in 1919 Kenneth won his colours in the Junior Cricket XI, showing early promise as a bowler. He also revealed a quick turn of speed on the athletics field, winning the Boys Under-12 100 Yards race.

During the summer he made steady progress in the Junior XI: 'Horne II and Wilkinson have proved reliable bowlers. For runs . . . Horne II [has] played useful innings.' That is more than can be said for his elder brother Ronald, who was dropped from the first XI with the withering critique: 'Has failed to retain his place in the team owing to atrocious fielding. Lacks keenness.'

In athletics, Kenneth again won the Boys Under-14 100 Yards, but he was also showing a flair for rugby and in the autumn term he played in the Junior XV at three-quarter back. There was more to life at St George's than sports, however, and Kenneth had become a member of the Debating Society.

On 6 December 1920 the motion before the house was 'That a King is necessary to Great Britain' and according to the school magazine:

Horne II proposed the motion in a well delivered but very short speech. He claimed that the King is one of the greatest assets to the empire, that having a King to look up to is an essential to the loyalty of India and other of our less civilised colonies. He showed how the tour of the Prince of Wales has inspired loyalty to the motherland in a way quite impossible for a president or other leader. He also stated that, as many European kings are related, the dangers of foreign wars are less in a monarchy than in a republic.

The motion was won by seven votes to three. Kenneth seemed to enjoy speaking in public and took part in several more debates, including one in which the house advocated the prohibition of alcohol in England and another which condemned the hunting of wild animals.

In the summer of 1921 Kenneth added tennis to his list of sports. In August, when he was fourteen, he went down to London to take part in the Public Schoolboys Lawn Tennis Championship at Queen's Club. He did not progress beyond the first couple of rounds, but one of the other competitors was a fifteen-year-old boy from Repton School called Henry Wilfred Austin, known to his friends as 'Bunny'.

Austin was a naturally gifted tennis player but for some reason he lacked confidence. He was small for his age and was described by *The Times* as 'not much bigger than his racket', but Kenneth was impressed with the young player and the two boys became life-long friends. Austin was encouraged by Kenneth to have more faith in his ability and years later he would pay tribute to the part Kenneth played during his early days, saying that Kenneth had more confidence in him than he did himself. Austin went on to win the Under-16 singles that year and he would be the national schoolboy champion for three consecutive years.

Back at school, Kenneth played rugby for the Under-15 XV and was beginning to make an impact as a place-kicker. In a match against Berkhamsted, he converted three tries and St George's won by 18–3. Another sport at which he excelled was lacrosse. Although the school was coeducational, the boys and girls generally played their sports separately, apart from the annual 'Boys v Girls' lacrosse match, which was one of the highlights of the school year. 'Once Kenneth got the ball,' said one old friend, 'no one had any hope of catching him from one end of the field to the other.' One of the advantages of being at a coeducational school, and of having four elder sisters, was that Kenneth was not intimidated by the opposite sex, unlike many of his contemporaries at all-boys public schools. He liked the company of women, which is why many of them found him so attractive.

It was when he was about fourteen that Kenneth acquired his

first 'girlfriend', Anne Moulsdale. He used to write to her at her boarding school at St Andrews, in Fife, and send her boxes of chocolates, which were strictly forbidden. They remained friends for several years and she recalled one of his favourite sayings as: 'It is better to keep silent and be thought a fool than to speak and remove all doubt.'

At fifteen, Kenneth moved up to the 2nd XI in cricket and in one match against the National Children's Home he took 6 wickets for 14 runs. He was now in the school XV for rugby and at the end of term *The Georgian* reflected: 'His place-kicking is, on his day, excellent.' However, it added, 'Tackling could be improved considerably.'

As well as his love of sports, Kenneth was also very fond of music, especially the works of Gilbert and Sullivan, which he had learned around the family piano at home. At the age of sixteen he already possessed a bass voice and it has been suggested that he might have been good enough to be a professional singer. In February 1923 a Gilbert and Sullivan concert was given in the Big Schoolroom to raise money for the Organ Fund. According to *The Georgian*: 'Gilbert's wit and Sullivan's melodies found some very able interpreters. Horne proved himself an efficient showman and introduced each number. Encores were freely demanded and the whole entertainment was very enjoyable.' It added, 'Horne [was] among the most successful performers.'

This is the first reference anywhere to Kenneth's abilities as a performer and he seems to have made quite an impression. He was now tall and good-looking, with an athletic build and a mass of curly dark hair, giving him the nickname 'Curly'. Towards the end of 1923 he would take part in another Gilbert and Sullivan concert in front of a large audience of members and friends of the school. Once again he acted as the compere and also sang several songs including the quartet 'A regular Royal Queen' from *The Gondoliers*, the trio 'A Paradox' from *The Pirates of Penzance* and the duet 'The Bridegroom' from *Ruddigore*. 'Horne sang the bass parts very efficiently,' reported the magazine, 'as well as acting as showman.'

He was now nearly seventeen but despite outward appearances he felt uncomfortable performing in public. Out of the seven Horne children, he was the shy one. He confessed in later years, 'I didn't enjoy myself like the others until almost the end of my teens, when I became almost human. I was very, very shy.'

One of the ways he gained confidence was through his success on the sports field. In the summer of 1923 Kenneth made it into the 1st XI and his batting feats that year became legendary. He had been known in the 2nd XI as a hitter, although he tended to get out from the occasional wild shot, but now he developed a range of defensive strokes, playing straight down the pitch with a perfectly upright bat. This made him difficult to get out and resulted in some great deeds for the side. He also cultivated his running between the wickets; his speed as a sprinter enabling him to pick up some quick singles. In addition, he was described as 'an excellent fielder, who can gather the ball and throw in on the run'.

In the last four matches of the term Kenneth averaged an hour at the crease, with two not outs. One match against Old Georgians was described by the school magazine as: 'The match of the season. We had hardly dared to think of winning, but an astonishing display of tenacity by Horne and Sealy-Allin, when 6 wickets were down for 38 and 53 runs were needed for a victory, pulled us through, to our delight. They played most carefully, straight down the pitch, smothered everything, and refused to be tempted. When they were separated, only 8 runs were required for a win.' After the match, both boys were awarded hat-bands and 1st XI caps.

The following match against Dunstable Grammar School, however, had the magazine reaching for its superlatives: 'The most sensational match of the season, possibly in the history of St George's. Horne did valuable work by running about 9 of his own brand of short runs. When the last over was called 11 runs were required. Horne had the bowling; he scored 2 off the first and third balls; off the fifth he got a single. The last ball of the over and 6 to make.' Kenneth's batting partner Murrell hit the ball straight over the fielders' heads into the pavilion and St George's won the match by 1 run and 6 wickets.

During the summer holidays in 1923 Kenneth again took part in the Public Schoolboys Lawn Tennis Championship at Queen's and this time he did much better, making it to the fourth round. In the early rounds the standard of tennis was not very high. 'It is worth pointing out, for their benefit,' commented *The Times* lawn tennis correspondent disdainfully, 'that most of the boys have rackets quite unfit for play.' In the first round Kenneth beat C.R. Lane from Westminster 6–0, 6–0 and he also won the next two rounds in straight sets, but in the fourth round he was beaten 6–3, 6–2 by G.S. Fletcher, the reigning Doubles champion.

In 1924 there were more thrilling exploits on the sports field. In the Lent term he played in the rugby XV and in a game against Merchant Taylors: 'Almost immediately after the kick-off, Horne took a difficult pass and ran half the length of the field for a try. Horne decided the match when about ten minutes later he again made a good run to score a try, which he converted.'

In the summer term he enjoyed mixed fortunes. He had his best season yet in athletics, winning the 120 Yards Hurdles and the High Jump and coming second in the 100 Yards, and throwing the cricket ball. He was runner-up for the Victor Ludorum prize, behind his friend and great rival Garth Wilkinson. But in cricket he had no luck at all. He was promoted to open the batting for the XI but failed to reach double figures in almost every innings. In the field, however, he saved more runs than he scored, and was described as being in a class by himself as a fielder, running in to the ball and picking it up at full speed. In the Public Schoolboys Lawn Tennis Championship that summer he entered the Doubles, partnered with his school friend Wilkinson, and they got through to the fourth round, where they were defeated by the holders of the championship.

Back at St George's in the autumn of 1924 Kenneth was entering his final year at the school. He had already been a house prefect and a school prefect. In recognition of his popularity he was now made Head Pupil, an early example of political correctness at the school – years later he would remark that at least it was not Head Girl – and he was also Captain of Games.

He was now seventeen and had grown to be 5 feet 11½ inches tall and weighed 12 stone. His speed meant that he had become a formidable rugby player; he was both the fastest and the heaviest man on the side but it was his place-kicking that was exceptional. He had reached a standard far higher than the average at the schools against whom he played. *The Georgian* wrote: 'Horne's place-kicking has been remarkable. He created a record at Dunstable by converting ten times in succession. Incidentally his place-kicking won us the Mill Hill match.' In October the magazine reported: 'Horne, discovering rather late – a fact he ought to have found out earlier – that his weight and pace would carry him through an average defence, scored three times under the posts.' Against Leighton Buzzard he scored another five tries.

His sensational sporting exploits began to produce other benefits. R.S. Postgate recalled: 'I knew him at school, and since I was precocious in Latin and Greek and he was not, I was allowed at times to help him with Greek sentences, which I felt to be an honour since he was something of a hero to me.' Kenneth may not have been an academic scholar but he was clearly an intelligent boy. He was hoping to go to university and in December 1924 he sat the Responsions exam at Oxford, achieving passes in Latin, English, French and Mathematics.

Pupils at the school were encouraged to learn wind instruments and in his final year Kenneth took up the clarinet. The pupils' concert took place in May and it was marked by the first appearance of the new wind-instrument ensemble, who played Rubinstein's 'Melody in F' and Offenbach's 'Barcarolle'. They seem to have acquitted themselves well and 'the concert was enjoyed by a large audience'.

In his final term in the summer of 1925 Kenneth carried on his sporting heroics. After a bout of influenza, and without any training, he climbed out of his sick bed to win the 120 Yards Hurdles and the High Jump, and came second in the 100 Yards. On the cricket pitch he continued to struggle as an opening batsman for the XI and after a few matches he was dropped down the order. The result was instant. In the next match he scored 44 against Harpenden 'A': 'Horne, second wicket, freed from the responsibility of first man in, started straight off at the bowling, jumped for and took every ball that came as a half-volley and gave a fine display of straight hitting on the off side.' The season ended in a blaze of glory with St George's winning successive victories by huge margins, and in the penultimate match against St Albans Grammar School Kenneth scored 65 not out and took 4 for 8.

He had become the hero of the school, an amalgam of Jonny Wilkinson and Andrew Flintoff. But it was the warmth and generosity of his personality that endeared him to his fellow pupils. R.S. Postgate recalled: 'His infectious good humour, his capacity to make you laugh and his total lack of meanness were all clear at that age, and remained with him all his life.'

After Kenneth left St George's, it was decided to knock down the partitions between some of the classrooms and to name the result in honour of the seven Horne children who had been taught at the school. Later Kenneth used to joke, 'They decided to name a room after us, and then it was the most repulsive room in the place – Horne Hall!'

Kenneth himself became a governor of the school between 1951 and 1961 and the family legacy lingers on at the school. A few years ago Horne Hall was divided into separate classrooms once again, which are now being used for IT, while the corridor outside the school archives room is still known as Horne Passage.

Cambridge Blues

FTER LEAVING ST GEORGE'S, in August 1925 Kenneth and Garth Wilkinson entered the Public Schoolboys Lawn Tennis Championship at Queen's for the last time. Had the draw been in their favour, they would undoubtedly have been the finalists, but they were beaten in the semi-finals after a hard-fought match in which they managed to wrest one set from the champions, the Repton pair Austin and Tickler. Kenneth also reached the seventh round of the singles, where once again he had the misfortune to meet the defending champion, the unstoppable Bunny Austin.

Now that Kenneth had left school, his mother was very concerned about his future. He had done well at St George's; he had been a popular Head Pupil and had excelled at sports, but he had no qualifications and he needed to earn a living. By this time she had moved back to her old house at 2 Campden Hill Gardens, just south of Notting Hill Gate, where she lived with her unmarried children. She decided that Kenneth's future lay in business and enrolled him at the London School of Economics, where it was hoped he would equip himself for a career in business.

Kenneth would rather have studied languages, which he enjoyed, but he accepted his mother's decision without question. In those days, children, and especially youngest sons, were expected to do as they were told by their parents.

There was also a certain amount of sibling rivalry involved. His elder brothers and sisters had all excelled at school and were going on to develop impressive careers. Dorothy was said to have been the most academically talented of the Horne children; she was a historian and the author of a history of Europe. After obtaining a good degree at Lady Margaret Hall, Oxford, she had entered the Civil Service, where she became an Inspector at the Board of Trade, before marrying the diplomat Sir Archibald Gordon. Oliver Horne had graduated from New College, Oxford, and was now a barrister and a well-respected banker, soon to be appointed Secretary of the Trustee Savings Bank Association. Bridget had attended the London School of Economics but was not interested in a career and had married John Bull, who ran the family jewellery and silversmith business, Walter Bull & Sons, in Liverpool Street.

Ronald Horne had studied Law at Balliol College, Oxford, and was now a barrister in chambers at 7 New Square, Lincoln's Inn, where his grandfather Lord Cozens-Hardy had practised earlier. Of the two younger daughters, Ruth Horne would marry Sir Archie Gordon's younger brother, Douglas; while Joan, being the youngest girl, remained unmarried and stayed at home to look after her mother.

Kenneth felt under pressure to succeed. He joined the LSE in October 1925 and became a member of the Ist XV, but, try as he might, he could not raise any enthusiasm for economics. 'When you're seventeen and someone is lecturing to you on economics,' he declared later, 'it can't be very interesting to anybody.' Two of his tutors were Hugh Dalton and Stephen Leacock, both brilliant men. Dalton went on to be Chancellor of the Exchequer in Clement Attlee's post-war government and Leacock was a renowned Canadian economist and humorist, the author of two bestselling books *Literary Lapses* and *Nonsense Novels*. The latter contains a wonderful oxymoron which became one of his most famous lines:

Lord Ronald said nothing;
he flung himself from the room,
flung himself upon his horse
and rode madly off in all directions.

Kenneth was unimpressed, describing poor Leacock as 'one of the most boring lecturers I ever came across!'

At the beginning of May, Kenneth's studies came to a temporary halt when the TUC declared the first General Strike in British history in support of the coal miners, who were fighting against a 13 per cent pay cut. It began at midnight on 3 May and many businesses and universities were forced to close after the transport network became severely disrupted. The government called for volunteers to help man the essential services and on 10 May more than six thousand men and women queued in the quadrangle of the Foreign Office to sign up with the Organization for the Maintenance of Supplies. They included stockbrokers, barristers and other city office workers in their pinstripe suits, as well as many under-graduates, perhaps looking for a bit of light-hearted relief.

Kenneth was among them and he was given the job of driving a London bus. Unfortunately he was nearly the cause of a riot after he took it upon himself to divert from the normal bus route to drop several passengers outside their homes. One woman passenger became so enraged that she threw her hairbrush at him. The General Strike was called off two days later and Kenneth returned reluctantly to his studies.

While he was living in London, at least Kenneth had the chance to indulge his lifelong enthusiasm for the works of Gilbert and Sullivan. He claimed to know most of their operas by heart, as did his brothers and sisters. When the D'Oyly Carte Company was performing Gilbert and Sullivan at the old Prince's Theatre (now the Shaftesbury Theatre), Kenneth would often queue outside the theatre in the West End for up to two days in order to get a seat in the gallery for the last night of one of its seasons. A typical season finale in December 1926 featured the first act of *Iolanthe* and the second act of *The Yeomen of the Guard*. It was worth the wait because in those days it was possible to buy tickets in the gallery for just fourpence, if you were prepared to join the queue.

Kenneth's mother Katharine had a younger sister, Hope Cozens-Hardy, who was married to Austin Pilkington, of the famous glass manufacturers Pilkington Brothers of St Helens. Uncle Austin had two daughters and three sons, including Harry, who was two years older than Kenneth and was at Magdalene College, Cambridge. The two families were quite close and Harry used to impress his cousin Kenneth with tales of the wonderful time he was having at Cambridge. Not surprisingly Kenneth began to wish he could go there too.

Uncle Austin seems to have had a soft spot for his wife's youngest nephew and he made some discreet enquiries. On paper, Magdalene College was a good choice for Kenneth. He was the son of a Congregationalist minister and several Fellows at the College were well-known in Congregationalist circles, such as the historian Frank Salter and the mathematician A.S. Ramsey, father of the future Archbishop of Canterbury, Michael Ramsey.

Kenneth's mother wrote to the Dean of Magdalene College, Frank Salter, to see whether there was any chance of Kenneth getting into the College in the autumn. She explained that he had already passed the Responsions exam at Oxford but, as he was not a classical scholar, she felt it might be better for him to take a degree in economics at Cambridge. She wondered whether the college was 'suitable for a boy with plenty of brains but no special strong point and with more interest in athletics than work – at present'. She added that there was a possibility he would be offered a job later at Pilkingtons and, in any case, his future would be in business.

The Dean replied that the Economics course would cost between £250 and £300 and requested a copy of the Responsions certificate, suggesting that she put Kenneth's name down for the College Entrance Examination in June. The certificate proved to be adequate and he was exempted from taking the similar 'Previous Examination' at Cambridge. On 20 June Kenneth travelled up to Magdalene and stayed overnight in the college before taking the College Entrance Exam the next day.

Meanwhile the Reverend Cecil Grant, his former headmaster at St George's, had been asked for a reference and he wrote what would prove to be a most perceptive letter to A.S. Ramsey, the President of Magdalene College:

> C. Kenneth Horne is a boy of very considerable promise and I shall watch his career with much interest and some anxiety. He is the seventh and last of his family to come to us and he suffered – I think – from the premature death of his father and from some temptation to spoil the youngest. His faults have been those of the boy to whom success and popularity come too easily and taste too sweet.
>
> 'Morally' his record is unstained. He shared the head-boyship with another for a year and came thro' creditably with signs of very real improvement at the finish.
>
> I am writing – as you will understand – rather to put you on your guard as to possible weak points than with any idea that you should hesitate to receive him. If he can be got to make good use of his time at Cambridge it should do very much for him and he should prove not only a very delightful member of his college but capable of a distinguished career. He should find no difficulty in reading for Honours.
>
> He is an unusually good athlete.

At the beginning of July they received the news that Kenneth had passed the necessary exams and had been accepted into Magdalene to read for an Honours degree in Economics. His mother was asked to send a cheque of £5 for the College Entrance Fee and £15 Caution Money, which was a refundable deposit for any unpaid bills.

Kenneth entered Magdalene College on 12 October 1926 and was allocated rooms in the college overlooking Magdalene Street, one of the main thoroughfares and a busy bus route. Kenneth was often distracted from his studies by the sight of pretty girls sitting on the upper deck of the open-top buses as they stopped outside his window at the corner of Chesterton Lane.

The actor Michael Redgrave went up to Magdalene a year later and encountered a similar problem. He had rooms a few yards further down the road in Bridge Street and the midday bus to Newnham used to stop opposite his window. In his autobiography *In My Mind's Eye* Redgrave recalled: 'The Newnham girls on the top deck would be able to look straight into my sitting room on the first floor, where they could see me . . . casually looking up to see if any one of them was interested. None of them ever looked back: I could not think why. Too well brought up, I supposed.'

Not that it took much to take Kenneth's mind off his studies. In fact he hardly seems to have done any work at all. He threw himself wholeheartedly into all the sports that Cambridge had to offer and over the next year he began to fulfil his promise as a first-class all-round athlete. Magdalene was one of the small colleges so Kenneth, as he put it, 'got roped into doing everything – soccer, hockey, the lot!'

At the end of his first term the *Magdalene College Magazine* reported: 'The College Trials revealed a considerable amount of talent among the Freshmen, notably in A.D. Bonham Carter, who won the Weight Putting in the Freshmen's Sports, and C.K. Horne . . . in the Sprints.'

Kenneth became a member of the Magdalene College relay team alongside the great Lord Burghley. David Burghley, who was two years older than him, caused a sensation the following year by running around the Great Court at Trinity College in the time it took the Trinity Clock to strike twelve noon, a feat that was re-created in a famous scene in the Academy Award-winning film *Chariots of Fire*. Burghley would go on to win the 400 metres hurdles Gold Medal at the 1928 Amsterdam Olympics.

In November 1926 Magdalene made it to the finals of the Inter-

College Relays Competition, and Kenneth ran the first leg of a 3 × 120-yard hurdles relay, with an Old Etonian called Charles Chichester and Lord Burghley, which Magdalene won. He also ran the second leg of the 4 × 150-yard relay with Philip Marchington, William Milligan and Lord Burghley, in which Magdalene came second, and the college ended the competition overall in joint first place with Kings.

In Rugby he was equally impressive: 'The presence of many Old Colours and a number of promising Freshmen led to considerable optimism at the beginning of term,' said the *Magdalene College Magazine*. 'The 1st XV, by 10 victories in 13 matches, have justified this hope. The backs do not often have the opportunity of playing together [but] Horne, when he has played, has been a tower of strength.' He now weighed 15 stone and, as he said once, 'You try and stop fifteen stone when it's ten yards from the line!'

One of Kenneth's great disappointments was that he never got a rugby blue at Cambridge, although he took part in a few games for the University in the Lent Term, playing at wing outside the formidable Carl Aarvold, who went on to be Captain of England and then the Lions on their 1930 tour of Australasia, where he scored a record three tries against the All Blacks.

Kenneth also represented Magdalene at athletics in the inter-college 'Cuppers' competition, which consisted of individual events rather than relays. In February 1927 Magdalene were drawn against Corpus Christi College in Division 2. Lord Burghley was ill and did not compete, but Kenneth came second in the 120 yards hurdles, the 220 yards hurdles and the shot, helping Magdalene to win the match by 58 points to 45.

During the Easter Term Kenneth also played cricket and he was said to be excellent at squash and pretty good at golf, although he once joked that he only played it 'for his own amazement'. He was, of course, an extremely talented tennis player and in early May he took part in the annual Cambridge Freshmen's Tournament. He made it to the final in the singles but was beaten in three sets by

N.G. Farquharson, a young South African from Emmanuel College. The tennis correspondent in *The Times* reported that 'C.K. Horne (Magdalene) the runner-up in the singles, played very well.' Kenneth also reached the doubles final but lost to the talented South African pair, Farquharson and Porter.

His performance was good enough to gain him a place in the Cambridge University Lawn Tennis team and in June he played in the annual match between Oxford and Cambridge on Oxford's new grass courts at Iffley Road. He was paired in the doubles with his former nemesis Farquharson and after losing their first rubber, they went on to win the next two, helping Cambridge to win the match by 13 rubbers to 8.

After the match Kenneth was awarded his half-blue for Lawn Tennis although later he would claim that he managed to obtain his blue only 'by taking the Captain out to lunch fairly often'. The Captain of the Cambridge University team was none other than his old friend Bunny Austin, so there may have been a small element of truth in his remark. Kenneth was obviously delighted to be given his half-blue but he was always disappointed that he did not achieve his real ambition at Cambridge, which remained to get a blue at rugby.

At the end of June 1927 Kenneth came back down to earth with a bump. He was required to take a preliminary first-year exam, known as the Economics Tripos Qualifying Examination. He failed it badly. Kenneth's tutor, Frank Salter, solemnly informed his mother: 'He failed on every paper and his marks and his supervisor's report indicate a low level of industry.'

His mother wrote back apologizing for Kenneth's failure and adding: 'I have felt all along that he was spending too much at time at athletics and twice I have tried to see his supervisor about his work but he was out.'

It was decided that Kenneth would retake the exam at the beginning of October. If he failed again he would have to give up his Honours course and, as a condition of him staying on at the university, he would have to pass an exam in his principal subject for the Ordinary Degree in December.

During the long summer vacation of 1927 Kenneth joined the rest of the team of the Cambridge University Lawn Tennis Club on a tour of Germany. The other team members were Bunny Austin, Russell Young, Bill Powell and Jack Baines, and they took part in a series of tournaments and exhibition matches. Kenneth, Bunny and 'Rusty' Young enjoyed each other's company and used to dine out together, so Kenneth came up with idea of forming a club. They had all been amused by the long German names for most of the dishes on the restaurant menus. One exception at the bottom of the menu was the word 'Obst' which they discovered meant 'fruit'. They liked it so much that they decided to call themselves The Obst Club.

The three members would be known as 'Ein' (Bunny), 'Zwei' (Rusty) and 'Drei' (Kenneth), and they arranged for a special club tie to be made which portrayed silver bowls of fruit on a green background with their individual numbers, 1, 2 and 3. They were supposed to appoint a President, a Secretary and Treasurer but no one was ever elected because the other two would always vote against him. There were several reunions over the years and they continued to meet at irregular intervals until 1961.

Bunny Austin and Kenneth became great friends. In 1926 Austin had reached the men's doubles semi-finals in his first Wimbledon. He would go on, with Fred Perry, to be a member of the legendary British team who won the Davis Cup for four consecutive years in the 1930s, and he would be the losing Wimbledon men's singles finalist in 1932 and 1938, the last British player to reach the men's finals.

Austin once said of Kenneth: 'He was a much better sportsman than many people realise. He already had the ingredients of his later character. Kenneth had the joyful gift of turning every occasion into a party and every party into an occasion.'

Another of Kenneth's best friends at Cambridge was Henry Pelham-Clinton-Hope, the eldest son and heir of the eighth Duke of

Newcastle. They were the same age and had been freshmen together at Magdalene the previous year. During the summer of 1927 Henry invited Kenneth to stay with the Duke and his family at their home in Dorking, Surrey. It was there that he met Henry's youngest sister, Lady Mary, who had recently turned seventeen and was three years younger than him. She was said to be something of a tomboy, with a great enthusiasm for cars, and had been taught how to drive at the age of fourteen by the family chauffeur on the ducal estate at Clumber, in Nottinghamshire. She and Kenneth seemed to hit it off right away.

In the first week of October he returned to Cambridge and walked straight into a crisis of his own making. He had missed his vital exam, which had been held a few days before. It seems almost unbelievable in view of its importance, but he had not bothered to check the actual date of the exam and had simply presumed it was going to be after the beginning of the term. As his tutor pointed out: 'I think he ought to have had the enterprise to find out for himself, if he did not know it, the date of the Examination. No one else made any mistake.'

As a final warning Kenneth was told he would have to pass the exam in his principal subject in December or face being sent down from the university.

Realizing that he was about to throw it all away, Kenneth finally settled down to his studies, although quite how much is open to question. Years later Kenneth would admit cheerfully that he attended precisely seven lectures in his entire time at Cambridge.

He still played rugby for Magdalene and was now also the secretary of the College Rugby Union Football Club. 'Horne was very strong on the wing,' enthused the college magazine that term.

Kenneth knew that anyone in residence at Magdalene for four terms without passing an exam in a principal subject was automatically ineligible for further residence. In early December he sat Part I of the Economics Tripos exam. He failed it badly. In fact, he did not pass in three out of the four papers and in two of them 'his marks were very poor indeed'. On 16 December 1927 the Governing Body informed him that he would not be allowed to return to the College. He had been sent down from Cambridge.

Two weeks later, Kenneth wrote to his tutor, Frank Salter:

I'm very sorry to have let you down so badly over the exam. I can't honestly think how it happened, as I really did work last term.

I know I have never had the exam temperament, but I feel I could have passed in almost any other subject, as I pointed out.

However I feel I've let you and my mother down very badly and I would be awfully grateful if you could use your influence to persuade the authorities to allow me to take the two exams at the end of the summer term, in order to try and make some amends for my failure.

Once again – I'm very sorry.

Kenneth's mother also wrote to Salter to say how very distressed she felt about what had happened. She put the blame on St George's School for not teaching Kenneth concentration and accused his tutors at Cambridge of not showing enough interest in the standard of his work. She complained that if she had been advised that Kenneth had needed extra coaching, the result would have been very different. She did finally admit, however: 'I think the mistake has been for him to take economics in which he is not really interested. I am told he put in a lot of work last term . . . but I fear he will never be a scholar.'

Salter's reply was blunt and unsympathetic: no extra coaching would have made any difference. The exam was not a difficult one and two men who were 'intellectually very weak' had both managed to get through. Kenneth should have had no difficulty at all but, according to Salter, he had suffered from ideas of self-confidence, thinking he would 'get through all right'.

Salter's letter to Austin Pilkington was even more succinct: 'I'm afraid that Kenneth has all along been extremely idle, but that is all.' He suggested that, sobered by this failure, Kenneth might do quite well if he found himself a job in business where he would be compelled to work definite hours.

Austin Pilkington was angry at being let down so badly and genuinely disappointed at the behaviour of his likeable nephew. 'I have really looked forward to the boy coming here,' he wrote. 'He has got his life before him and this may shake him up in a way that nothing else would do. What an awful pity, but I'm afraid he's been a bit spoilt by the others. It often happens with the youngest one.'

The plan had been for Kenneth to start at the bottom at Pilkingtons, working his way upwards, with the intention of eventually becoming a director of the company. But without a degree or any other academic qualification to his name, even Uncle Austin did not feel able to nominate Kenneth for a job with the family firm. The offer was withdrawn. As a final favour, however, Pilkington mentioned Kenneth to one of his customers, a friend of his called Colonel Clare, who was a director of the Triplex Safety Glass Company Limited.

He left it up to the colonel whether he considered the charming but impetuous boy suitable for a job. From now on, Kenneth was on his own.

4

Breaking Glass

THE TRIPLEX SAFETY Glass Company Limited was founded in 1911 to manufacture a revolutionary new type of glass that did not shatter on impact, but merely cracked without breaking. It was developed by coating two sheets of glass with cellulose-acetate, placing a sheet of celluloid between them, and then compressing the sheets together. During the First World War Triplex supplied the Royal Flying Corps with laminated glass for windshields in the open cockpit aircraft and for pilots' goggles. Then in 1926 the company signed a major contract with the Austin Motor Company to produce safety glass windscreens for their production cars. A new Triplex factory was built at King's Norton, not far from the Austin plant at Longbridge, Birmingham, and it was about to start production in early 1928 when Kenneth arrived for his job interview.

He was seen by the Works Manager, Major Dick, who was rather surprised to learn that his job applicant had not only failed to earn a degree at Cambridge but had no other academic qualifications at all. The major perked up visibly, however, when he discovered that Kenneth had won a half-blue at tennis and had played rugby for Magdalene. The Triplex works were trying to start up a rugby team and they were one man short. Kenneth was hired on the spot.

He started work the following Monday at a wage of thirty shillings (£1.50) a week. He began on the factory floor as a trainee, learning everything about the glass business from the bottom up, or as he once described it, 'cutting glass, polishing glass, storing glass, sorting orders, chasing orders, doing anything I was told to do'. He must have been a quick learner, because soon after production started at the King's Norton factory in May, Kenneth was made the manager of the new Order Office. His former assistant, Reg Anscombe, then aged sixteen, recalled that their first order came from the Bean Motor Company.

At first Kenneth stayed with Major Dick and his wife until he found rooms with a Mrs Dawson in her house in Middleton Hall Road, King's Norton. Before long, he got to know the family next door, Ernest Burgess and his wife, their twelve-year-old daughter Joan, and her younger brother. Burgess was chairman and managing director of a well-established company of brass founders called Harrison's Limited in Birmingham. Joan was a pretty girl, with an easy smile and a lively sense of humour, and even though she was nine years younger than Kenneth, she became friends with her good-looking neighbour.

On one occasion Kenneth took Joan and her parents to see Fred and Adele Astaire in their new Gershwin musical *Funny Face* at the Theatre Royal in Birmingham. Joan was a keen tap-dancer and the excitement of seeing the Astaires on stage, and her first grown-up show, made a lasting impression on the young girl. After that, Kenneth became a frequent visitor at the Burgesses, and whenever Joan answered the door he would perform a little tap-dance on the doorstep before entering the house. Later that year, however, Joan went away to boarding school at Cheltenham Ladies' College and they lost touch with each other.

During the summer of 1928 Kenneth invited his friend Henry Pelham-Clinton-Hope and his sister Mary for a tennis weekend at the White House. Mary arrived in a brand new eight-horse-power Rover, which her father, the Duke, had given her as a seventeenth birthday present the previous year. In those days you were not officially allowed to drive until you were eighteen but she had acquired a driving licence by lying about her age.

Kenneth was suitably impressed by her new car but noticed that it was not fitted with Triplex Safety Glass. In an effort to impress her with his new-found influence at Triplex, he offered to have the car fitted with the glass at Kings Norton. On the Monday they set off to Kings Norton in pouring rain, with Mary driving, and were going down a narrow country lane when a cow ran out in front of them. Mary could not avoid the cow, which somehow escaped unhurt, but the car was badly damaged. After a few roadside repairs, they managed to get to Kings Norton, where Kenneth used all his charm to persuade his colleagues at Triplex to fit the safety glass and repair the damage. The Rover was returned to Mary looking as good as new, and she was suitably grateful.

In 1929 Kenneth moved out of Mrs Dawson's and into a flat in Sherlock Street, King's Norton, which he shared with Hugh Borley, a work colleague at Triplex. Hugh was the son of a wealthy farmer in Dorset and he and Kenneth would remain friends for many years.

Although he was slowly climbing the executive ladder at Triplex, Kenneth's weekly wage was barely enough to live on. His pay had gone up to £3 a week or, as he put it, 'thirty shillings for the digs and thirty shillings for wine, women and song – and you can get a lot of wine for that!' He tried to make a little extra money on the side by opening a small shop selling gramophone records in The Cotteridge in King's Norton. It must have been difficult for him to run a shop at the same time as his regular job and after a while his bosses at Triplex persuaded him to close it down. He was needed at the factory. By the second half of 1929 the sales figures of 'Triplex Safety Glass' had soared and leading car manufacturers were now fitting it as standard for the first time. Annual turnover had increased to £427,000, and the King's Norton factory was having difficulty meeting demand.

Kenneth also became involved with a local dance band. A friend at the Triplex works called Norman Aylward, known as 'Bo', played the alto saxophone and wanted to start a band. He already had a pianist and a drummer and when he heard that Kenneth could play the clarinet, he encouraged him to learn the tenor saxophone as well. Kenneth bought himself a tenor sax and after work he used to go round to Bo Aylward's house every night for lessons.

After a while he was judged to be good enough and they called their new band 'Bo Aylward and his Rascals'. They played at the Triplex Social Club and even managed to get some gigs in Coventry, Oxford, Warwick and Church Stretton, where Kenneth was hailed as a 'local boy made good'. He certainly looked the part, fronting the band with his saxophone and his immaculate white tie and tails, although he had no illusions about his musical prowess and once confessed that he tried to 'pretend I was an expert without destroying the illusion by actually blowing!' He also used to sing through a megaphone, in those pre-microphone days, and had quite a pleasant baritone singing voice, which he would use to great effect in his future broadcasting career.

While all this was going on, Kenneth was also beginning to see more of Lady Mary. He had enjoyed a fleeting romance at Cambridge with a girl called Marjorie French, but this was his first serious relationship. It is easy to see why Mary was interested in Kenneth: he was tall and good-looking, a superb athlete and he had a relaxed, easy charm. What attracted him to Mary, however, is less certain: she had an engaging personality but was not conventionally pretty, with crimped, dark curly hair and a short, rather dumpy figure. But they developed a close and loving friendship and after about eighteen months they became officially engaged.

Lady Mary was still only nineteen but she was determined to get married. Her elder sister Doria and her brother Henry had already wed and Mary did not want to be left behind. She and her father are said to have 'fought like cat and dog', but the Duke was clearly fond of his headstrong daughter and he usually gave in to her demands. The Duke also liked Kenneth but he believed the couple were far too young, and he arranged a meeting over luncheon with Kenneth's mother Katharine to discuss how they might resolve the situation. It was to no avail. Mary's mind was made up and she was used to getting her own way. Kenneth does not seem to have had much of a say in the matter. In hindsight, it seems doubtful that he was ever passionately in love with Mary. It may be that he felt powerless to

resist in the face of her stubborn determination but he also felt
intimidated by the Duke. According to Mary, Kenneth was terrified
of her father.

Kenneth and Lady Mary Pelham-Clinton-Hope were duly
married on 20 September 1930 in a quiet ceremony at the Holy
Trinity Church in Hampstead, north London, with the Duke giving
the bride away. Mary was twenty and Kenneth was twenty-three.
They spent their honeymoon in the elegant seaside resort of Dinard
on the Emerald Coast of Brittany. Back home, however, Mary had
to face the realities of married life to an impoverished Triplex junior
manager.

They moved into a furnished semi-detached house in Solihull,
not far from Kenneth's office. He went off to work every weekday
and Mary was left at home alone. She was bored. She did not enjoy
doing the housework and would often spend her afternoons visiting
one of the many cinemas in Birmingham or going for a spin in her
new car, a Hudson coupé, which had replaced the Rover.

Kenneth did not own a car but had a motorbike and sidecar,
which was his pride and joy. He tried to teach Mary how to ride it
but he gave up after one occasion when she drove at high speed
through a twelve-inch-deep ford, drenching Kenneth in the open
sidecar.

They used to play tennis together, although Kenneth was a much
better player than her, and he still kept in touch with the other
members of the Obst Club. In April 1931 he wrote a typically light-
hearted letter from his office at Triplex to Bunny Austin:

du bist mein ein,
I have yours of the ult; and am completely obst by your inst;
Much as I should like to visit you on Saturday, I cannot, as I don't
finish work here until one of the clock and I am going out in the
evening.
Couldn't you manage to come to Town Sunday afternoon, and have
a Comic Tennis match with Phyllis against Mary and I, at the

Campden Club, and a meal and Cinema afterwards?
An early reply will oblige,
Yours, for and on behalf of the OBST Club,
C. Kenneth Horne (Drei)
President and Secretary.

Le ver Triplex est encore bon, merci. Comment Allez, dit-il, le, 4½%
preference stock d'almalgamated Moustaches et Cie?
Il reste a 85¾ – non?

Later that year Mary managed to obtain some money from her
trustees and they bought a small house on the outskirts of
Solihull. They furnished it with regular shopping expeditions into
Birmingham.

The D'Oyly Carte Company used to visit one of the theatres in
Birmingham every so often and Kenneth would save up enough
money from his meagre wages to go and see several performances.
After the show he would always stand outside the stage door in the
hope of catching sight of his favourite members of the cast. One
evening in 1932, during one of the intervals, he met a friend called
Eddie Williams who asked him if he would like to meet some of the
company. The answer was, unsurprisingly, 'Not half, I wouldn't!'
and next thing Kenneth knew he was shaking hands with the
legendary Sir Henry Lytton, who had been one of the most popular
stars of the D'Oyly Carte Company for more than a quarter of a
century. Many years later Kenneth would recall that meeting as 'a
tremendous thrill' and 'never to be forgotten', and it heralded the
start of a long association and friendship with several members of
the company.

Sometimes at weekends Mary would drive the two of them down
in the Hudson to stay with the Duke of Newcastle in Dorking, or
with Kenneth's mother at Campden Hill Gardens in London. At
Christmas Kenneth and Mary would join the rest of the Hornes for
a family reunion and the traditional Christmas Show. Kenneth

would help to write and produce it and Mary would be persuaded to take part.

They seemed to be happy and had a loving friendship, but underneath it all there was something terribly wrong with their marriage. In September 1932 they celebrated their second wedding anniversary. Not long afterwards, Mary wrote to her father, pouring out her unhappiness and frustration. The Duke was so shocked by the contents of her letter that he wrote straight back to her, asking her to come and stay, alone.

Kenneth had no objection, so she agreed to drop him off at his mother's house in Kensington on her way down to Dorking. When he entered the house he found a letter addressed to him from the Duke. It announced that Mary would not be coming back to him.

Kenneth was stunned. He tried to telephone her at Dorking but his calls were intercepted. Mary was forbidden to answer the telephone or to communicate with him in any way at all. The Duke kept her under a virtual house arrest.

Kenneth appears to have accepted the sudden breakdown of his marriage without putting up any kind of resistance. He made no attempt to contact the Duke or to persuade his wife to return. This seems remarkably spineless, but of course he would have known the reason for her departure and perhaps he recognized that his words would have no effect. On 21 November 1932 Lady Mary filed a petition in the High Court for the annulment of their marriage and six months later, on 29 May 1933, the marriage was officially dissolved.

Kenneth never talked about this period of his life and Lady Mary died at the age of seventy-one in 1982, so it is impossible to discover what really happened between the two of them. But when writing his book *Solo For Horne*, published in 1976, Kenneth's friend Norman Hackforth talked to Lady Mary about her marriage to Kenneth. She told him there had been 'some physical incompatibility' between them, which was irreconcilable. My curiosity aroused, I consulted the Principal Registry of the Family Division in

London's Chancery Lane and managed to obtain a copy of the official certificate of annulment, which reveals the shocking truth behind the collapse of their marriage. In plain black and white it declares the marriage to be 'absolutely null and void . . . by reason of the incapacity of the respondent [Charles Kenneth Horne] to consummate the marriage'.

It seems almost incredible that the couple were married for more than two years without once having sexual intercourse. No wonder the Duke was so outraged when he read his daughter's letter that he demanded she return home immediately. The question is, *why* was the marriage not consummated?

He was certainly not impotent. In his second marriage his wife became pregnant within weeks of their wedding. Lady Mary would go on to marry twice more, to Romaine Alphonse Stemmer in 1939 and then, after a second divorce, to William Serge Belaieff in 1947, but she would remain childless. Who knows what goes on behind closed doors in any marriage? The truth about what really happened – or did not happen – between Kenneth and Mary will have to remain a mystery.

The annulment of her marriage would have been embarrassing enough for Lady Mary but Kenneth must have felt humiliated. There are not that many legal reasons for an annulment and most of them are scandalous, from bigamy or fraud to someone being under-age or mentally ill; and, of course, non-consummation. Rumours among his friends and work colleagues at Triplex must have been rife.

Kenneth needed to put the whole experience behind him and move on. After all, he was still only twenty-six. For the next few years he threw himself into his job at Triplex, where he was determined to succeed, and he was appointed Midland sales representative for the company.

He also played hard. He was still a supremely fit all-round athlete and he became closely involved with the Triplex Social and Athletic Association, serving on the committee and later holding the office of

Chairman. He used to play cricket for the Triplex Club and was renowned as a tremendous hitter. He was not the most stylish of batsmen but with his quick eye gained from years of playing tennis and squash, he could pick up a ball very quickly. One year the club was playing Small Heath on a ground surrounded by houses and gardens. Kenneth hit three sixes in one over, sending the balls soaring into the nearby gardens, never to be seen again. The desperate Small Heath captain had to beg him to stop, because they had only one ball left! He also played rugby for Kings Norton in the seven-a-side league and one year he even won the Worcestershire Squash Championship.

It was at Triplex that Kenneth developed the art of entertaining an audience. His job required him to demonstrate the strength of Triplex Safety Glass at motor shows and he would do it with infectious enthusiasm, throwing a succession of objects at a large plate of Triplex glass to prove that it would not break. Many years later, after the war, his godson Tim Murdoch recalls seeing Kenneth in front of a large crowd at the Motor Show in London, immaculate in his business suit with a red carnation, hurling things at a sheet of glass and finally attacking it with a car jack.

Kenneth also gained his first experience of speaking over a microphone at Triplex. As a member of the committee, he was asked to be the announcer at one of the Association's annual fetes. He turned out to be a natural, with a clear, warm and friendly voice, and he became their regular announcer. Without realizing it, he was about to embark on a whole new career.

5

Ack-Ack
Beer-Beer

DURING HER LAST term at Cheltenham Ladies' College in May 1933, Joan Burgess was sent a press cutting by her mother. It had been taken from a Birmingham newspaper and it announced the end of Kenneth's marriage to Mary. Half in jest, Joan scribbled on the bottom: 'A chance for me yet!'

The following year she was driving through King's Norton in her new, pale green Austin 10 'Swallow' drophead coupé, a Christmas present from her generous father, when she saw an identical 'Swallow', only pale blue, coming towards her. It came to a halt and out stepped Kenneth. It is hard to say who was the more surprised. Joan was thrilled to see Kenneth again but he could hardly believe his eyes. The last time he had seen Joan she had been the gawky schoolgirl next door, but now she was eighteen years old, blonde, petite and extremely pretty.

Joan took Kenneth back to meet her parents at their new home, called The Dell, in Northfield. They were also delighted to see him again. It turned out that the young couple shared much more than cars in common. Joan was also an excellent racket player, playing squash for her county; she played tennis and golf, and she loved dancing. Perhaps for the first time in his life, Kenneth was truly smitten.

They were married on 5 September 1936, one month before Joan's twenty-first birthday. They had a traditional white wedding in Edgbaston Parish Church, followed by a big reception at The Dell. Kenneth's old flat-mate Hugh Borley gave them a golden cocker spaniel puppy as a wedding present, which they called 'Snip'. They spent their honeymoon at the sumptuous Palace Hotel in Jersey and returned home to begin married life in a pretty house called White Lodge at Burcot, a little village on the edge of the countryside near Bromsgrove, and about seven miles from Kings Norton.

Six weeks after their wedding Kenneth had to go down to London for the Motor Show at Olympia, where Triplex had a stand. One afternoon he was leaving the main hall through a pair of swing doors when he literally bumped into Mary coming in the opposite direction. She was looking for some friends but he invited her to join him for a cup of tea. They talked for a while, and laughed a bit, and then they went their separate ways, as friends.

At first Kenneth and Joan were perfectly happy. In contrast to his first marriage, Kenneth became quite domesticated. They entertained frequently, holding several cocktail parties, for which Kenneth would prepare the snacks. He even made Joan a triple mirror, an unheard-of event for him. They became members of the nearby Barnt Green Sports and Social Club and joined in their events enthusiastically. Joan was still a good tap-dancer and at one of the club dances she performed a cabaret dressed as Minnie Mouse, with a dummy Mickey Mouse as her dancing partner. It was so popular that she was asked to repeat the routine at the next dance and this time she persuaded Kenneth to wear a special Mickey Mouse costume, which she had made herself. They danced the routine together, much to the amusement of the crowd, with Kenneth as a giant Mickey towering over his petite wife.

Whenever the D'Oyly Carte Company was in Birmingham, Kenneth would get up teams to play them at golf. They would have a round in the morning, followed by a heavy lunch, and another round in the afternoon. The lunches could be fairly riotous affairs. One of the principal tenors was John Dean and one day he teed off after lunch with a ball still wrapped in its paper. Afterwards the players would gather back at Kenneth and Joan's house, where they would eat sausage and mash, and end the evening with a game of darts.

The newlyweds had another reason to be happy. Within two months of their marriage, Joan had become pregnant. Like most young couples, they looked forward eagerly to the birth of their first child. Then on 21 July 1937 Joan gave birth to a baby boy. He was stillborn.

They were devastated. Kenneth did what he could to comfort Joan but his world had been turned equally upside down. When Joan felt well enough to travel, Kenneth arranged a motoring holiday to Germany and they drove through the Black Forest for three weeks, trying to come to terms with their terrible loss.

Back home at Burcot they tried to put their lives back together. Kenneth was slowly climbing the executive ladder at Triplex. The previous year Triplex had bought a plastics moulding business called H.E. Ashdown Limited and in the summer of 1937 Kenneth was offered the post of sales manager at Ashdown's. Subsequently it was decided that he should remain in his existing job at Triplex and the offer was withdrawn. He was earning considerably more than his original thirty-bob-a-week but he always had expensive tastes and money was tight. Early in 1938 he heard a rumour that Triplex was going to lose its contract with Austin Motors and it was going to be awarded to another firm called the Lancegaye Safety Glass Company, which had been formed in 1928 with money won from backing a horse of that name. The news was due to be announced at the next Austin board meeting in two weeks' time.

He told a friend called Edmund King, a young chartered accountant, and over a drink one evening they hatched a plan to make a swift killing on the stock market. Neither of them had any money, but King contacted a broker he knew in Birmingham and bought ten thousand Lancegaye shares at sixpence-farthing (about 2.6p) each, which came to £260. The plan was simple. They had three weeks before they would have to settle their account with the broker. When the new Austin contract was announced, the price of Lancegaye shares would rise, the pair would sell them quickly, pay off the broker and clear a handsome profit each. It was foolproof.

One week later, on 14 March, Adolf Hitler annexed Austria. The Stock Market slumped and Lancegaye shares dropped to fourpence. A week after that, the Austin Motor Company held its board meeting at which it was announced that the Triplex contract was being *renewed*. Lancegaye shares dropped to threepence. After three weeks Kenneth and Edmund's account became due and, after they had sold their shares, the pair received a bill from their broker which showed a loss on the deal of £127.

The following week Triplex took over Lancegaye.

The two men simply did not have the money, the equivalent of several thousand pounds at today's prices. King had to explain their embarrassing situation to his broker, who kindly allowed them to pay off the account in instalments, but it took them nearly a year to clear the debt.

After Neville Chamberlain returned from Munich at the end of September announcing that he had secured 'peace in our time' many were convinced that, on the contrary, another war against Germany was only a matter of time. Soon afterwards, Kenneth joined the auxiliary airforce. He enlisted in the RAF Volunteer Reserve on a part-time training scheme and on 28 April 1939 he was granted a commission as Acting Pilot Officer in No. 911 (County of Warwick) Squadron. It was a Barrage Balloon unit attached to No. 5 Centre at Sutton Coldfield.

He reported for training after work but at first there was not much for him to do; there was a shortage of equipment and the unit had only one balloon. So Kenneth used his organizational skills to put on some entertainments for his fellow volunteers, at which he joined in enthusiastically, singing comic songs and playing the saxophone.

He was called up for service on 24 August and bid a fond farewell to his friends and colleagues at Triplex, where he had recently become the new Midland sales manager. After war was declared ten days later, Kenneth and Joan closed up their house at Burcot, putting their furniture into storage. They moved in with Joan's parents who were now living in Edgbaston, conveniently close to A. Flight Headquarters, where Kenneth was based.

His war got off to an inauspicious start at the end of October when he was put on the injury list; his medical records report him as having a 'dislocated and sprained ankle' while playing organized games. But in December he was confirmed in his appointment and graded as Pilot Officer. He was given the title of Flight Commander and put in charge of a barrage balloon called Agnes, which was flown from a site near the Wolverhampton Road.

Barrage balloons were temperamental affairs. They were known by aircraft pilots as 'Silver Monsters' – majestic but deadly. The huge balloons were more than 60 feet long and 30 feet high, and weighed about 600 pounds. They were filled with hydrogen gas and could fly at a height of up to 5000 feet, supporting a strong steel cable which was attached to the ground. The idea was that fear of hitting the cables, which would fatally damage an aircraft, would force enemy bombers to avoid the area, or at least force them to fly so high that they could not bomb their target accurately.

Sometimes the balloons would leak. They attracted bullets from passing enemy aircraft, but also insects, and many holes in the fabric were the result of birds pecking at them. When that occurred they would lose height and often swerve dangerously out of control, dragging the cable behind them and causing damage to buildings. One night Agnes drifted towards a local factory and the cable sliced the top off the factory chimney.

During the early months of the war, official transport was scarce, but now that he was a Flight Commander, Kenneth was appointed a driver, Aircraftman Edward Wilkinson, whose main qualification would appear to be that he owned a Jaguar. Notwithstanding the difference in rank, he and Kenneth soon became good friends and they held a number of parties at Wilkinson's flat near the A. Flight Headquarters.

By now Kenneth had become quite an accomplished cook and prepared some 'sumptuous repasts' at the parties, with the help of a friendly butcher called Len Houghton, who had a shop in Broad Street, Birmingham. Kenneth and Edward Wilkinson used to invite the butcher to join them at the Crown pub opposite the shop, where they would ply him with drink, and he would return the favour by staggering back to the shop and telling them to 'Help yer bloody selves!' from his cold storage room.

One of the main problems during the early days of the war was boredom, with not enough work to keep the men busy, so Kenneth set about organizing a concert party. He enlisted all the talent available in A. Flight, including singers, dancers and comedians, and even Joan, who helped out with a tap-dance routine. Edward Wilkinson played the part of a volunteer striptease artist, peeling off his clothes to music until he was left in his long woollen combination underwear with an L-plate on his bottom. Kenneth wrote some topical jokes and sketches and acted as the compere of the show, which was put on at the Talbot Hotel at Oldbury, where it was judged to be a 'riotous success'.

In early 1940 Wilkinson received his commission and was posted to Liverpool. He and Kenneth would not meet again until after the war, with memorable consequences.

In July Kenneth was promoted to Flying Officer and a month later he was sent on an administration course with the temporary rank of Acting Squadron Leader to 966 Squadron based at Newport, Monmouthshire. Joan went with him and they lived on the base in a married-quarter house, where they were given a full-time batman to look after their every need.

In November Kenneth was promoted again to Flight Lieutenant and then in April 1941 he was posted back to No. 31 Group Headquarters in Birmingham, where he was responsible for organizational duties.

The men and women of the Anti-Aircraft and Barrage Balloon Commands were the unsung heroes of the early part of the war. They were often sited in isolated places around the country and during the blitzes they would be on duty day and night in all weathers, sometimes up to their knees in mud. They felt unappreciated and neglected and, with some encouragement from the Air Ministry, the BBC attempted to raise their morale by introducing a new twice-weekly radio series to be called *Ack-Ack Beer-Beer*, the abbreviation for the Anti-Aircraft and Balloon Barrage Commands in the phonetic alphabet then in use.

At the outset of the war, the BBC had compressed all its National and Regional Programmes into a single BBC Home Service. In January 1940 the Corporation launched an alternative service called the Forces Programme, specifically aimed at the armed forces, although its steady diet of light entertainment, dance bands, comedy shows and quizzes soon attracted millions of civilian listeners as well.

The first edition of *Ack-Ack Beer-Beer*, described as 'a radio magazine with sports, news, interest and entertainment', was broadcast on the Forces Programme on 1 July 1940. It was a forty-five-minute programme which went out every Monday and Thursday evening between 5.15 and 6 p.m. The early editions received a mixed reaction. The original compere was Lionel Gamlin, who introduced such features as Sandy Macpherson at the BBC Theatre Organ, a boxing serial, a topical talk, and 'These You Have Loved – a gramophone recital by Doris Arnold'.

The items were considered too worthy and not relevant enough to the men and women at whom they were aimed. After a number of complaints the producers decided to encourage the members of the Anti-Aircraft and Balloon Barrage units to contribute more to their own programme. Letters were sent to units around the country asking whether they had any singers, musicians, comedians, actors, authors or poets among their ranks.

In June 1941 Bill MacLurg, the producer of *Ack-Ack Beer-Beer*, wrote to the Entertainments Officer at No. 5 Centre in Sutton Coldfield to enquire if he could find out who might be available: 'a good band or orchestra and choir – and doubtless any amount of individual talent'.

Kenneth was given the job of finding the talent. In October he contacted MacLurg, who sent a memo to W.K. Stanton, the Programme Director of the Midland Region, saying; 'Squadron Leader Horne, RAF Balloon Command, has a show in Birmingham on Oct 23 which he says is very good and would like somebody from the BBC to see it. We wonder whether anybody from the M.R. staff could have a look at it?'

Stanton replied that he was extremely sorry but he had no one available to see the show: 'It is the old story: shortage of staff.' The concert went ahead as planned, but without anyone there from the BBC.

A month later, at the end of November 1941, Kenneth was transferred from Birmingham to No. 32 Group Headquarters at Claverton Manor, a large country house about two miles east of Bath, and his rank was confirmed as Acting Squadron Leader. Joan went with him and they moved into a very attractive house almost opposite the RAF station.

Kenneth was attached to the personnel office and his duties involved the legal aspects of service life, such as courts martial and courts of enquiry. When a local farmer demanded compensation for an injured horse after airmen had left open a gate on his land, Kenneth wrote in his official report: 'Judging by the value he puts on his horse, I can only assume that it is the original Weston super mare.'

He was required to serve his turn as Orderly Officer and one of his duties at Claverton Manor was a regular inspection of the fire escapes. One of them was a fixed metal ladder which ran from the roof of the dining hall up to a bathroom window on the top floor of the mansion. This was where the WAAFs were stationed and Kenneth was supposed to inform the WAAF Duty Officer whenever he was about to undertake an inspection. One day the message failed to be passed on. When Kenneth reached the top of the ladder he flung open the bathroom window to be greeted with a loud shriek from a totally naked WAAF about to enter her bath. In the Officers' Mess later that evening, Kenneth entertained his fellow officers with the story, concluding, 'She was a very smart girl, you know, she just grabbed a sponge and covered her face!'

In early 1942 the Commanding Officer at No. 32 Group was contacted by Bill MacLurg from *Ack-Ack Beer-Beer* to see whether the RAF station could put on a radio show using local talent, and Kenneth was ordered to organize it. Not only did he have to audition and select all the acts for the show but he also had to introduce them. It was to be the turning point in his life.

Kenneth made his broadcasting debut on 16 April 1942 from the BBC studios in Bristol in a special edition of *Ack-Ack Beer-Beer* called 'A Cable to the Sky' featuring 'artists from the personnel of a South-Western Group of the Balloon Barrage. Presented by Squadron-Leader Kenneth Horne assisted by Sergeant Bill Hall, under whose supervision the "Ballomets" provide the music throughout the programme.' The guest artist was John Dean, Kenneth's close friend from the D'Oyly Carte Company.

The standard of the amateur talent in the show was not exactly high and afterwards the West Region Programme Director wrote to Bill MacLurg: 'I must say I was not impressed.' MacLurg agreed and replied that he had gone lightly in his letter about the programme to Kenneth because he did not want to discourage him. But he added that it had been their first show and he felt the next one would be much better.

MacLurg may have had reservations about the local talent but he had been very impressed with the way Squadron Leader Horne had presented the show, and in particular the quiz. A few weeks later, on 28 May, he invited Kenneth up to London to take part in the 200th edition of *Ack-Ack Beer-Beer* at the Paris Cinema in Lower Regent Street. As Kenneth described it, 'I was roped in to do the quiz and it went from there.' Over the next two years he would present nearly fifty quizzes on the series. Without planning it, he had stumbled onto a new career.

Later he would comment, 'It certainly was never my intention to go into showbiz. I was a very serious young lad, educationally not very bright, not very erudite, but I did laugh at things all the time. The idea of standing up in front of an audience and trying to make people laugh, or thinking I was being funny at all, honestly didn't occur to me until it was forced on me.'

Kenneth was that great rarity, a natural broadcaster. He sounded confident and relaxed, talking to the contestants in the studio and the listeners at home in a warm, friendly voice. He also possessed an aura of authority gained from his experience as an officer and a sales manager. He attributed his easy microphone and stage manner to 'the Grace of God', his grandfather Lord Cozens-Hardy, the former Master of the Rolls, and the hard training of being 'a jovial chap among the golf and motoring fraternity'.

In August he presented a second edition of *Ack-Ack Beer-Beer* from Bristol called 'Going Up', featuring both Balloon Barrage and Ack-Ack personnel from the south-west in an effort to improve the standard of the talent. Kenneth covered most of the Division auditioning and choosing the best acts, and presented the programme with Lieutenant Sir Thomas Hood. This time the programme received some praise from the BBC top brass, who noted how much effort Kenneth had put into the show.

One night during the summer of 1942 Kenneth and Joan went out for dinner at the Swan Hotel in nearby Bradford-on-Avon. There was a party of WAAF officers sitting at one of the other tables and after a while Joan turned to Kenneth and confessed that she wanted to do more to help the war effort; she was thinking of joining the WAAF. Kenneth was quiet for a moment. They had been married for nearly six years and had spent barely a night apart from each other. They had a happy marriage. He may have had misgivings about how a separation might affect their relationship but he could hardly disagree with her motives and told her that he thought it would be a good idea.

The next day she telephoned an old school friend called Valerie St Ludger who was serving in the First Aid Nursing Yeomanry in Wiltshire, but not enjoying it. Joan persuaded Valerie to leave the FANYs and join her in the WAAF. A few days later Valerie and Joan went up by train to Birmingham, where they were met by their parents and taken to lunch at the Grand Hotel. It was an uneasy meal. Joan's mother supported her daughter's admirable desire to enlist but at the same time she felt dismayed about it, perhaps sensing that it would turn out to have unforeseen consequences.

Joan drove with Valerie up to RAF Bridgnorth in Shropshire, where they had been instructed to enlist. Within a few days, however, Valerie came down with mumps, so Joan had to join the WAAF on her own.

Her first posting was to an RAF station at Coleherne, near Bath, only about five miles from Claverton Manor. Now that she was an airwoman she was required to live on the station, but she was able to see Kenneth fairly regularly. At the earliest opportunity she applied for a commission and was selected for 'Administration'. She was sent to Windermere on a commission course, the first time she and Kenneth had been separated for any significant period.

After she was granted her commission, Joan was posted back to Fighter Command at Rudloe Manor, near Bath, and, as an officer, she was able to live with Kenneth once again in the nearby village of Corsham.

One of Kenneth's fellow officers at Claverton Manor was Edmund King, his partner-in-crime in the Lancegaye share debacle. King had been persuaded by Kenneth to join the RAFVR on the outbreak of war and had been posted to a Balloon Barrage unit in Smethwick. In 1942 he was transferred to No. 32 Group Head-quarters where, to his delight, he found that he was to share an office with Kenneth and a Flight Lieutenant Bazely. He was even more delighted on his first morning in the office when he discovered that the bottom drawer of the filing cabinet was packed with bottles of beer.

Kenneth enjoyed a laugh with his fellow officers but he took his responsibilities seriously and the successive promotions which took him from Pilot Officer to Wing Commander in less than four years could not have been achieved if he had not been extremely efficient at his job. His experience as a businessman meant he was used to making quick decisions but it had also taught him how to inspire loyalty among his men. In particular, he did not believe in too much pomposity among officers. One of his duties as Orderly Officer was to visit the Mess Hall with his NCO to oversee the meal of the other ranks. Other Orderly Officers would wear their hats while in the Mess Hall but Kenneth would always remove his and carry it under his arm. As he pointed out, he would not like anyone to walk through *his* dining room wearing a hat, so he was not going to do so either.

King recalled that period as his happiest year of the war and described Kenneth as the most popular man on the station, loved by everyone, from the officers to the other ranks.

Kenneth presented two more special editions of *Ack-Ack Beer-Beer* from Bristol in October and December 1942, which seem to have been well received, although there were some complaints about the tone of the comedy quiz, which involved a female officer having to simulate the sound of a kiss. A meeting was held between the BBC and the War Office at which it was decreed that 'a certain residuum of dignity must be retained by serving officers and men at the microphone'.

In January 1943 the BBC decided to update the series and make it more professional. From now on it would be a weekly broadcast on Mondays only, and would be produced in London, instead of twice-weekly from the regions.

Kenneth was invited to become one of the regular comperes on the new-style *Ack-Ack Beer-Beer* and on 25 January 1943 he presented the whole show for the first time from the Monseigneur

Studio in London. As a serving officer he was not supposed to be paid by the BBC, so he received thirty shillings in expenses and a donation of five guineas was made to the Air Officer Commanding's Benevolent Fund on his behalf.

Over the next five weeks he compered the show on three more occasions and also performed a five-minute comedy spot. He was spending more and more time in London, so it was probably no surprise when he was officially transferred on 29 March from Claverton Manor to the Administrative and Special Duties Branch at the Air Ministry in London.

Within a year his whole life would change.

6

Men from the Ministry

I<small>T WAS THE FIRST TIME</small> Kenneth had ever worked in London. He found himself a small flat in Kensington Close for a few weeks and then moved out to a new home at The Tiled Cottage at Beaconsfield, in Buckinghamshire, where Joan was able to visit him on the few occasions when she was allowed home on leave.

His first job at the Air Ministry was as an assistant to Wing Commander Christian Stock, who had also been at Claverton Manor. Meanwhile he continued to make regular appearances on *Ack-Ack Beer-Beer* as the compere and the question-master for the comedy quiz, which rapidly became one of the most popular parts of the show. He also wrote some comedy and dramatic sketches for the programme. Now that he was classified as a writer he was allowed to receive payment for his contributions, and in May he received his first official payment from the BBC, a fee of six guineas (six pounds and six shillings) for one of his scripts.

On 7 May 1943 Alfred Dunning, the producer of the series, sent a memo to the BBC Copyright Department:

> We are using a short dramatic sketch in 'Ack-Ack, Beer-Beer' on Monday 10 May written specially for this programme by S/Ldr Kenneth Horne.
>
> I should be glad if you could arrange fees for this sketch on the basis of eight minutes duration and the fact that S/Ldr Horne has on

several occasions in the past written and broadcast material for this programme and is a very capable writer.

Three weeks later another payment was requested for an eight-minute sketch by Kenneth entitled, 'Oh Haricot Where Have You Been?' or 'Curse You, Archibald'.

Now that he was based in London, Kenneth offered his services to a wartime organization called the Overseas Recorded Broadcast Service (ORBS), which recorded programmes for transmission to the allied forces in the Middle East. His experience on *Ack-Ack Beer-Beer* proved to be invaluable and he was taken on as a general announcer. The Controller of the ORBS was Harry Alan Towers, a prolific scriptwriter with more than two thousand radio programmes to his name, who was also the head of the RAF Radio Production Unit. He was impressed with his new announcer and in October Kenneth was booked to be the compere on the Air Force version of *Middle East Merry-Go-Round*, a weekly radio variety series that, uniquely, was devised and presented by the services themselves, with the Army, Navy and Air Force each taking turns.

The programme was recorded during the lunch hour at the Fortune Theatre in Covent Garden and on one show he had to introduce the well-known actor and comedian Richard Murdoch, who was now serving as a Flight Lieutenant in the RAF. To his surprise, Murdoch heard Kenneth announce, 'And now that you are round your radio sets, let's go over again to that well-remembered RAF station, which tonight comes off the secret list again, Much-Binding-in-the Marsh. And waiting at the gate to welcome you is its station commander, Flight Lieutenant Richard Murdoch . . .'

This was the first time Murdoch had ever heard of Much-Binding-in-the-Marsh. After the programme Kenneth invited him out to lunch, in the hope that Murdoch might be able to advise him about his radio career. They discovered that they had a lot in common; they were the same age, from upper-middle-class families with clerical connections, and they shared the same sense of humour. Murdoch had also been up at Cambridge, at Pembroke College, at the same time as Kenneth, although their paths had never crossed. Their experience there was remarkably similar. Murdoch used to say that his time at Cambridge was taken up with 'drinking, golf, cross-country running and the Footlights, although not necessarily in that order'. Like Kenneth, he got a half-blue, for athletics, and he was also sent down from the university for not doing enough work. Kenneth used to joke that 'Dick and I came down from Cambridge minus two degrees.'

Kenneth had recently been promoted to Acting Wing Commander and when Murdoch disclosed that he was not exactly happy in his present job, Kenneth mentioned that his Squadron Leader's post at the Air Ministry was up for grabs. Would Murdoch consider taking it? When it dawned on him that the promotion would mean not only a new rank but also more money, Murdoch answered, 'By Jove, yes!' It was the start of a great partnership.

Richard 'Dickie' Murdoch had started out in the 1930s as a song and dance man and juvenile lead in musical revues, and graduated to radio in the hugely popular pre-war radio series *Band Waggon*, in which he played the straight-man to the pint-sized Liverpudlian comedian Arthur Askey. Murdoch co-wrote the series, which ran from January 1938 to December 1939 and was the first regular weekly show on the BBC. It made household names overnight of Askey and Murdoch, who were supposed to be the official custodians of the Greenwich time-signal pips, living in the Top Floor Flat at Broadcasting House with their two pigeons, Basil and Lucy, and Lewis the Goat. The show also featured an assortment of memorable characters such as Mrs Bagwash, the charlady, and her daughter Nausea, who were often referred to but never heard.

Band Waggon was the first series to be designed specifically for radio, making good use of sound effects, and it was also the first to develop catchphrases, like Askey's 'Big Hearted Arthur, that's me!' and Murdoch's 'You silly little man'. It was Arthur Askey who gave Murdoch the nickname 'Stinker', which stayed with him for the rest of his life. The series came to an end when Askey became too busy with his films and stage shows, for which he was being paid up to £600 a week. The last broadcast on 2 December 1939, with its realistic departure of 'Big' and 'Stinker' from their famous flat, left many listeners in tears. A stage show toured the country for a while and they even made a film version in 1940 produced by Gainsborough, but then Richard Murdoch joined the RAF and *Band Waggon* was over.

Askey used to tell a story about how, after the evacuation from Dunkirk in June 1940, he went to entertain at an army hospital in Preston. He took along his entire stage show including the orchestra. It went down like a bomb with the patients, and at tea after the performance the commandant took Askey on one side and thanked him profusely for coming. Askey replied modestly, 'We don't want thanking after all those lads did for us at Dunkirk.'

'Dunkirk?' said the boss. 'None of this lot has been further than Blackpool. This is a VD hospital!'

At first Murdoch was a junior intelligence officer at Bomber Command before being posted to the Department of Allied Air Force and Foreign Liaison at Turnstile House in Holborn, where his job was to help in the administration of the Czechoslovak and Belgian squadrons. However, he was not very happy there. After having lunch with Kenneth in 1943, he agreed to join him at the Air Ministry in King Charles Street, off Whitehall, where they shared an office in a department called The Directorate of Administrative Plans. Their particular section was responsible for the supply of aircraft and spare parts to Russia. These were a gift from the Allies to assist the Russians on the Eastern Front and the job involved a lot of liaison work with the Russian Supply Missions. This meant that Kenneth and Richard were constantly being invited by the Russian Trade Delegation to drinks and parties at the Russian Embassy in Kensington Gardens.

After a while Kenneth thought they ought to reciprocate and he applied to the Finance Department at the Air Ministry for an allowance. He was granted a small amount per head from the Ministry and he and Richard took three Russians off to lunch at a restaurant in Charlotte Street, accompanied by Squadron Leader Pennington, who spoke Russian and would act as an interpreter.

The allowance from the Ministry was used up on the pre-lunch vodkas alone and Kenneth and Richard had to pay for the rest of the meal themselves. The party ended with numerous toasts of vodka and an exchange of dirty stories which kept Pennington busy with the two-way translation.

Back at the office they both felt rather the worse for wear and tossed a coin to see who would have the first nap. Kenneth won and was catching forty winks when the telephone rang. He awoke and lifted up his extension in time to hear an angry voice demanding, 'What about those Spitfires for Russia?' Richard, feeling tired and emotional, managed to mutter, 'Do nothing till you hear from me,' before he hung up the phone.

One day when Kenneth was on leave, Richard had to brief Quintin Hogg MP (later Lord Hailsham) with the exact number of tons of small arms ammunition and gallons of lubricating oil they had sent to the Russians, and then accompany him to a meeting of the War Cabinet chaired by Oliver Lyttelton, the Minister of State for War Production. Richard looked on in admiration as Hogg trotted out the figures as if he had compiled them himself.

The third member of their office was Squadron Leader Paul Bazely who, according to Richard, 'gave us a lot of laughs'. Kenneth was normally unflappable but one day a serious crisis blew up which even he felt unable to resolve. Bazely saved the situation. 'I know,' he said, as all eyes turned towards him, 'what about . . . a quick game of shovers?' The crisis was immediately forgotten as out of the filing cabinet he produced a shove-halfpenny board.

In June 1943 Kenneth heard the good news that his eldest brother Oliver had been awarded the MBE for his services to charity and to the banking industry. He sent him a note from Tiled Cottage:

My Brother Excels,

I am, of course, very annoyed that you should beat me to it, but in true British Sportsmanlike fashion (Schola Georgianae), I congratulate you! Ad hoc – sic transit & what ho.

Oliver Horne replied: 'My Brother Exaggerates, Many Better Entitled.'

Kenneth was continuing to appear weekly on *Ack-Ack Beer-Beer* and in October he was listed for the first time in the *Radio Times* as the Question-Master on 'Quiz Time', in a light-hearted contest between a team of three AA gunners and three female physiotherapy nurses from the Middlesex Hospital. A month later another team of nurses was pitted against a celebrity trio of Arthur Askey, Richard Murdoch and Charles Shadwell, the conductor of the BBC Variety Orchestra. The Comedy Quiz was now being described by listeners as 'one of the funniest moments of the week'. The BBC acknowledged that its growing popularity was due entirely to Kenneth, who had to devise all the questions as well as to ask them, and they increased his fee to seven guineas a programme.

Back in the office, Richard was intrigued by Kenneth's idea of a remote RAF station somewhere in England and thought there might be some mileage in it. The title was based on RAF slang. Anything tedious was often referred to as a 'bind', whereas 'binding' meant complaining or grumbling. In those days the RAF had numerous isolated country stations with names like Little Rissington, Upper Heysham and Moreton-in-Marsh, and so 'Much-Binding-in-the-Marsh' was born.

Together they developed the idea and expanded it, writing gags and situations which they would try out on the people in the office next door. One of them was Kay Bagley, a former WAAF Flight Officer who had been with Kenneth at Claverton Manor and had followed him to the Air Ministry. Later she would recall fondly, 'Ten minutes with Ken was better than a tonic. In that rich fruity voice of his he would make the dullest routine matter sound funny.'

The first public airing of their new 'Much-Binding-in-the-Marsh' routine was in *ENSA Half Hour* on 4 January 1944. Murdoch was the Station CO (Commanding Officer) at their imaginary RAF station in 'Laughter Command' and Kenneth was his superior, the rather dim-witted AOC (Air Officer Commanding), who visited the station weekly. The AOC was full of his own importance and liked to tell boring stories which would always begin, 'When I was in Sidi Barrani . . .', later to become a popular catchphrase. He also repeatedly stressed that he was 'a very busy man', but events always conspired to deflate his ego. On one of his first visits, the opening dialogue went:

HORNE: Sorry I'm late, Murdoch. I had a puncture.
MURDOCH: Oh, bad show, sir.
HORNE: Yes. Nearly threw me clean over the handlebars!

Some of the exchanges had a wonderful sense of the ridiculous about them:

MURDOCH: This is the cookhouse, sir.
HORNE: By Jove, it's hot in here. Do you mind if I take my other sock off?

Their routine must have gone down well because the ORBS encouraged them to do some more together. Kenneth's skill at handling quizzes was also being noticed and in February he began a new weekly series for the ORBS as the Quiz Master on *The Overseas League*.

Meanwhile *Ack-Ack Beer-Beer* was coming to an end and it was broadcast for the 324th and final time on 27 February 1944. The programme had enjoyed the longest run of any BBC variety series at that time, but the powers-that-be felt that it had served its original purpose and they wanted to redirect their programming towards the general armed services.

Kenneth compered the final edition, which included Gunner Moss, a singer, and Corporal Bill Waddington, a wise-cracking comedian. As usual Kenneth was the quiz-master and introduced the Comedy Quiz, which involved several amusing challenges. One was to sing the popular song 'Daisy, Daisy' in four different styles – soprano, dialect, hoarse and as a foreigner. Another was to recite the tongue twister 'A bike, a bagpipe and a pike'. One contestant had to make the sounds of a man pouring a drink: popping the cork, pouring the liquid from the bottle, adding a splash of soda from a siphon, and then drinking it – only to be told it was vinegar. The final challenge was to sing 'I've got a sixpence' while eating a mouthful of cake, with predictably hysterical results.

The General Officer Commanding made a speech praising the quality of the talent: 'The series was put on as a medium in which these men and girls doing no "cushy" job but serving their country in isolated places, facing blitzes, up to their knees in mud, could find expression. And what a number of musicians, artists, authors and poets have been discovered among them!'

At the end of the programme Kenneth said a fond farewell to the listening audience and the series was over. He had served his radio apprenticeship on *Ack-Ack Beer-Beer* and it was now time to move on.

Middle East Merry-Go-Round had been so popular with the troops abroad that the BBC decided to introduce it to home listeners as well. In March the series was broadcast for the first time on the new General Forces Programme, an expanded all-day version of the Forces Programme. Two weeks later, as the focus of the war moved towards Europe, the title of the series was changed to *Mediterranean Merry-Go-Round* but with the same personnel. The signature tune was 'The Army, the Navy and the Air Force', whistled by a forces audience at the start of each show, and it was billed as the series which 'week by week goes round the services bringing music and fun to boys and girls in khaki and two shades of blue'.

The amateur aspect of the series now began to be replaced with a more professional attitude, and the three service shows gradually evolved into regular formats. The Army segments starred Sergeant 'Cheerful' Charlie Chester from the Royal Irish Fusiliers in 'Studio Stand Easy', an energetic mixture of high-speed gags, sketches and songs, which featured recruits from 'Stars in Battledress'; while the Navy segment became 'HMS Waterlogged at Sinking-in-the-Ooze', starring Sub-Lieutenant Eric Barker and his wife, Wren Pearl Hackney, with Petty Officer George 'Hair' Crow and the Blue Mariners Dance Band.

The first broadcast of 'Much-Binding-in-the-Marsh' in the Air Force segment of *Mediterranean Merry-Go-Round* was on 31 March 1944. At first it had to share the airwaves with other RAF shows such as 'Ralph Reader and his Gang Show' and 'Café de NAAFI'. As a result, the second edition of 'Much-Binding' was not broadcast until six weeks later and the next edition was another twelve weeks after that. It was not exactly an overnight sensation, but the producer of the series, Leslie Bridgmont, liked the idea and it slowly began to catch on. Following the fourth programme at the end of October, the show was broadcast every six weeks.

This early series featured Kenneth and Richard with a number of guest stars, including Joyce Grenfell, Joan Winters and Binnie Hale, who used to be incorporated into the scripts and were always delighted to join in. One of the most popular characters was Flight-Officer Flannel, a hefty, hoarse-voiced WAAF officer, played originally by the vocalist Dorothy Carless and later by Binnie Hale and Doris Hare. The versatile Carless, in reality an attractive blonde, also played the Honourable Babs du Croix Fotheringham, known as Queenie for short, another WAAF stationed at 'Much-Binding' whose main dialogue was 'Okay, ducks!' The show was introduced by Flight Sergeant Anne Grisewood and the all-star RAF Orchestra was directed by Sidney Torch.

A popular feature was the 'Double or Quits Cash Quiz' conducted by Pilot Officer Roy Rich, in which contestants from the audience answered questions supplied by members of the three armed services. Competitors could select a subject from a list including: Animals, Current Affairs, Films, Food and Drink, Geography, History, Lucky Dip, Music, Radio, Sport, Theatre, and Tune Titles. The signature tune was 'We're In the Money' and the prize for the first correct answer was half-a-crown, doubling to five shillings, then ten shillings, and finally one pound, with the whole amount being forfeited if a wrong answer was given.

Another vital member of the 'Much-Binding' cast was to join the team during these early programmes. Leading Aircraftman Sam Costa had been a singer before the war, recording with some of the leading British bands such as Ambrose, Jack Hylton and Lew Stone. After joining the RAF, he had been posted to Iceland for ten months, which he found particularly depressing. Thinking that his singing days were probably over, he had decided to make a new start as a comic, and on his return to England had taken any broadcasting work he could find, more to break the monotony of his job and to get a trip to London than to make any money, as he was only being paid a nominal subsistence allowance of one guinea.

In 1943 he was booked to appear on a programme starring Richard Murdoch on ORBS. Richard's 'stooge' – the comedian meant to feed him his lines – had failed to turn up. Costa persuaded Richard to let him take the part of his stooge and Richard was impressed. Afterwards he told Costa that he was working on an idea with a chap called Kenneth Horne and there might be something in it for him.

A few months later Richard rang him and invited him to take part in 'Much-Binding'. Kenneth and Richard played the RAF officers but they needed someone to represent the other ranks. They had written some dialogue for an airman and Leading Aircraftman Sam Costa fitted the bill perfectly. Known on the show simply as 'Costa', he was the amiable chump who always got things wrong, driving his superiors mad. He became an essential member of the cast and his opening words, 'Good mornin', sir. Was there something?' soon turned into a national catchphrase.

In May 1944 Kenneth was booked to appear in another radio series called *Navy Mixture*. Now that he was becoming better known, he felt it was time for a pay rise from the BBC and he wrote to Arthur Brown, the Variety Booking Manager:

> I am returning the enclosed contract [for *Navy Mixture* at seven guineas] duly signed, but should be grateful if you would give consideration to my request that my fee should be increased to ten guineas.
>
> I have done a lot of work for the BBC, in 'Ack-Ack Beer-Beer', 'Mediterranean Merry-Go-Round' and other programmes, which necessitate not only a personal appearance, but also a great deal of scriptwriting.
>
> I am doing a 'Music Hall' during June and I am sure that you will agree that the work that I have done justifies an increase in fee.

His request was granted and Kenneth's new fee was fixed at ten guineas. Throughout his broadcasting career Kenneth never used an agent to negotiate his contracts and always dealt with the BBC booking managers personally. This meant that he was frequently paid less than his colleagues with aggressive agents, but on the other hand he developed good relationships with the all-important booking managers and he probably gained more work as a result.

During the summer of 1944 Kenneth appeared as a compere or quiz master in several variety series such as *Music Hall*, *Shipmates Ashore* and *Atlantic Spotlight*. At that time Richard Murdoch was the chairman of a weekly quiz called 'Puzzle Corner' in the popular series *Monday Night at Eight*. The fifth series was due to start on the Home Service in October and Murdoch persuaded the producer of the show, Harry S. Pepper, to book Kenneth as a writer, supplying gags, puzzles and ideas for the show. Eventually Kenneth would take over as the presenter of 'Puzzle Corner'.

In June the first German V-1 flying bombs landed on London, causing a considerable number of casualties. Air Ministry personnel were advised not to travel home at night and for a while Kenneth and Murdoch had to sleep in the sub-basement at King Charles Street. They called it 'The Dorm' and, apart from camp beds, it also contained a NAAFI canteen and a club bar decorated with murals by the *Punch* cartoonist David Langdon.

One night they returned to the Air Ministry after a late meal, turned down a wrong corridor and found themselves in the Ministry of Health building next door. Through an open office door they spotted a desk with an in-tray full of files. Together they sat down and went through the files, forwarding them to spurious departments and scribbling silly comments on the minute-forms. Next morning they felt rather embarrassed about their drunken escapade and thought they ought to apologize, but neither of them could remember the location of the office or how to find it.

On another occasion Kenneth and Richard were thrown into a panic when they heard that the Air Officer Commanding was on his way to make a surprise inspection of their office. Within minutes typewriters were clattering, signals were being sent to Archangel, and Kenneth and Richard were busy making phone calls to the Spitfire factory, the docks, the Ministry of Aircraft Production and even Moscow. The AOC made his inspection and was so impressed by the level of activity that he decided they must be understaffed and posted two additional WAAFs to help them handle the work.

Another prank that nearly backfired was when in an idle moment they filled out a form for a new course entitled 'Celestial Navigation', supposedly connected with teaching air crew to fly, and invited applications from WAAF officer cadets. They sent the form to another department, never expecting it to go any further, but it was passed from one office to another until it ended up being published in Air Ministry Orders.

Only one unsuspecting WAAF took the bait: LACW (Leading Aircraftwoman) Constance Weston, based at the RAF station at Boscombe Down in Wiltshire, spotted the new commission in the latest Air Ministry Orders posted on her station notice board. She duly attended a Selection Board at the Air Ministry in London but was surprised to find that they knew nothing about this new post. They advised her to find someone who would recommend her for it. She made enquiries around the Air Ministry but no one had ever heard of Celestial Navigation.

Eventually someone suggested that she might try Room 200. The two officers inside seemed to be rather amused when she explained her interest in Celestial Navigation but were very helpful and the senior officer happily signed her application form: C.K. Horne. W/Cmmdr. Orgs.

LACW Weston sent off the completed form and returned to Boscombe Down to await news about her application. She never heard another word and after a few months she was commissioned into the Intelligence Branch.

Some time later, another Air Ministry Order was published, cancelling the original one asking for officer cadets to apply for Celestial Navigation. It was only after the war, when Constance Weston read a newspaper interview with Horne and Murdoch which revealed the whole story, that she realized the whole thing had been a hoax.

7

Merry-Go-Round

T HE SUCCESSFUL LAUNCH of 'Much-Binding-in-the-Marsh' was not the only event that was to change Kenneth's life irrevocably in 1944. The other was totally unexpected. One day he opened a letter in his office at the Air Ministry from a woman inviting him to come round for a drink. Her name was Marjorie Thomas and she explained that they had been introduced at a cocktail party a few months earlier. Kenneth was not a great party-goer so he was fairly certain that he had never met this woman in his life, but his curiosity was aroused, so he rang the telephone number at the top of the expensive headed notepaper. When Marjorie Thomas answered the phone it soon became obvious that she had mistaken him for somebody else. 'You're not Wing Commander Kenneth Horne!' she protested. When he insisted that he really was, she recalled later that she was thinking, I wonder who I've written to?

Kenneth realized instantly that he had never met her before but he liked the sound of her voice and joked, 'I suppose that means the drink is off then?' Now it was her turn to be curious. He sounded pleasant and she had her daughter's nanny in the flat with her to act as a chaperone, so she told him, 'Come round and have a drink anyway.'

As soon as she had put down the phone Marjorie dashed along to the nanny's room in her large mansion flat in Kensington and told her to put on a clean dress and make herself look respectable.

When Kenneth arrived an hour or so later, however, it was not exactly love at first sight. She thought he was too tall, his feet were enormous, and the state of his shoes was 'shocking' – later she used to call them 'the boats'. But he did have a friendly manner and a good sense of humour so, perhaps intrigued, she agreed to join him for dinner and soon they were seeing each other on a fairly regular basis.

The mystery of the mistaken identity was easily explained when it transpired that Marjorie had heard Kenneth on *Ack-Ack Beer-Beer* and written to the BBC thinking that he was the dramatist Kenneth Horne, whom she had indeed met at a cocktail party. 'A friend had sent me some wonderful daffodils from the country – fifteen bowls of them,' she explained later, 'and it seemed a pity for them not be admired.' The BBC had forwarded her letter to the Air Ministry, where by an amazing coincidence the other Horne also worked as a Wing Commander. In 1942 Horne had enjoyed a successful West End run with his play *Love in a Mist* at St Martin's Theatre and he was to be frequently mistaken for Kenneth, and vice-versa.

Since Kenneth's promotion to the Air Ministry in March 1943, he and Joan had been leading virtually separate lives. Her duties as a WAAF officer meant that she was able to spend only the occasional leave at Tiled Cottage in Beaconsfield with him. It was during her second leave in 1944 that she realized something was wrong. It became obvious that Kenneth had fallen for someone else. Kenneth and Joan had been married for eight years and she was no longer the impressionable schoolgirl he had first met. Joining the WAAF, and being forced to live apart from him for the past year, had made her more resilient and independent. She had enjoyed the odd flirtation during their separation but these had been merely wartime romances and she still thought of herself as being firmly married to Kenneth. When the war was over, she expected them to resume their married life together. She had believed that Kenneth felt the same way.

After she had got over the initial shock, Joan thought long and hard about their future. She still loved Kenneth and would have been prepared to forgive him if he had shown any desire to continue with their marriage. Eventually she decided to confront him and ask if he wanted a divorce. To her surprise and dismay, he replied, 'I suppose it would be best.'

For the second time in his life, rather than try to save his marriage, Kenneth had given up without a fight. A friend who knew Kenneth later in his life believes that it would have been a different situation if his and Joan's baby had lived; he would have had a family and responsibilities. As it was, he felt able to leave Joan without looking back.

When Kenneth's mother heard the news she was distressed. For such a religious family, a second divorce after yet another brief marriage was considered to be both unacceptable and deeply embarrassing. His eldest brother Oliver was despatched to London to read Kenneth the riot act. It had absolutely no effect and Oliver's son John, who was sixteen at the time, thinks his father probably explained to Kenneth why he had come to see him and then took him out to dinner. On the journey home, Oliver Horne had a narrow escape when his train was machine-gunned by a German fighter plane and a bullet went right through his compartment.

A few weeks later Kenneth rang his old friend Edmund King at Claverton Manor. He explained that Joan had agreed to divorce him on the grounds of adultery but, in the legal requirements of the time, he had to supply her with the necessary evidence. There was no way he would allow Marjorie's name to be dragged through the courts so he needed to set up an assignation with a girl in a hotel bedroom. He wondered if King could suggest a suitable hotel near Bath and, more importantly, a girl who would be willing to be his co-respondent.

A few minutes after Kenneth had put down the phone, Edmund King heard a knock on his office door. It was the WAAF corporal who operated the telephone switchboard. She confessed rather sheepishly that she had been listening in to their conversation and volunteered her services as Kenneth's 'girlfriend' in his divorce case. She got the job.

The evening went off without a hitch and, on the morning after, Kenneth rang King to thank him for setting it all up so efficiently. 'What a jolly nice little girl,' added Kenneth. 'We played gin rummy all night and, do you know, she beat me hollow!'

At first glance, Kenneth's attraction to Marjorie Thomas is difficult to fathom. She was a petite brunette, even smaller in stature than Joan and very slim, with sharp, angular features. She was thirty-six years old, the widow of Second Lieutenant George Thomas of the Rifle Brigade, who had been killed at Calais in May 1940 during the evacuation from Dunkirk. She also had a young daughter, Susan, who was born in 1939 and never knew her father.

George Thomas had come from a family of wealthy wool brokers, originally from Yorkshire, and grew up in a large house called The Doune (now Broadlawns) in the village of Elstree, in Hertfordshire. By contrast Marjorie was from more humble origins. Her grandfather had been a missionary in China and her father, about whom she never spoke, was believed to have been an accountant but also an alcoholic. Her mother had died when Marjorie was fifteen and, curiously, it was the teenage girl who had to register her death; the whereabouts of her father at such an important time is unknown. Later Marjorie had met George Thomas on board a ship to New Zealand, where he was going to learn more about the wool business, and where she was going, with her sister, probably in search of a husband.

George Thomas had left Marjorie very comfortably off. She lived with Susan and a nanny-cum-housekeeper, whom she called 'Nurse', in a large luxuriously appointed flat at No. 10 Cottesmore Court in London W8. She was always immaculately dressed and gave the impression of being used to wealth and all its trappings. Perhaps she had simply grown accustomed to it.

Marjorie expected only the very best and from the outset Kenneth did his utmost to indulge her. Even though it was wartime, at least twice a week he would hire a Rolls-Royce and a chauffeur, Percy Millea, to take them out in the evenings to dinner and to the theatre. He must have been determined to impress her. Marjorie admitted later that she had not fallen for Kenneth straight away. She had been a widow for only five years and she was ambivalent about remarrying so soon. 'If your first marriage has been a success,' she observed, 'you've got to be pretty careful about the second one.'

She was also not convinced that her husband was dead. At the end of May 1940 she had received a telegram from the War Office informing her that Second Lieutenant George Thomas was 'Missing, presumed dead'. His body was never found, and for a long time Marjorie fantasized that he must have been badly burned and was being kept hidden away in a hospital somewhere.

Kenneth courted Marjorie assiduously for nearly two years during 1944 and 1945 before she finally agreed to marry him. His friends did not want him to wed her at all. They could tell that they were two very different people. Underneath his jovial exterior, Kenneth was a serious-minded businessman, whereas Marjorie was described as 'a bit of a flapper' and a 'flibbertigibbet', someone who loved gossip and cocktail parties. But she was stylish and elegant, perhaps more suited to his ambitions in life than Joan. She was also a mother, and Kenneth may have been attracted to the idea of acquiring an instant family.

At the beginning of 1945 his broadcasting career really began to take off. During the year he would make regular appearances on his own, or with Richard, on *Monday Night at Eight*, *The RCAF Show*, *Music Hall*, *The Will Fyffe Programme*, *Workers' Playtime*, *With a Difference* and a dozen other programmes. This is as well as co-writing and starring in 'Much-Binding-in-the-Marsh' every six weeks. His fee went up accordingly, from ten guineas to fifteen guineas. It was a good thing the war was drawing to a close, because he could hardly have spent much time behind his desk at the Air Ministry.

One of the most important programmes of the year was *Victory Night at Eight*, which was broadcast after VE Day on 14 May 1945. The show was actually recorded at the Paris Cinema a month earlier

and it was a remarkably lacklustre affair. One of the problems must
have been that everyone involved with the broadcast, from the cast
to the audience, knew that it was being recorded under false
pretences; victory in Europe was certainly drawing near but even at
that stage no one knew exactly when it was going to happen.

The cast included Kenneth and Richard, Arthur Askey, Ann
Todd, Cyril Fletcher and Joyce Grenfell. Listening to the programme now, the most noticeable aspect is the difference in comedy
styles. It was almost like a changing of the old guard. The show
started with Arthur Askey and Richard Murdoch reviving their old
partnership from *Band Waggon*, with Askey as the cheeky comedian
and Richard playing his straight-man:

MURDOCH: Now, can you sing Handel or Bach?
ASKEY: Well, I can sing Handel but I can't bark very well, I'm
afraid – I'll do my best. Woof, woof! My next, a blue Alsatian chow
hound – woof, woof! My next, a very small dog in America!
MURDOCH: Don't be funny.
ASKEY: Who's being funny?
MURDOCH: That's a matter of opinion.

And so on for several minutes. None of which produced much
laughter from the audience. This was followed by some very 'Odd
Odes' from Cyril Fletcher, including 'The Tale of Fanny Fannit'
(who had a set of teeth like granite). After a musical interlude, it was
the turn of Kenneth and Richard. Unlike the earlier music hall
routine with Askey, their humour was unforced, calmer and more
sophisticated, and they sounded so natural together, chatting like
two old friends, trying to do a crossword:

MURDOCH: Now then, here's one I'm absolutely stumped over.
Twenty-nine across. It's a three-letter-word beginning with 'F' and
ending with 'X', and the clue is 'Animal that steals chickens in
farmyards and is sometimes hunted by hounds.'

HORNE: Beginning with 'F' and ending with 'X', eh? What about Phoenix?

MURDOCH: 'Fraid not – one letter too many.

HORNE: 'Animal that steals chickens and is hunted by hounds' – it must be Dog.

MURDOCH: Well I tried that, but it made 'game played at the Wembley Cup Final' – Dootball!

Later the two of them introduced 'Puzzle Corner', which featured a typical mix of mystery voices, tongue twisters, spot the tune, and some clever quick questions:

Q: How do you pronounce CHO, PHO, USE?
A: Chophouse!
Q: How many months have thirty days?
A: All except February.
Q: A car and a train approach a level crossing – both are 100 yards away and going at 40 mph. How did the driver get across?
A: His widow bought one!

Kenneth's divorce case was heard on 13 April 1945. By then Joan had been demobilized from the WAAF and had returned to live with her parents in Birmingham. Her father took her down to London and after the decree nisi was granted successfully, he treated her to a week at the Imperial Hotel in Torquay to raise her spirits. In an extraordinary twist of fate, while she was there Joan met a young RAF bomber pilot who was convalescing in Torquay, and fell in love with him. They were married later that year and enjoyed a long and happy life together.

After the end of the war with Germany the BBC disbanded the General Forces Programme and on 29 July it was relaunched as the Light Programme (now Radio Two), the entertainment alternative to the existing Home Service (now Radio Four), which contained more high-brow news and talks programmes. When Japan surrendered on 14 August, Kenneth returned instantly to civilian life. The end of the war meant that his job at the Air Ministry no longer existed. Two days later he took part in a special *Victory Party* on the new Light Programme and at the end of August he was officially released from service with the rank of Wing Commander. After the war all businesses were required by law to provide work for former employees who had been called up to the armed forces. Kenneth was now free to return to Triplex in his new position as General Sales Manager, no doubt awarded to him on merit, although it cannot have done any harm that his cousin Sir Harry Pilkington served on the board of Triplex and was also a member of its sales committee. Kenneth notified the BBC that with immediate effect his contracts were to be addressed to Kenneth Horne Esquire, at 1 Albemarle Street, W1.

The Triplex head office was at the corner of Albemarle Street and Piccadilly, in a historic building which had once been the exclusive Albemarle Hotel, whose most famous resident was Lillie Langtry, known as 'The Jersey Lily', the mistress of King Edward VII.

Kenneth threw himself into his work. He was determined to succeed in business and he took his job at Triplex very seriously. As far as he was concerned, his radio career was still a hobby; the money and the prestige lay in his position at Triplex. He was reported to have turned down an offer of £250 a week, a significant amount of money in those days, to become a full-time professional comedian, touring the music halls and variety theatres. 'I have seen too many stars come and go to be attracted to the footlights,' he said. Kenneth was once asked why he pursued both careers simultaneously and his reply was that he loved doing them both, but he admitted freely that if forced to choose, he would have given up radio first. At first it was relatively easy to combine the two. He worked from 9 a.m. until about 5.30 p.m. every weekday at Albemarle Street and then wrote the 'Much-Binding' scripts with Richard Murdoch at the weekends.

After the end of the war the BBC decided to cancel the other Air Force programme in the *Merry-Go-Round* series, which had featured the RAF Orchestra directed by Flight Lieutenant Sidney Torch, with various guest artists, and from the end of September 'Much-Binding' was broadcast every three weeks.

Richard once described writing scripts with Kenneth as 'pure joy'. He had exactly the same kind of humour and they used to write down pages of funny material in long hand, taking it in turns with a pen or pencil. One afternoon at about four-thirty, Kenneth suddenly said, 'Wouldn't it be fun if we had a song that began "At Much-Binding-in-the-Marsh" and went on from there?' Richard thought it sounded like a good idea and, between them, they knocked together a tune and each wrote two verses.

That evening they were due to broadcast 'Much-Binding' at the Paris Studio and when they arrived at six o'clock they hummed the melody to Sidney Torch, who worked out some chords for it on his Hammond organ. He scribbled out a top-line and that night at about seven-thirty, they sang it live on the show for the first time. From then on the song would end every programme and they would eventually write more than five hundred verses for it.

At Much-Binding-in-the-Marsh,
Our aeroplane's a thing we're very keen on,
At Much-Binding-in-the-Marsh,
It's used for WAAFs and bicycles to lean on,
Although the undercarriage isn't what it used to be,
And though the rudder blew away in 1943,
The radiator still provides hot water for our tea,
At Much-Binding-in-the-Marsh.

At Much-Binding-in-the-Marsh,
Security has never been neglected,
At Much-Binding-in-the-Marsh,
We're careful that our station's not detected,
To camouflage the aeroplane instead of using net,
The other day we painted it and much to our regret,

We did it so successfully we haven't found it yet,
At Much-Binding-in-the-Marsh.

Later they added a few extra touches to the song. Before the war Richard had appeared in the West End musical *Over She Goes*, which featured a song by Billy Mayerl called 'Side by Side'. It had four verses, with the music rising by half a tone each verse to give it some brightness. They borrowed that idea for their 'Much-Binding' song and also added two 'dog-ears' at the end of the final verse, two complete non-sequiturs such as 'What's for breakfast?' or 'Splice the main brace!' or 'How's your father?' – anything that would fit the metre.

On one show Richard sang 'Tumby Woodside', which mystified the comedian Bob Monkhouse and probably most of the audience. Afterwards Richard explained to Monkhouse that he often had to look up trains to Tunbridge Wells and had noticed that the next station listed in the ABC railway timetable was Tumby Woodside. He always thought it sounded rather a nice place, so he had simply put it in the song.

The pair became so adept at writing verses for the song that they could make them up on the spot if necessary. During one programme they suddenly realized that they had written only three verses instead of the usual four. They waited until Stanley Black and the orchestra were playing a musical number and then huddled together in a corner of the studio, scribbling words frantically on the back of a script. Within three minutes the verse was written and about ten minutes later they were singing it on air.

Sometimes they simply could not make the verses rhyme, which led to the following wonderful example:

At Much-Binding-in-the-Marsh,
We're very keen on higher education,
At Much-Binding-in-the-Marsh,
We always try to learn something that's useful.

We're very keen on languages, we often study Greek,
Experiments in science keep us busy every day,
And when we're in despair we often make up rhymes like this,
At Much-Binding-in-the-Marsh.

The show began to attract some favourable reviews in the national press. One uncredited press cutting pasted into Richard's scrapbook from that period declares:

'Merry-Go-Round' lives up to its name. It does go round, and it is certainly merry. This show moves steadily up in order of merit. When it is as good as it was last Friday the category becomes No. 1. Perhaps it is that Dickie Murdoch and Kenneth Horne can not only write a good script, but one which fits their own personalities like a glove. Here, obviously, are a pair of first-class scripticians (oh, my word!) Other artists might take the hint. Write your own stuff and you can't put the blame on the gag merchant!

After six months Kenneth's decree absolute from Joan came through at the end of October and he married Marjorie Thomas on Friday, 2 November at Caxton Hall in Westminster. It was a very quiet wedding. Percy Millea collected them in his Rolls-Royce and drove them to the Bristol Grill, where they were supposed to meet Richard Murdoch, who was their best man. However, Richard never turned up and they had to leave without him. In the end, they were married in the presence of Percy Millea and the Registrar's clerk.

Three weeks later Kenneth and Richard were guests on *Vic Oliver Introduces* – a 'Programme of Stars, Personalities, Songs and Music' – hosted by the popular comedian, who gave them an enthusiastic introduction: 'Two guests for the price of one – and WHAT guests! They're crazy – they're original – they're funny – and their double-act has been one of the greatest radio discoveries of the war.'

On Christmas Day 1945 there was a special edition of 'Much-Binding':

HORNE: Well, that was a wizard lunch, Murdoch.

MURDOCH: I am glad you enjoyed it, sir.

HORNE: By Jove, yes! One of the nicest sandwiches I've ever had. What was in it, Murdoch?

MURDOCH: Well, there was – er – have you read any good books lately?

HORNE: I thought it tasted something like that.

Since their first meeting at the end of 1943, Kenneth Horne and Richard Murdoch had become the most popular new comedy double-act on the radio. They had come a long way in only two years.

8

Much-Binding-in-the-Marsh

THE LAST EDITION of 'Much-Binding-in-the-Marsh' as part of the *Merry-Go-Round* series was broadcast on 1 February 1946. It ended with Richard and Kenneth saying goodbye to each other as civilians once more and walking off in different directions.

There had been only twenty editions in all, but the RAF station in 'Laughter Command' had cemented itself so firmly into the public consciousness that the BBC was anxious to turn the idea into a series of its own. When Richard Murdoch told them he would be unavailable for several months because he was embarking on a nationwide tour, in a musical revue produced by the theatre impresario George Black, BBC officials seriously considered doing the series without him.

The Acting Controller of the Light Programme, T.W. Chalmers, sent a memo to the Director of Variety, Pat Hillyard, saying that he was 'most loath' to let the idea of 'Much-Binding' go by default simply because Richard was no longer available. He asked Hillyard to see whether he could devise a treatment for a series based on the title 'Much Binding Enterprises Ltd.' which would be set in a factory.

Chalmers suggested that they could create a perfectly good comedy show by teaming Kenneth Horne and Sam Costa with Eric Barker, from the Navy edition of *Merry-Go-Round*, or even the veteran comedian Robb Wilton, who would play a resident government inspector or factory-personnel-and-entertainments-

manager. The factory location would give them plenty of opportunity for importing guest artists to entertain the workers and
Richard would be reduced to being a 'sleeping partner', always
sending letters of advice and making telephone calls, but never,
except perhaps once a year, coming down to the factory itself.

With the BBC uncertain about whether or not to commission a
new series and Richard away on tour, Kenneth found himself in
demand on his own. In February 1946 he signed a contract to supply
ideas and gags and to attend script conferences for the radio series
Howdy Folks Again, a satirical revue devised and produced by Leslie
Bridgmont. It was a revival of a series originally broadcast in 1940,
and starred the comedy double-act Nan Kenway and Douglas
Young playing several roles, including the food-conscious Mr Grice,
an ancient rustic with the catchphrase, 'Very tasty, very sweet!'

He also took on a new role in the popular series *Monday Night at
Eight* as host of 'Monday Birthday Party', in which well-known
personalities celebrating a birthday that week were given 'The
Freedom of the Air' to fulfil a personal wish or ambition. Their
wishes could be anything from hearing a favourite song to riding on
a rollercoaster, and during the series they included a broadcast from
down a coal mine, a trip to Paris, and even a visit to South Africa.

In March Kenneth was booked to co-star with Arthur Askey in a
new comedy series called *Forever Arthur*, which was set in a
lighthouse. Despite an increasing demand for his services as a writer
and performer, the BBC was reluctant to increase Kenneth's fee.
They seemed to consider that his business career meant they could
get away with paying him less than his colleagues. In March he fired
off a letter to the BBC's Variety Booking Manager, Arthur Brown:

Like a good boy I have signed and returned the contracts for
'Monday Night at Eight' and the 'Arthur Askey Show'.

I had hoped that, as a result of our last talk, during which we
agreed to defer any discussion on sordid financial details until after
'Howdy Folks' [then scheduled for six broadcasts only], some

suggestion about an increase in payment might have emanated from the BBC.

In my business, if I think one of my employees is doing well and is worth the money, I offer him an increase <u>before</u> he approaches me to ask me for one.

It may be, of course, that the powers that be do not think I am worth more than my present fee – if that is so, then there is no more to be said.

Let it be quite clear, however, that the fact that I have another job cannot conceivably make any difference to your decision – nearly everyone who performs for the BBC has another job, some on the 'Halls', some on Films. The fact that my alternative job happens to be a normal business one does not alter the position one whit.

Will you think the matter over please, because I do feel just a fraction upset about the whole thing.

After further heated correspondence, the BBC finally agreed to increase his fee to twenty guineas per programme. Meanwhile Kenneth wrote another letter to Arthur Brown, this one rather more tongue-in-cheek:

I have noticed recently that almost all the well known BBC artists are now announced as appearing by kind permission of someone, presumably their agent. Alternatively, they are billed and announced as at present appearing in such and such a show.

Under the circumstances, I would be grateful if you could arrange that when my name is mentioned on the air in future, it should be followed by a statement to the effect that I am appearing by kind permission of the Chairman and Managing Director of the 'Triplex' Safety Glass Company. May I have your confirmation that this is in order.

Kenneth's letter was only half-serious but Arthur Brown dismissed his suggestion out of hand, urging him not to 'press your request'.

Faced with such a total lack of humour, Kenneth threw in the towel: 'With regard to the question of any acknowledgement in the programmes, as this seems to be of great worry to you I shall not press the matter any further, at the moment.'

It was a difficult period of transition at Triplex. After the war the company had faced the challenge of having to re-equip its factories, in some cases dismantling machinery which had been manufacturing munitions for seven years, and change them over from wartime to peace production; extra staff had to be recruited and existing staff retrained. There was no shortage of orders from car manufacturers but the costs of glass, labour and manufacturing had increased by up to 60 per cent since before the war, while the price of the new Triplex toughened glass had been raised by less than 20 per cent. For the year ending 30 June 1946 the company announced a substantial net trading loss of £26,847. Westcote Lyttleton, the co-founder of the Triplex company in 1912, decided to retire, and his place on the board was taken by Kenneth, who was promoted to Sales Director.

The BBC was still trying to come up with a format for a series based on 'Much-Binding' and in August the producer Michael North wrote to the Acting Assistant Director of Variety, C.F. (Mike) Meehan, suggesting a series for Kenneth and Richard running a crammer for backward boys, with Richard attending to the scholastic side and Kenneth to the administration. The pair would be 'very nice rogues'. The school would be by the seaside and enormous fees would be charged from unsuspecting parents. He added that Kenneth and Richard 'seem very attracted to the idea'.

This new proposal met with instant approval and three days later Meehan gave the go-ahead for a series of twelve programmes of *Crammers* to begin in January 1947 on the Light Programme.

After *Forever Arthur* ended its run in September, Kenneth was booked to take part in a brief series called *Heigh Ho*, which was intended as a showcase for Peter Waring, a conjuror-comedian who had been a big success at the Windmill Theatre. Written by Frank

Muir, the series also included Charmian Innes and Maurice Denham, and featured Kenneth as 'Uncle Eustace'. Peter Waring was a so-called 'sophisticated' comedian who had acquired the mannerisms of a languid man-about-town, complete with a long cigarette holder, and was being hailed as a great new talent. Shortly before the first broadcast, however, the BBC discovered that in reality Waring was an ex-jailbird who had once worked for the BBC in the accounts department before disappearing with the funds. It was too late to cancel the series, which had been booked for an initial six programmes, but after that, the BBC felt they could no longer employ him. Waring was later convicted of fraud and sent to prison, where he committed suicide.

In October Kenneth began another series of *Monday Night at Eight*, which would run for several months, and he was also due to start the new series of *Much-Binding-in-the-Marsh*, which had now reverted to its original title. In previous years he had politely requested an increase in his broadcasting fee from the BBC but now he was no longer prepared to negotiate, especially with Arthur Brown. In November he wrote to Brown to inform him that, with effect from 1 January 1947, his normal fee would go up from twenty guineas to thirty guineas. For scripted shows such as *Much-Binding*, he would also expect an additional fee of twenty-five guineas for scriptwriting.

This put the cat among the pigeons at the BBC. Kenneth was hoping for a rise from twenty to thirty guineas, whereas Richard Murdoch was already being paid forty guineas a programme and, unknown to Kenneth, his agent Julius Darewski had just demanded an enormous increase to a hundred guineas for his performance and for co-writing the scripts.

In a revealing memo to Pat Hillyard, the Acting Director of Variety, Arthur Brown described Kenneth as being 'not of course a professional artist; he is in effect an amateur', although he went on to concede that the success of *Much-Binding* was due equally to him and to Richard. In the end the BBC acquiesced to both requests and paid Kenneth a fee of thirty guineas per programme and Richard a fee of a hundred guineas, out of which he was expected to pay Kenneth twenty-five guineas for his share of the script. This arrangement lasted for about a year but Kenneth was never happy about receiving his script fee from Richard's agent, and in the end he insisted that it be paid direct to him by the BBC.

Richard was notoriously shy when it came to discussing money. His son Tim recalls an occasion when the comedy writer Frank Muir came round to the Murdoch home to talk about a new script. When the subject of money came up, Richard was so embarrassed that he drew all the curtains in the sitting room, turned off the lights, and insisted that the two of them sat there in the dark while they negotiated the fee.

The first series of *Much-Binding-in-the-Marsh* started on 2 January 1947. It consisted of thirty-eight weekly half-hour shows and an August Bank Holiday special and was transmitted on Thursday evenings, generally at 7.30 p.m. The cast was Kenneth and Richard, with Sam Costa, Marilyn Williams, Vivien Chatterton, Maurice Denham and Dick Griffin, with music provided by the Augmented Dance Orchestra, conducted by Stanley Black.

Music played a very important role in the programme. In those days almost all radio comedy shows were divided into three segments with a musical interlude between each part, often featuring a girl singer, or a vocal group, and a full orchestra. Even *The Goon Show*, which broke all the other rules of comedy, had two musical interludes. Many comedians and writers believed that audiences needed a break after eight minutes of laughter to recharge their batteries, and the practice would continue until the days of *Round the Horne* in the late 1960s, when BBC cutbacks forced producers to dispense with their resident singers and bands.

The idea of setting the series in a crammer for backward boys had eventually been rejected in favour of a return to basics. After all, why change a winning formula? The premise of the opening programme was that the old RAF station at Much-Binding-in-the-Marsh was being put up for sale at auction, and the two former RAF officers, Murdoch and Horne, were both interested in making a bid for it. By coincidence, they travelled together in the same railway carriage on the way to the auction, although at first they failed to recognise each other:

> MURDOCH: ... Well, it takes all sorts to make a world.
>
> HORNE: I suppose it does. Mind you, when I was in Sidi Barrani ...
>
> MURDOCH: Good heavens! I know a chap who used to say that.
>
> HORNE: Oh, who was he?
>
> MURDOCH: Oh, rather a pompous old poop – RAF type. Mind you, I must confess that if it wasn't for your moustache you would be quite like him.
>
> HORNE: But I haven't got a moustache.
>
> MURDOCH: Good heavens, then it must be – I say, sir, surely you remember me? I used to be under your command.
>
> HORNE: Why, of course, it's Corporal Spenlove-Enthover.
>
> MURDOCH: Not exactly, sir. I'm Murdoch.
>
> HORNE: Well, aren't I a silly old fossil?
>
> MURDOCH: Yes, sir. You haven't changed a bit.
>
> HORNE: Nor have you, Murdoch. I would have recognised you anywhere.
>
> MURDOCH: So would I.

They ended up buying the dilapidated old RAF station and set about turning it into the Much Binding Country Club, which they ran from an old Nissen hut, with the 'help' of the faithful Costa. The *Radio Times* of 27 December 1946 said of the new series: 'Richard Murdoch has decided to convert his once famous aerodrome into a roadhouse and from what we remember of the flying field this can be used as the bathing pool – a building permit won't be necessary.'

In the early days of the series, the senior member of the partnership was undoubtedly Richard, because of his previous radio experience, and he always got top billing. In fact the first editions of the series were listed as: 'Richard Murdoch in *Much-Binding-in-the-Marsh*, with Kenneth Horne'. Soon the pair would be regarded more as equals but the opening format of the show remained essentially the same.

After the signature tune, the announcer, usually Philip Slessor, would declare, 'Much Binding takes the air!' Kenneth would then make a brief introduction, before saying, 'Here he is, your old friend, Richard Murdoch!' Richard would do his solo spot outlining the 'news' that week in Much Binding, followed by a piece of music from Stanley Black and the orchestra. Then Kenneth would enter, greeted by Richard with the words, 'Good morning, sir. It *is* good to see you,' and they would be off, gradually bringing in the other characters one by one.

The scripts were so well written that many listeners thought the cast made them up as they went along. Sam Costa once described being on the programme as 'money for old rope', because they all enjoyed themselves so much.

HORNE: Why has this chap Costa been allowed to meddle with the accounts?
MURDOCH: Well sir, we thought he was the ideal man to deal with figures on account of his peacetime occupation.
HORNE: Oh, and what was his peacetime occupation?
MURDOCH: Stagehand at the Windmill Theatre!

In the seventh show the cast were joined by Maurice Denham, once described by Richard as a 'vocal chameleon', and while the rest of the cast effectively played themselves, he took on more than sixty different roles. He played almost every other character on the show including Group Captain Funny-Bone, Lieutenant-General Sir Harold Tansley Parkinson, Ivy Clingbine, Winston the dog, Gregory the sparrow, Nigel the silkworm and Mr Blake the Sexton (after the radio detective Sexton Blake), an incomprehensible country yokel whose entire vocabulary seemed to consist of 'Ooh-argh-um-er-ee'.

Denham could change voices so quickly that he would often play several different parts in one sketch. When he received a new script, sometimes he would turn over a page to find he had to play the part of a pregnant yak. 'It was bit disconcerting,' he remarked later, 'but it was definitely a challenge!'

In one episode Kenneth and Richard walked down the street from the Country Club to the Everything Shop in 'Little Binding', saying hello and good morning to a number of villagers in quick succession, all played by Denham: Mr Blake the Sexton, the Vicar, Miss Ivy Clingbine, Percy, and Mrs Dimsdale. Then Richard added an unscripted, 'Good morning, Mr Denham,' and there was a momentary pause as Denham tried to remember how to answer in his own voice.

His most popular character was the well-spoken Dudley Davenport, who had a wonderful laugh, written in the scripts as 'Keogh-keogh-keogh!' He used to announce himself briskly with the words, 'Dudley Davenport at your service, sir!', and his closing remark was always an embarrassed, 'Oh, I say, I am a fool!'

Kenneth usually played himself because he was notoriously bad at doing accents. Denham recalled, 'If Kenneth had to play, for instance, a Scot or a foreigner, he'd become so Scottish or so foreign it was ludicrously funny. The voice sounded so wrong coming out of him.'

The strength of the series lay in the comic personalities of Kenneth and Richard, once defined as being 'a pair of intellectual buffoons'. Kenneth was stolid and reliable, whereas Richard was more light-hearted and frivolous. The comedian and scriptwriter Bob Monkhouse used to listen to the programmes when he was a teenager during the war, and he recalled in admiration, 'You could laugh at "Much-Binding" for half an hour and yet find no lines, other than catchphrases, that you could repeat to your friends and get a laugh with.'

Every member of the cast had their own catchphrase. Vivien

Chatterton used to play the frail old spinster Louisa Goodbody, who was always ready to 'have a bash', while Richard had 'Read any good books lately?' which was usually muttered when he wanted to change the subject, and 'It takes a long time to warm up!' He would also announce suddenly, 'I have an idea, sir,' to which Kenneth would always exclaim, 'You haven't, Murdoch!' before receiving the hesitant reply, 'Yes, I have, sir – I think.'

Kenneth loved to use long words and would slip one into the script whenever he could – one of his favourites was 'floccinaucinihilipilification'. His most famous phrase was 'Not a word to Bessie about this, Murdoch', referring to his wife, who was never heard. Similarly Sam Costa used to mention his wife, Emily, and her 'twinges' every week, and another character called Charlie Farnsbarns, whose name became a part of the language, although he never actually appeared on the programme.

He was not the only character who was never heard. Towards the end of 1945, Kenneth had been sitting on board a train at Manchester Station when a man entered his carriage and lifted up his suitcase onto the luggage rack. 'I'm afraid, sir,' Kenneth had informed him with a smile, 'you will have to get out of this carriage. It's reserved for women only!' It was Edward Wilkinson, his RAF driver from the early days of the war at A. Flight Headquarters in Birmingham. They had renewed their friendship during the train journey and after that, whenever he was in London, Wilkinson would call in to see Kenneth at his flat.

One evening Wilkinson was listening to one of the *Much-Binding* programmes when he was amazed to hear Kenneth ask Richard, 'By the way, Murdoch, have you seen Edward Wilkinson lately?' There was a fractional pause before Richard replied, 'No, I haven't, sir. I think he's probably wintering in Sidi Barrani.'

After that obviously unscripted moment, the name 'Edward Wilkinson' seemed to crop up without any explanation in almost every programme. Puzzled listeners began to write in to the BBC, wondering who this chap was or whether he even existed. It got to the point where Wilkinson had only to give his name for people to ask, 'Oh! Are you *the* Edward Wilkinson from "Much-Binding-in-the-Marsh"?' Kenneth kept a file of letters from all over the country by people named Edward Wilkinson, demanding to know why he kept mentioning their name on the programme.

Because Kenneth was so busy working at Triplex, the only time he and Richard could write the scripts together was at the weekends. Sometimes they would meet on a Saturday at the Royal Automobile Club in Pall Mall, where they would sit at a small round table in the writing room and stare bleakly at each other, trying hard to come up with something new. Occasionally Richard would visit Kenneth at Cottesmore Court, where Marjorie was careful not to interfere. 'Only twice did I offer suggestions to Kenneth and Richard when they were writing scripts,' she would reveal later, 'but they told me my ideas were no good. However, to my surprise, they did use them in their next radio show and I've been teasing them ever since.'

More often than not, on Sundays Kenneth would drive down to the Murdoch family home in Staines, and later Tunbridge Wells, where Richard's daughters Belinda and Jane would be waiting at the gate for him. After Sunday lunch the two men would go into Richard's study and the family would be asked to keep the noise down while they were working. As Belinda remembers, 'You'd hear quiet voices and then Kenneth's deep laugh, and they'd be off.'

Richard once admitted that he was the one who always wanted to do something else and it was Kenneth who kept him working and made him do it. Occasionally they would take a break and ride around the garden on a little Corgi motorbike, but eventually the script would get written.

Maurice Denham recalled, 'Richard was a very witty man and had this butterfly mind, with wonderful flights of fancy. The trouble was, he used to turn up with odd bits of paper and the backs of envelopes with all these ideas on, and Kenneth had the job of trying to pin him down and get a coherent script.'

Sometimes invention would flag and the script would just say 'Village Concert' and underneath, 'Costa–solo piece', or 'Dudley Davenport–solo piece', which meant that Costa and Denham had to write their own party pieces. It gave the other cast members a chance to shine and Denham once said that he found many of his characters that way. Richard's speciality was to sing rapid parodies of fast tunes such as 'Sabre Dance' and 'Nola', with titles like 'My Aunt's name is Ella Wheeler Waterbutt.'

After a while Kenneth and Richard developed a shorthand for some of their catchphrases and the script would read simply 'GMSIIGTSY' for 'Good morning, sir, it is good to see you' or 'OISIAAF' for 'Oh I say, I am a fool'. If Kenneth was required to do his silly laugh they would put 'LLD' for 'Laughs like a drain'. Leslie Bridgmont's secretary Margaret Hearne became adept at deciphering their scribbled hieroglyphics and notes which were often pencilled on the backs of envelopes. One which defeated even her, however, was 'ATDSTWADHF' which meant: 'Angry Taxi Driver Shouting Through Window and Demanding His Fare.'

The first series of *Much-Binding-in-the-Marsh* was a triumph. By the end of its run in September 1947 it had overtaken the most famous comedy show of the war years, *ITMA,* or *It's That Man Again,* starring Tommy Handley, to become the most popular series on the BBC. The success of the show meant that Kenneth and Richard were forced to cut back on some of their other radio programmes. With its two repeats, *Much-Binding* was heard three times a week and a memo was sent out that the pair were not to be booked for any other programmes until further notice, although Kenneth's regular booking on *Monday Night at Eight* would be allowed to continue. This led to an unexpected twist one week when the 'Birthday Star' was his namesake Kenneth Horne, the playwright with whom Marjorie had once confused him when she wrote to the BBC.

In the final 'Monday Birthday Party' of the series, one of the guests wished to hear his old regimental march played on the bagpipes, which was followed by Kenneth attempting to play the bagpipes himself, with predictably disastrous results. The final 'request' (surely with a little prompting from the producer) was to hear Richard Murdoch up in an aeroplane – in all the wartime episodes of *Much-Binding*, even though he was the CO, he had never actually managed to fly because their aircraft were permanently grounded, 'due to the tremendous shortage of elastic'.

Richard was sent up in a de Havilland Dragon Rapide, a twin-engine biplane, and 'live' on air, circling over Herne Hill in south-east London, he had to sing a duet of the 'William Tell Overture' from the plane with Kenneth back in the studio. Somehow the two of them made the whole crazy idea work.

Now that he was a radio celebrity Kenneth received frequent letters from people wanting to know how to break into broadcasting. In June 1947 he forwarded a typical letter to David Manderson, the Drama Booking Manager and received the following reply:

> My in-tray overflows with similar enquiries to the one which I now return to you. Our 'official' reply in such instances is to regret that 'applicants for auditions for the London wave-lengths must be full-time professional artists. As you do not come into this category, there is nothing we can do to help you.'
>
> At least one recipient of such a note rang me up and said, 'Ah well! What about Kenneth Horne?' So you see the sort of thing you have let us in for! You will appreciate that we are closely watched by the Actors' trades union organisation, which is trying hard to create a 'closed shop' – of that there is little doubt.

By the end of June 1947 Triplex had staged a dramatic recovery. After the losses in the previous year, the company was able to announce a profit of £91,000. Sir Graham Cunningham, the Chairman and Managing Director, declared that, as a result of the efforts of Sales Director Kenneth Horne and his general sales manager Jack Follett, the company now counted among its customers nearly every car manufacturer in Britain, more than two dozen of them, from Alvis, Austin and Bentley to Triumph, Vauxhall and Wolseley. Kenneth was on his way to becoming one of the most influential figures in the motor industry.

After only a two-month break, the second series of *Much-Binding-in-the-Marsh* began on 26 November 1947. It was reduced to thirty shows, with an Easter special, and the transmission time was switched to Wednesday evenings, in a slot varying between 7.30 and 10 p.m. on the Light Programme. It went out at so many different times during the first twelve weeks that in February 1948 Kenneth wrote to the BBC saying that he had been inundated with complaints from listeners. The BBC replied citing 'technical reasons of programme planning' as the cause of the variations in transmission time but it was eventually fixed at 7 p.m.

In the second episode the new Much Binding Country Club was officially opened by the glamorous British film actress Patricia Roc, who had recently starred as the tragic heroine of the film *The Brothers*, with Maxwell Reed and Duncan Macrae. At this time Kenneth and Richard both had a reputation for having 'an eye for the ladies', which it appears may have been well-deserved in Richard's case. Although happily married to the actress Peggy Rawlings, a former member of 'Mr Cochran's Young Ladies', he was said to have enjoyed a succession of affairs. 'It wouldn't surprise me about either of them,' says Richard's eldest daughter, Belinda Innes, 'although it is not the kind of thing a father would ever talk about with his daughter. I think Richard was congenitally unfaithful, and Kenneth probably was too, but people were just not as nosy in those days. In general, the press left them alone.' In a later programme Kenneth and Richard would discuss whom they should invite to open the 'Bindbourne Music Festival':

HORNE: Have you thought of Patricia Roc?
MURDOCH: I very seldom think of anyone else, sir.

HORNE: Anyhow, Murdoch, it's a first class idea. I'd like to see Patricia Roc in Much Binding.

MURDOCH: Yes, sir. Not *too* much, you know . . .

'Ah yes, Patricia Roc!' said an old friend of theirs, when I mentioned her name. 'They both had her.'

Of the original cast, Sam Costa and Maurice Denham remained, but the second series of *Much-Binding* also featured Janet Davis, and the coloratura soprano Gwen Catley, once known as 'the highest voice in the land', although she was only 4 feet 11 inches tall. Kenneth had heard her singing at a Proms performance and during the interval he had begged her on bended knee to come on *Much-Binding*. She took a singing part as 'the vet's niece' but left after only six programmes, because she received the music and scripts only on the day of the recording and did not think the music suited her voice.

Once the second series had settled into a regular slot the show went from strength to strength. In April the Acting Controller of the Light Programme, T.W. Chalmers, wrote to Kenneth: 'Your impassioned appeal on the 'phone last Tuesday gave me no chance to say that I thought "Much Binding" had been getting better and better of recent weeks – months, rather. Last Wednesday's was quite the best ever, and it takes a lot to make me laugh; after all, I listen to practically every radio comedy show. By the way, what <u>was</u> it that Dickie found in your ticket pocket?'

Not everyone was so happy, however. In May the Assistant Controller of General Overseas Programmes registered a strong complaint that there were too many 'house jokes and inter-show' jokes in *Much-Binding*, which made it virtually incomprehensible to anyone listening abroad who was not familiar with a wide range of BBC variety programmes.

Meanwhile the BBC was threatened with a lawsuit by Lt. Col. The McGillicuddy of the Reeks, DSO, who, according to his solicitors, took 'serious exception' to a gag in the programme about 'McGillicuddy's reeks', especially as he had been similarly libelled in

1930, 1944 and 1946! The threat of High Court action was discontinued only after the BBC apologized profusely and agreed to issue a strict ban on the use of the name McGillicuddy in all future BBC programmes. The ban was included in the BBC's list of broadcasting guidelines, the 'Producer's Bible', and remained in effect for many years.

Even though they were required by the BBC to limit their radio work, Kenneth and Richard were allowed to appear on the fledgling television service and in October 1947 Kenneth made his first TV appearance, with Richard Murdoch and Sam Costa, in a live broadcast from the Radiolympia Exhibition in London. A month later he and Richard were two of the guests in a Jubilee Variety Gala at His Majesty's Theatre in London to celebrate the twenty-fifth anniversary of broadcasting in Britain. The two-hour show featured more than a dozen stars, including Charlie Chester, Vera Lynn, Tommy Handley and Vic Oliver and, in an unusual move, it was broadcast simultaneously on radio and television to give viewers a chance to see how a radio programme was performed.

Some of Kenneth's other radio work was rather less glamorous. In December he had to make the journey down to Bridport in Dorset to take part in the programme *Whatever Next* on the West of England Home Service, where he was booked to make a special guest appearance as the mystery 'Body in the Bag'!

At the beginning of 1948 Kenneth continued to develop his television career, making half a dozen appearances on a series called *Kaleidoscope*. Then in June he and Richard wrote and starred in their first television special, *At Home*, a forty-five-minute sitcom which also featured Sam Costa as the 'odd jobs man' and other special guests, and was broadcast live from Alexandra Palace.

When the second series of *Much-Binding* came to an end on 16 June, T.W. Chalmers requested permission from the BBC to give a small party for the cast and the production staff. 'Cost: £15 – number of people: 35.'

Permission was granted.

9

By Royal Command

IN APRIL 1948 the BBC launched a new weekly variety series called *Show Time*, introduced by Dick Bentley, which was designed to act as a showcase for up-and-coming talent. The BBC producer was Roy Speer and one day his secretary informed him he had a telephone call from Kenneth Horne.

'Hello, Roy,' said Kenneth. 'Dickie and I saw a young fellow the other evening, he was extremely good. He would be marvellous on your "Show Time", this boy. His name's Peter Sellers.'

After a brief conversation, Speer thanked Kenneth for taking the trouble to call him, and he replied, 'Trouble? It's no trouble at all, Mr Speer, because I *am* Peter Sellers. I've been impersonating Kenneth Horne because I couldn't get in to see you.'

Sellers had been doing an act impersonating film stars at the Windmill Theatre. Roy Speer was so impressed by the sheer nerve of the twenty-three-year-old comedian that a few weeks later he gave him a three-minute spot on *Show Time* and the rest is history.

In August Kenneth and Marjorie went on holiday to Bermuda. On their return journey, they stopped off for a week in New York, where they were shown around the city and introduced to local radio and television people by Bill Reid, the head of the BBC office in New York. In an introductory letter to Reid, T.W. Chalmers described Kenneth as 'an astonishing fellow; by day he is a very high official of the Triplex Glass Company, but by night he and Richard

Murdoch join forces in one of the funniest, wittiest and most devastating comic turns on the air'.

Kenneth was discovering that fame could have some beneficial side effects. One evening he was feeling particularly pleased with himself after he had used his name to secure a private room for dinner at the Savoy Hotel in London. After the meal, however, his self-esteem slipped slightly when a waiter approached him respectfully and said: 'I wonder if I might ask a personal question, Mr Horne. Which of your branches would be best for getting a stiff collar?' [Horne Brothers (no relation) chain of shops was a popular men's outfitters in the late 1940s.]

Much-Binding returned for a third series on 21 September 1948 and this time it was extended to a remarkable forty-three weekly shows, running until July 1949 and followed by a Christmas Day special. The regular cast of Kenneth, Richard, Costa and Denham were joined by the soprano Helen Hill and the talented actress Maureen Riscoe, whom Richard had met while they were touring after the war. Riscoe had a flair for dialects and languages, particularly Italian, and would introduce several new characters such as Hyacinth Meadows and Mr Blake the Sexton's daughter Bluebell. Kenneth and Richard sounded happy to be together again after their holidays:

MURDOCH: Ah! Good morning, sir. It is good to see you. Oh, sir, aren't you looking sunburned.

HORNE: Am I Murdoch, that's very nice of you. Does it suit me?

MURDOCH: No, sir, but it makes a change. Tell me, sir, how was Bermondsey?

HORNE: Bermuda, Murdoch.

MURDOCH: I am so sorry, sir, I forgot you'd been to foreign parts.

HORNE: Bermuda isn't exactly foreign, Murdoch. It's a British possession.

MURDOCH: Oh, we've still got one left, have we? Oh good. But sir, honestly you are looking sunburned, all except the top of your head.

HORNE: Well, Murdoch, it was pretty hot on the beach in Bermuda so I kept my bowler on most of the time.

MURDOCH: Very wise of you, sir.

HORNE: Yes, what's more it came in pretty useful on the boat coming back.

MURDOCH: Why, did you have to bail?

HORNE: Don't be silly, Murdoch. The captain does that. What I mean is, it was a great protection in the swimming bath when I dived in at the shallow end.

MURDOCH: I'm sure it was, sir. Oh, sir, you are looking sunburned. Are you like that all over?

HORNE: (pause) There's one little place that you really must see when you go to Bermuda, Murdoch . . .

The programme was now so popular that it attracted guest appearances from several international film stars, usually in London for their latest film premiere. A particular favourite was the young British actress Jean Simmons, the beautiful star of *The Blue Lagoon*, who joked that if Kenneth and Richard ever made a film it should be called *The Blue Baboon*. Another star guest was the husky-voiced Glynis Johns, who had been a mermaid in the film *Miranda* and, with the aid of a sound-effects man and a bucket of water, was heard 'splashing her tail' as she swam down the River Bind.

In November the programme featured two guest stars, the BBC radio and television personality Richard Dimbleby, playing himself as 'Richard Bumblepuppy' doing a broadcast of 'Up Your Alley' [*Down Your Way*] from the village of Much Binding, and the Hollywood film star Alan Ladd, the tough-guy actor who was visiting London to promote his new film *The Great Gatsby* and to appear at the Royal Command Film Performance of *Scott of the Antarctic*. In the programme, Ladd was supposed to be a guest staying at the Much Binding Arms.

MURDOCH: How do you do, Mr Ladd. My name's Murdoch and this is Mr Horne.

LADD: Glad to know you, Mr Horne.

HORNE: Oh, this is indeed an honour, sir. I did enjoy your performance in *Laddie Come Home*.

MURDOCH: Sir, that wasn't Alan Ladd, it was a horse.

HORNE: Oh, was it? Well I was sitting a bit at the side, it was difficult to see.

Ladd entered into the spirit of the programme, referring to Kenneth as 'Baldilocks' and Richard as 'Stinky', uttering the catchphrases 'Good morning, was there something?' and 'Oh I say, I am a fool', and even engaging in a garbled conversation with Mr Blake the Sexton.

The show was now at the height of its popularity, with a total listening audience of twenty million. It was a particular favourite of King George VI and towards the end of November 1948 Kenneth and Richard were invited to take part in the cabaret at the annual Staff Ball at Windsor Castle. The cabaret was organized each year by the ventriloquist Peter Brough, famous for his schoolboy dummy Archie Andrews, and it was never known in advance which members of the royal family would be there. Marjorie Horne and Peggy Murdoch were also invited to the event, and after they were escorted to the front row of the audience, they were joined by Queen Elizabeth (later the Queen Mother) and Princess Margaret, although the King was ill and unable to attend.

Everyone was required to wear full evening dress and Kenneth and Richard were kitted out in immaculate white tie and tails. They raised a huge laugh when Richard said, 'I saw some marvellous socks in Windsor today,' lifting his left trouser leg to show the sock, 'only five shillings a pair.' He then lifted his right trouser leg to reveal he was wearing no sock at all. 'Unfortunately, I only had half-a-crown on me at the time!' Not perhaps the funniest of jokes, he admitted later, but at least it was clean.

After the cabaret there was a ball and Richard was informed by Peter Brough that Princess Margaret would like to dance with him. The band was playing a slow waltz at the time, so the Princess suggested that they wait for something more lively. She led Richard to a chair at the side of the ballroom where he suddenly found himself sitting alongside the Queen and had to apologize for wearing only one sock. When the band picked up the tempo, Princess Margaret danced with Richard, while his wife Peggy danced with the King's equerry, Group Captain Peter Townsend.

Richard had heard from Joyce Grenfell that *Much-Binding* was a particular favourite of the royal family and they were regular listeners to the programme. So he asked the Princess whether she would like to attend a broadcast of the show at the Paris Studio; she replied that she would, and later the Queen added that she would like to come as well. Kenneth and Richard quickly wrote a letter to Major Harvey, the Queen's private secretary, giving him a few possible dates.

A few days later the telephone rang at Richard's home in Staines and his cleaner answered it. She told Peggy that it was a lady-in-waiting from Buckingham Palace. Kenneth and Richard always used to start their telephone calls to each other by saying, 'The Archbishop of Canterbury speaking' or 'Hello, this is the Pope here,' so Peggy thought it was Kenneth having a joke, but it really was the Palace.

As Richard was out, Peggy referred the lady-in-waiting to Kenneth. She told him that the Queen would like to bring a party of ten or twelve to the broadcast at the Paris on the following Tuesday and wondered if he could organize some tickets. Kenneth promptly rang Leslie Bridgmont at the BBC. When he asked him if he could manage twelve extra tickets for next week's show, Bridgmont told him brusquely that all the tickets had been allocated weeks ago.

'Oh, what a pity,' murmured Kenneth, 'I shall just have to ring the Queen back and tell her she can't come.'

Bridgmont nearly exploded. Tickets were hurriedly arranged and the front row of the audience at the Paris Studio was reserved for the royal family. On 28 December a red carpet was laid out at the entrance in Lower Regent Street, while flowers were displayed on the staircase down to the auditorium and all around the stage. Before the doors were opened, the cast held a special rehearsal and afterwards Kenneth was making a final check in the auditorium when he spotted some cigarette ends in the ash-trays. He turned to an attendant standing nearby and said, 'Get these ash-trays emptied, would you?'

The 'attendant' was in fact William Haley, the Director-General of the BBC, but he cleaned out all the ash-trays just before the royal family arrived; soon afterwards he was awarded a knighthood, and Kenneth used to joke that the two events were not unconnected.

There were several knowing references in the script to their royal guests in the audience:

DENHAM (Dudley Davenport): Miss Riscoe, may I snatch this speaking opportunity of telling you how 'jolly D' I think you are.
RISCOE: Oh, Dudley, I like you too.
DENHAM: Yes, so do I. I mean, every time I see you at the club I think of . . . I mean, sometimes, you see, when I see you I feel quite speechless, Miss Riscoe, I feel almost as if I was in the presence of . . .
well, as it I was about to be presented to . . .   Oh! I say, I am a fool!

The royal party had been joined at the last minute by Princess Elizabeth (now the Queen) and the Duke of Edinburgh. It was her first appearance in public since the birth on 14 November of her first son Charles, now the Prince of Wales. At the end of the programme Richard brought the house down when he added three extra words to the last verse of their signature tune:

At Much-Binding-in the-Marsh,
Today we're thrilled about this special visit,
At Much-Binding-in-the-Marsh,

It's not an everyday occurrence, is it?

R: I still can't quite believe that this has happened, sir, can you?

K: Quite frankly I'm so shaken that I haven't got a clue.

R: Perhaps we're dreaming.

K. No, we're not, down there!

R: Oh, sir, it's true!

At Much-Binding-in-the-Marsh,

K: (Say it, Murdoch)

Much-Binding-in-the-Marsh,

K: (Go on, Murdoch, say it. You must say it, go on.)

R: (Oh, shall I? All right, then.) Good old Char-lee!

At Much-Binding-in-the-Marsh.

In February 1949 the series hit the headlines for different reasons when a joke backfired badly and caused a storm of protest in the national press. It all started when Sam Costa arrived for rehearsals one day to read in the script that Richard was supposed to become so exasperated with him that he gave him the sack, saying, 'This time you've gone too far, Costa. You'll simply have to go.'

It was meant to be a bit of harmless fun to attract some publicity. Costa would be left out of the next programme, but then the following week he would be welcomed back with open arms. Costa was not happy with the idea but he went along with it for the sake of the series.

The cast were sworn to secrecy but Costa began to worry that there was more truth in the script than he had been led to believe. He confided his fears to a friend, who told another friend, and two nights later the headline in the evening paper read 'COSTA' FIRED FROM 'MUCH-BINDING'. The following day the national press picked up the story and suddenly Costa's telephone was red hot with calls from an inquisitive press, as well as other radio programmes wanting him to join their shows. One of his calls was from Kenneth who demanded to know what the hell was going on. When Costa explained, Kenneth reassured him that there had never been any intention to get rid of him and that he was back on the programme the following week.

On 7 March the radio critic of the *Daily Mirror*, Robert Cannell, fulminated in his column:

> The BBC's biggest and silliest leg-pull – the 'Much Binding' mystery of Sam ('Wos there somethink?') Costa – ends tomorrow night. And it has taught the BBC a lesson. The lesson is that gags of this kind on the radio are dangerous – easy to start and difficult to stop. That not only do they anger the audiences – they harm the people who are innocently concerned in them.
>
> But it mustn't happen again. For the cynics along Radio Row have been only too quick to set going the vicious rumour that there 'is something in it, old man'. Had Costa REALLY got too big? Were Murdoch and Horne REALLY jealous of Costa's popularity? Everybody in the secret knows that there is no foundation of truth in these rumours whatsoever.
>
> Who examined this 'idea' before it was given the okay for the air? Whose was the JUDGEMENT that went so stupidly awry in deciding to perpetrate this serial gag on a listening public which only asks for entertainment?
>
> THE BBC MUST TAKE THE CULPRITS TO TASK. OTHER-WISE NOT ONLY IDEAS BUT THE BRAINS OF THOSE CONCERNED MUST COME UP FOR KEENER EXAMINATION TOO!

There were some red faces in the corridors of the BBC at that last remark. A flurry of memos was exchanged by the department heads who all agreed that Leslie Bridgmont should have informed his superior, Michael Standing, before embarking on such a stunt and Standing, in his own words, 'admonished him accordingly'. On 8 March Sam Costa returned to the programme as originally planned and did not miss another single episode.

To see *Much-Binding* being recorded was often funnier than to hear it. One observer described the cast as 'a lot of big, grown-up boys having the whale of a time'. One of the running gags was the fact that Kenneth was supposed to have difficulty understanding Richard's jokes. He would 'get' a punch-line about two minutes after everyone else, resulting in an unexpected 'Ho! Ho! Ho!' which always produced a big laugh from the audience:

MURDOCH: Mr and Mrs Cobean had a son, what was his name?

HORNE: I've no idea.

MURDOCH: Harry, sir.

RISCOE: Ha, ha, that's very good.

HORNE: I'm afraid I don't quite see it, Murdoch.

MURDOCH: Oh, sir. Harry Cobean – haricot bean, d'you see?

HORNE: Oh yes, that's very good I'm sure.

RISCOE: Now I've got one, I think.

MURDOCH: Good, let's have it, Miss Riscoe.

RISCOE: Mr and Mrs Pelago had a son. What did they call him?

HORNE: Well, er, Bruce?

RISCOE: Why Bruce?

HORNE: Well, why not? I knew a Bruce Pelago out in Sidi Barrani, and he had a brother called Archie.

MURDOCH: Oh, that'll be it, Miss Riscoe. Jolly good.

HORNE: I don't see that Murdoch.

MURDOCH: Archie, sir. Archipelago.

HORNE: Yes, that was his name, and many's the time that Archie Pelago and I have . . . Ho, ho, ho, ho, ho . . .

MURDOCH: Oh, you've seen it, sir. I'm so glad.

HORNE: Oh, yes it's darn clever. Haricot bean! I must tell Bessie.

Kenneth was now at the peak of his profession in two different careers and in early 1949, in a business move which must have made him chuckle at the reversal of fortune, he was appointed to the board of Lancegaye Safety Glass (1934) Limited, the company in whose shares he had so disastrously speculated before the war.

Most people in the entertainment business knew vaguely that Kenneth was a 'director of Triplex' but they were not really interested. On the other hand, his business colleagues were much more likely to be impressed by his fame as a broadcaster. He would often go to a meeting as Sales Director of Triplex and his opposite number would greet him with a cheerful, 'Do come in, Mr Horne. How is Sam Costa?' and immediately the ice would be broken.

It undoubtedly helped him to open doors, enabling him to call on the biggest motor manufacturers and to be shown straight into the Chairman's office. Among his close friends in the late 1940s and early 1950s were giants of the car industry such as Sir Donald Stokes of Standard Triumph, Sir George Harriman of the British Motor Corporation, Sir William Lyons of Jaguar and Sir Alec Issigonis, the designer of the Mini, as well as Lord Sieff of Marks and Spencer and the Cabinet Minister Lord Mancroft.

Within the office at Albemarle Street, however, Kenneth tried to keep his two careers strictly separate. On the morning after a radio show, if one of his staff commented, 'Enjoyed it last night, sir,' Kenneth would reply, 'Good show! We thought it was great fun. Now, what have we got today?' Then it would be straight back to work.

Kenneth's nephew Richard Bull, the son of his elder sister Dilly, was a teenager in the late 1940s and remembers Kenneth at that time as 'an incredibly genial and glamorous figure, who rushed whirlwind-like through our lives. He was a kind of outsize personality, a burly figure, with a big voice. If he came into a room, you knew it. He was tremendously good fun to have as an uncle, both kind and generous.'

Another nephew, John Horne, the eldest son of Kenneth's brother Oliver, was at Cambridge University in the late 1940s and has never forgotten the day Kenneth was staying at the University Arms Hotel and invited him to supper. Afterwards Kenneth pressed what seemed to be a crisp one-pound note into his nephew's hand, but when John got back to his lodgings he discovered he had been given *two* one-pound notes. He endured a crisis of conscience wondering whether Kenneth had made a genuine mistake, but his weekly expenses amounted to about two pounds a week, so he kept them both!

At a time when people were generally smaller than today, he cut an impressive figure. He was six-foot tall and weighed about fourteen stone and was described in one newspaper article as 'an immaculately attired giant'. He always wore a red carnation in the buttonhole of his jacket. 'I've worn one every day since I was twenty-one,' he explained. 'My father loved flowers. I think a small splash of colour each day looks cheerful. It's swank too!'

He inspired devotion amongst his employees. Ralph Hewson joined Triplex Safety Glass in September 1946, recruited by Kenneth himself, as the progress controller at the Willesden factory. Later he rose to become the Sales Director of the company in the 1970s and said of his former boss, 'I would have gone to the ends of the earth for him.'

He recalled an incident in the winter of 1947, one of the severest of the century, when the factory at Willesden was completely frozen up and unbearably cold, with the workforce having to wear over-coats. On one of the coldest days of the winter, Kenneth made a point of leaving the warmth of his office in Albemarle Street and going to visit the workers at the factory, where he stayed for the whole day.

Hewson was promoted to Sales Manager and travelled with Kenneth on many occasions to meet important customers and attend sales conferences. With petrol still in short supply after the war, they frequently went by train and Kenneth was an enthusiastic sender of telegrams. He seemed to know the porters by name at virtually every station along the way. As the train drew into the platform, he would often stick his head out of the carriage window and shout, 'Fred! Hey, Fred!' When the porter came running up, Kenneth would ask him to 'be a good chap and send off this telegram for me,' before pressing a pound note into his hand. It is no wonder they were always so keen to assist him.

Much-Binding celebrated its one hundredth edition on 12 April 1949, but by the end of the series in July, all was not going well. The success of the show meant that Kenneth and Richard were required to stick to a rigid formula. It was a challenge to write and perform forty-three editions for ten months and towards the end the standard began to falter noticeably. To make matters worse, *ITMA* had finally come to an end in January 1949 with the death of its star Tommy Handley and it had been replaced by a brilliant new comedy series *Take It From Here*, written by Frank Muir and Denis Norden and starring Jimmy Edwards, Dick Bentley and Joy Nichols. Within six months it had overtaken *Much-Binding* at the top of the listening figures.

In June, C.F. Meehan, the Assistant Head of Variety, wrote to Leslie Bridgmont: 'In view of the considerable drop in listening figures and the somewhat adverse criticisms on recent programmes, Light Programme consider it essential that the next series starting in the spring of 1950 should have a completely new set-up. May we discuss?'

The programme may have needed a rethink but its catchphrases were now part of the national fabric. At the Radiolympia Exhibition in September the BBC stand featured a special disc which visitors could hear by pressing a button. It contained a selection of half a dozen catchphrases which had been made famous on the radio, and one of the most popular was a recording of Kenneth saying, 'Not a word to Bessie!'

All involved needed a bit of a break from the programme. Richard Murdoch signed up to do a pantomime at Christmas, which meant he would not be able to start a fourth series of *Much-Binding* until the spring.

In early November Kenneth went to Sweden on business for a week, and after a brief visit to the Scottish Motor Show in mid-November, he hosted a new radio series called *Spot the Winner*, an amateur talent contest which featured Charles Shadwell and his Orchestra and was arranged by the Carroll Levis Organization. The weekly series ran for four months and one of the early winners was the comedian Charlie Drake, who went on to become a major television star in the 1950s with his catchphrase 'Hello my darlings!'

On his return from Sweden in November, Kenneth had done a trial recording as chairman of the popular radio panel game *Twenty Questions*. A fortnight later he was offered the job and on 22 December 1949 he took over as the new question master. He would be associated with the series, on and off, as chairman or panellist for the next twenty years.

Twenty Questions

BASED ON THE old parlour game of 'Animal, Vegetable or Mineral' (to which they added 'Abstract') in which contestants had to guess a mystery word or phrase, *Twenty Questions* had become immensely popular since its first broadcast in March 1947. The original chairman was the fast-talking Canadian sports commentator Stewart MacPherson and the panel consisted of the former BBC war correspondent Richard Dimbleby, singer and actress Anona Winn, the comedian Jack Train from *ITMA*, and Olga Collett. After a few programmes Miss Collett became unwell and was replaced by Daphne Padel. The Mystery Voice, who would announce in a low whisper, 'And the next object is . . .' was Norman Hackforth, a pianist who had formerly accompanied Noël Coward.

Within a few months *Twenty Questions* became the most popular programme on the radio with an audience of about fifteen million. Columns of print in newspapers and magazines were devoted to describing the different skills of each panellist, and when the panel scored their first outright victory over Stewart MacPherson it was treated as a major story in the national press.

MacPherson had made his name as a war correspondent and later as a boxing commentator with a quick-fire delivery: 'He throws a right to the head! Another right to the head! Wham! A left to the body! That one went in right up to his elbow!' When the panel on *Twenty Questions* became too boisterous he would shout 'Shud-dup!' which soon became an unlikely catchphrase. The success of the series made him one of the most famous voices on British radio but his fame went quickly to his head. In February 1948 the producer of the series, Alick Hayes, wrote in a memo: 'I admire his work and like him personally but I think he is getting swollen headed, and unless kept in check, will become a menace.'

MacPherson shared an office in the BBC Outside Broadcasting Department at 55 Portland Place, opposite Broadcasting House. Just along the corridor were John Ellison, the presenter of *In Town Tonight*, and the cricket commentator Brian Johnston, who had originally met MacPherson during the war while he was serving as a Technical Adjutant in the Grenadier Guards. Johnston had a favourite routine when he thought 'Stewie' was getting above himself and others were in the office.

'I say, Jack,' he would start, 'did I ever tell you about the big retreat?'

'No,' Ellison would reply innocently, 'I can't say you did, Brian.'

'Well,' Johnston would continue, 'we were going back like mad when one of my men said to his mate, "I say, Bill, isn't that the famous war correspondent Stewart MacPherson over there?"

'"Blimey, so it is," said Bill. "I didn't know we'd gone back that far!"'

When the programme returned for a new series in January 1949 Richard Dimbleby filled in as the chairman for a few weeks but the BBC received a number of telephone calls complaining that his answers were misleading and spoilt the programme. The position of chairman was more complicated than it appeared. As well as being quick-witted, he needed to have an excellent grasp of the English language so that he could assist the panel to discover the mystery object by answering their questions correctly and precisely. One of the problems was that Dimbleby was better read and more erudite than anyone else on the panel and without his help they struggled to guess even one of the objects.

MacPherson returned as the regular chairman but he was increasingly out of his depth when trying to answer the panel's questions. He used to protest to the producer Alick Hayes that he was not a walking encyclopedia and sometimes he would make an elementary howler, which Hayes ascribed to 'his crashing ignorance'. In March Hayes was forced to intervene during a broadcast when MacPherson gave an incorrect answer and was told brusquely by the Canadian to 'get back to your kennel.'

In September Stewart MacPherson accepted an offer to work on radio in America and the BBC breathed a collective sigh of relief. Alick Hayes was replaced by Ian Messiter as the producer of *Twenty Questions* and Kenneth was offered the role of chairman. The trial recording in November was a success and he was booked to take over as the permanent chairman for the new series. Before it started, the BBC issued a carefully worded press release to explain the changes:

'Richard Dimbleby excels as a member of the team itself,' says Ian Messiter, the producer, 'and as such he is practically irreplaceable.' Dimbleby with his analytical turn of mind and sense of humour is of more value asking questions than answering them. So Kenneth Horne, with his long experience of impromptu broadcasting, comes in and the team remains intact.

Kenneth made his first appearance as the chairman of *Twenty Questions* on 22 December 1949 and he immediately induced a major controversy. One of the objects was 'Father Christmas' and Anona Winn quickly asked him whether it was fact or fiction. Kenneth was feeling rather nervous, as it was his first programme, and without thinking, he replied, 'Fiction'. When he got home there were three reporters waiting outside his flat demanding to know how he could dare to disillusion all the 'dear little children' so close to Christmas. He had to admit he had made a mistake, but in his defence he protested, 'How dare parents allow their dear little children of disillusionable age to stay up and listen to *Twenty Questions* at 8.30 p.m.!'

Apart from that, Kenneth's chairmanship of the programme was well received by the listeners, and in January he hosted a Royal Command broadcast of *Twenty Questions* from the ballroom at Windsor Castle, with the King and Queen, Queen Mary the Queen Mother, and the Princesses Elizabeth and Margaret sitting in the front row of the audience for the programme, in which the panel scored full marks.

Towards the end of the series, however, there were rumours that Daphne Padel was going to be dropped from the panel. Kenneth was always very loyal to his colleagues and believed in keeping a team together if at all possible. In February 1950 he wrote to the Assistant Head of Variety, C.F. (Mike) Meehan:

> I would like to put in writing the plea that I made to you this morning about the retention of the 'team' in its present form, even tho' I realise that anything I say comes from a 'new boy'.
>
> I honestly believe that Daphne is really a tower of strength to the team and the programme and I think it would be an awful pity if she were to be shelved for someone else.
>
> It is fairly easy for me now to be able to indicate to the listeners the difference between Anona's and Daphne's voices, and as far as ability is concerned, Daphne is almost in the Dimbleby class. I don't know why I should be pleading for her, except that I should be loath to break the happy spirit now so inherent in the team.

His pleading fell on deaf ears. When the programme returned in April, Daphne Padel had been replaced by Joy Adamson, who would remain a member of the panel for the next twenty years. In an unexpected twist, Stewart MacPherson returned from America, where his radio career had failed to take off, and in December he launched a rival series of *Twenty Questions* on Radio Luxembourg, sponsored by Craven A Cork Tips, with a panel featuring Richard

Murdoch, Daphne Padel, Frances Day and Ex-Detective Super-intendent Fabian of Scotland Yard.

With the BBC series of *Twenty Questions* running until the end of August and *Much-Binding* starting up again, Kenneth was now involved in two long-running series every week. As a result he had less time for doing other radio programmes, although he made the occasional guest appearance in popular shows such as *Music Hall* and *Variety Bandbox*.

In May 1950 he was the guest star on a unique programme called *Ladies Please* – 'an all-woman revue, about women, for women' – which featured Cicely Courtneidge, Jeanne De Casalis and Doris Hare, among others, and was also produced and written by women. The only male on the programme was Kenneth, who was the victim of the feature spot 'Men On Trial'!

The fourth series of *Much-Binding* was slightly shorter than before, consisting of twenty-seven shows, and was broadcast on Wednesdays at 8 p.m. from 15 March until 13 September 1950. Diana Morrison, formerly of *ITMA*, was brought in to add some variety to the programme with her repertoire of funny voices and the vocalist was Barbara Leigh. Years later, Diana recalled 'the warm, embracing way' that Kenneth welcomed her at rehearsals on her first day. He walked up to her with his hand outstretched, saying, 'Diana, how lovely to meet you!' and when they shook hands, he put a set of chattering teeth into her right palm. As she looked at the teeth in amazement, he chuckled, 'Sorry, I must have them back. Dickie has to have them for the show!'

A gradual fall-off in the number of listeners was only to be expected over such a long series, but the decline in the weekly audience for *Much-Binding* was beginning to cause alarm. The average weekly total of listeners in 1949 was 53 per cent of the overall radio audience and in 1950 it was 49.9 per cent – a drop of only 3.1 per cent. Not bad when taken overall but the drop in listeners from the start to the end of each series was considerable. The first nine programmes in 1949 had been highly successful, but aggregate audiences then fell from 74 per cent in March, after the 'Costa' incident, to only 39 per cent by the end of June. The fourth series in 1950 had started from a lower point than the previous year but had continued to decline as sharply as before.

T.W. Chalmers, a former champion of the programme, summed up the concerns of many in the BBC hierarchy when he described Kenneth and Richard as having become prisoners of the characters they had invented for themselves, unable to invent new situations in the *Much-Binding* framework. He concluded: 'There is no doubt that the public has got tired of it. The aggregate audience has fallen astonishingly.'

In the original contract for the fourth series of *Much-Binding* there was an option for a further thirteen programmes but in August the BBC decided to terminate the series when its initial run of six months ended in September. The BBC wrote to Kenneth, Richard and Sam Costa to inform them that, while no firm decision had been taken as to when, or whether, the series might return, they were prepared to offer them a different series involving the three of them in the New Year. The intention was to get Kenneth, Richard and Costa to commit themselves to doing a new series on BBC radio and to prevent them from looking elsewhere for work. It had the opposite effect.

Faced with the series being off the air for at least six months, possibly for ever, Kenneth accepted an offer from the producer Harry Alan Towers, the former Controller of the Overseas Recorded Broadcast Service, who had become the biggest producer of commercial radio shows in Britain with his company Towers of London. In mid-September Kenneth made a verbal agreement with Towers to record thirty-five shows for broadcast only on Radio Luxembourg, starting the following month.

When the BBC found out, there was uproar. In all BBC contracts there was a restrictive clause that forbade artists from working simultaneously for the BBC and any other broadcasting organiza-tion. But Towers had found a loophole. Now that the series had come to an end, none of the cast was under contract with the BBC and therefore there was no restrictive clause. There was nothing the BBC could do to prevent them recording for Radio Luxembourg.

Kenneth had consulted Leslie Bridgmont who advised him that the clause applied only to simultaneous *work* for the BBC and Luxembourg, whereas the Chief of the Light Programme had presumed it to mean simultaneous *broadcast*. The question remained whether the BBC could allow recordings made by Kenneth and the others while they were *not* under contract to the BBC to be broadcast on Luxembourg during a period when they *were* under contract to the BBC.

The BBC had only two alternatives: (a) to withhold all future engagements until the recordings ceased to be broadcast on Luxembourg or (b) to accept the situation of the recordings being broadcast during part of the period of the new contract.

When he was asked by the Chief of the Light Programme why he and Richard were bothering with commercial radio, which never had an audience of more than a million, Kenneth told him that such a small audience could do him and Richard no harm, and at least they would benefit financially.

The BBC promptly cancelled its offer of a new series in the New Year. Kenneth's contract as chairman of *Twenty Questions* was also not renewed and he was replaced by Gilbert Harding for the remainder of the series. Harding, a former schoolmaster, was the chairman of *Round Britain Quiz* and *Brains Trust* and was initially reluctant to appear on *Twenty Questions* because he considered it beneath him intellectually. He had gained a reputation as a 'cantankerous, opinionated bachelor' who was unable to disguise his disdain for people whom he did not respect. Unfortunately this included everyone on the panel.

Harding referred to Richard Dimbleby, famous for his commentaries on royal and state occasions, as 'obsequious granite' and considered him to be unforgivably pompous. Jack Train, on the other hand, was well known for his terrible puns, which used to get on Harding's nerves. Train would often prepare his puns methodically beforehand. On one programme he asked, 'Could you find it in a bird sanctuary?' to which Harding replied, 'Yes.' 'Sanctuary much,' said Train, to audible groans from the audience. Harding became so irritated by Train's contrived puns that he once told him, 'Punning is like masturbation. It brings pleasure only to the person who is doing it.'

Harding also had a drinking problem which had started early in his career when he knocked back a stiff brandy before doing a broadcast which went extremely well. He reasoned that if he did well after one brandy, he would do twice as well if he drank two. Two became three, and three became four, and soon he was unable to go on the air without imbibing several drinks beforehand. He never caused a 'live' broadcast to be cancelled through being drunk but sometimes it came pretty close. On the day of a programme the panellists would ask nervously, 'Has Gilbert arrived yet, is he . . . all right?'

His fondness for the bottle did nothing to improve his temper and his unpredictable behaviour made *Twenty Questions* more popular than ever. Harding's rudeness to the panel was half the fun of listening, but more than once he had to be 'rested' from the programme following an incident during a live broadcast. On one occasion he did not realize his microphone was switched on and was so irritated by the introductions of the panellists to the studio audience that he growled: 'This is the last time we have any of this nonsense . . . now let's see what we can make of this show after this horrid and unsettling start.' Next day the newspaper headlines read HARDING IN TROUBLE AGAIN and he was taken off the programme for the following week and replaced by the cricket commentator John Arlott.

After Harding's enforced absences from the programme, the BBC hoped he would see the error of his ways but he continued to drink heavily and in April 1951 it led to the famous occasion which came to be known as 'the night Gilbert was drunk on *Twenty*

Questions'. Later Harding would claim that he 'was perfectly sober that night, but had had a frustrating, wearing day during which everything seemed to have gone wrong'. Others said that, on the contrary, he gave the impression of being very drunk indeed.

Harding arrived at the studio very late and sat down in his chair only thirty seconds before the broadcast was due to begin. He reached for his headphones but the cord was tangled and while he was trying to sort it out the red light on his desk came on to signify that the studio was 'live' on the air. In a panic he dropped the headphones altogether. The continuity announcer had already introduced the programme and millions of listeners heard only the bang and clatter of Harding's headphones. The announcer blustered, 'They don't seem to be ready for us in the *Twenty Questions* studio,' and the programme was hurriedly cut off the air while Harding sorted himself out.

A minute later the programme started again but the incident had aggravated his temper to the point of no return. The programme descended into further confusion when Jack Train guessed one of the objects quickly but Harding failed to hear him. After the panel had exhausted their twenty questions and Harding gave the correct answer, Train protested indignantly that he had guessed it earlier, but Harding dismissed him with a curt 'Let's move on.'

Relations between the chairman and the panel gradually deteriorated from bad to worse and at the end of the programme, instead of announcing the result as usual, Harding said: 'I suppose I ought to let you know the score. If you've been listening you won't need it, and if you haven't you won't want it anyway!'

After the broadcast a furious row ensued in the studio, with Jack Train protesting about his disallowed answer and Richard Dimbleby arguing with Harding about his drunken behaviour. Many of the studio audience stayed behind to watch the entertainment.

The next morning Michael Standing, the Head of Variety, had a meeting with Harding who admitted openly to having been drunk and expressed his great regret. The BBC was so aghast at this debacle that the two recorded repeats were cancelled because, in an official explanation, they were 'not satisfactory' and Harding was suspended from *Twenty Questions* for several months.

To his surprise and delight, Kenneth was invited to take over from Gilbert Harding as the chairman of the programme, which he continued to do for four months until a penitent Harding was allowed to return.

After the BBC had accepted defeat, *Much-Binding* moved to Radio Luxembourg for thirty-four shows from 30 October 1950 to 17 June 1951. The series was sponsored by Mars Limited and was broadcast on Sunday afternoons at 3 p.m. The cast was Kenneth and Richard, with Sam Costa, Maurice Denham and Dora Bryan, and for the first three editions the musical accompaniment was provided by the Skyrockets Dance Orchestra, conducted by Woolf Phillips. For the remaining shows, Patricia Hughes joined the cast, with music from the Squadronaires Dance Orchestra, conducted by Ronnie Aldrich.

The compere was Bob Danvers-Walker, who made the announcement each week that the show was sponsored by Mars Bars. In those post-war days, sweets were still on ration, and one of the fringe benefits of the series was that the cast were given free supplies of chocolate by their sponsors, which at least made them popular with their children.

Later Richard confessed, 'It wasn't really a great success – even my mother said it was rotten, and she was my greatest fan.'

Meanwhile in May 1951 the Festival of Britain was officially opened by the King and Queen on the South Bank of the Thames. One of several radio programmes designed to celebrate the event was *Festival Music Hall*, which ran fortnightly from May until mid-August, and was introduced by Kenneth and Richard, with guest stars including the singers Anne Ziegler and Webster Booth, pianist Charlie Kunz, Arthur Askey and Diana Morrison.

When his stint on *Twenty Questions* finished in September, Kenneth became one of the regular panellists in an amusing new radio game called *One Minute Please*, in which personalities had to talk on different subjects for sixty seconds without pausing, repeating or deviating. The chairman was Roy Plomley and the two teams consisted of 'Gents' and 'Ladies', with the first programme pitting Kenneth, Gilbert Harding and Reggie Purdell against Yvonne Arnaud, Valerie Hobson and Nan Kenway.

One of the early favourites on the series was the musical cartoonist Gerard Hoffnung, who held the highest score of seventeen points, against an average score of only four, and he first related his famous 'Bricklayer's Story' on it. If the concept sounds familiar it is because the series was revived in 1967 as *Just a Minute*, chaired by Nicholas Parsons, and it is still as popular as ever.

This was a punishing schedule. Kenneth once described this period as 'probably the most complicated part of my life'. He would start in his office in Albemarle Street at 8.55 a.m. precisely every morning, answering his correspondence and setting up meetings. He once said that he put in about sixty hours of work for the company every week. This seems a remarkable number of hours but his job involved a large amount of travel around the country, visiting the various motor companies or taking clients out to dinner, and there were no motorways or high-speed trains available in those days. Despite his schedule, he always made a point of attending the Triplex board meetings in London once a week.

Sometimes he had to take extreme measures to honour all his work commitments. In the early 1950s Kenneth and Murdoch used to perform occasional Sunday concerts at theatres around the country. In July 1951, for example, they starred at the Shanklin Theatre in the Isle of Wight, in a show which also featured a fifteen-year-old Julie Andrews, accompanied on the piano by her mother Barbara.

These Sunday concerts were extraordinary affairs. There were usually five in their company, including Kenneth, Richard, and John Dean, the tenor from the D'Oyly Carte Company. Sometimes they would be booked to do five shows in one night. In order to play to as many people as possible, if they were appearing at a Butlins holiday camp they would perform two shows in each theatre at Butlins and another show at the theatre in town. The company would have to take it in turns. Kenneth would start his act at one theatre and carry on until he saw Murdoch or Dean waiting in the wings, then he would dash off in his car to the next theatre, and so on.

One weekend they went to the Isle of Man but because there was no scheduled flight back to the mainland on a Sunday evening, Kenneth had to charter a small plane, at a cost of more than his fee for the concert. Kenneth sat in the front of the plane holding his tenor saxophone, with Marjorie alongside him, while Richard sat in the back playing tunes on his piccolo.

They were supposed to be flying to Liverpool to catch a British European Airways flight back to London but their pilot got lost over the Lancashire coast. He kept staring at his map and then looking helplessly out of the window trying to find out where they were. At one point he shouted, 'Ooh, I think we've gone too far!' and they narrowly missed hitting the Blackpool Tower. Finally they landed at Speke Airport, where BEA had held their plane for them for half an hour, and Kenneth just made it into his office on time on Monday morning.

It had been desperately close, but later he would disclose proudly, 'I got away with it!'

Over to You

FTER AN ABSENCE of a year, the *Much-Binding* team returned to the Light Programme for a fifth BBC series on 30 September 1951, and the show ran for the next twenty-eight weeks, going out at varying times on Sundays. The cast and the format remained essentially the same but, confusingly, the BBC decided to liven up the series with a new title, *Over to You*, and a new signature tune. In recognition of their need for some fresh ideas, the scriptwriting duties for this series were shared between Kenneth, Richard, and Anthony Armstrong, with additional material by Talbot Rothwell, who would go on to write many of the *Carry On* films.

That was not their only source of new ideas. In early 1952 Kenneth received a letter at home from a Miss Mollie Bernard, enclosing about two dozen comic verses which she had written for the *Much-Binding* signature tune. They were surprisingly good and he wrote back to her:

> Thank you very much for your letter, and for the material which you enclosed. I have shown this to Richard Murdoch and we both agree that it is very promising. We shall hope to use some of your ideas in forthcoming programmes of 'Much-Binding-in-the-Marsh', and I enclose a cheque as an advance payment, which I hope you will find satisfactory. If you would like to come to a broadcast, perhaps you would contact my secretary, Miss Davis, who will be pleased to arrange to send you tickets.

The verses were so funny that Kenneth and Richard included four of them in the next programme. The following week Miss Bernard went along with three of her friends to the Paris Studio to watch a recording of *Over to You* and afterwards she introduced herself to Kenneth. He was astounded to discover that she was a seventeen-year-old pupil from Rochester Grammar School in Kent and her real name was Mollie Sharp.

'I was an absolute fan of "Much-Binding-in-the-Marsh" from about the age of twelve,' she recalls. 'I had three friends at school and we used to talk about it every week. We were guinea pigs for the first-ever "O" levels and after they were finished we had time on our hands, so I used to make up the verses for fun.' Her friends had dared her to send some of her material to the BBC and, unknown to her parents, she had found out Kenneth's home address and written to him under an assumed name.

When they had got over their surprise at her age, Kenneth and Richard had to agree that Mollie had a flair for writing comedy and shared their particular offbeat sense of humour. They encouraged her to submit more work and sent her copies of the *Much-Binding* scripts so that she could see how they were put together. For the next two years she contributed a large number of ideas for verses and sketches which they incorporated into their programmes.

Mollie continued to use a pseudonym and never told her parents that she was being paid for writing comedy scripts. She knew they would not have approved and would have insisted that she complete her education first.

Years later, in a letter to Doreen Forsyth, a producer on *Woman's Hour*, Kenneth recalled how one day he had received Mollie's original letter:

This was not unusual. But what was unusual was that it made us laugh like drains. We asked the sender to come and see us. She was a very plain, dumpy girl of about seventeen. We asked her if this was a 'flash in the pan' or could she repeat it. She could. And for the penultimate series of MB she provided some very good stuff for us. The next year we asked her if she would repeat the arrangement. The reply? 'I've had to consider seriously whether to continue with my present work (typist) plus a bit of scripting for you, or follow my vocation, and I've decided on the latter.' And what was the latter? A permanent official of the Salvation Army.

By 1954 Mollie had become a student at the Salvation Army Training College. One day Richard wrote to her inviting suggestions for an appearance on *Henry Hall's Guest Night* but his letter was opened by Mollie's training officer, Lieutenant Colonel Winifred Haynes. She allowed her to submit some ideas for that programme but persuaded her that it must be her last writing assignment. Mollie's parents never found out that she had been writing jokes for Kenneth Horne and Richard Murdoch until several years later.

Meanwhile, a month after the start of the *Over to You* series, Kenneth and Richard had another royal engagement when they were booked to appear in the annual Royal Variety Show at the end of October in the presence of the King and Queen at the Victoria Palace. They were to take part in a sequence called 'Radio Times' which also featured Jimmy Edwards, Arthur English and Sally Ann Howes. It turned out to be an emotional occasion. A few weeks earlier King George VI had undergone a serious operation to remove his left lung and the Archbishop of Canterbury had led prayers across the nation for his recovery. The Royal Variety Show was known to be one of the King's favourite events but two days beforehand it became clear that he was not going to be well enough to attend the performance.

The BBC agreed to set up a special land-line between the Victoria Palace and Buckingham Palace and the commentator Brian Johnston was positioned in one of the boxes in the theatre, opposite the Queen and Princess Margaret, with a BBC engineer and a telephone. The King's customary souvenir programme, printed on blue handmade paper, bound in silk and embroidered in gold – with all the advertisements removed – was delivered to him at Buckingham Palace.

When the show started, Johnston had to act as the eyes and ears of the King, who was listening to the show in bed, and describe everything that was happening on the stage. At one point Bud Flanagan of the Crazy Gang stepped up to the microphone and said, 'His Majesty is listening. Let us make him feel a bit better with some community singing.' He then led the audience of 1500 in a hearty rendition of 'Daisy Bell'.

King George VI died only three months later on 6 February 1952 and that evening, as a mark of respect, the broadcast of *Over to You*, along with many other BBC programmes, was cancelled. With the series nearing the end of its run, Kenneth began to think about the future. The previous series of *Twenty Questions* had ended in December and he was eager to resume as the chairman. In February he wrote to the Head of Variety, Michael Standing:

As you know, 'Over to You' finishes on March 21st, and naturally Dickie and I will be wracking the old brains to try and devise something to sell to you. Keep me in mind though, will you, if you have any Quiz type programmes which need a Q.M. because I love that sort of work.

My ambition needless to say is to get back into '20 Questions' which I believe was going really well when I left, and was on the up and up. Perhaps there's a chance of that job for me when it comes back?

To his great disappointment, *Twenty Questions* returned in July with Gilbert Harding as the chairman.

Meanwhile *Over to You* was extended by another three weeks until 14 April. A week later Kenneth and Richard were the joint castaways on the long-running radio series *Desert Island Discs*, the 133rd celebrities to be invited by Roy Plomley to choose eight records and a luxury object. Kenneth's eclectic choice included an aria from 'Carmen' sung by Enrico Caruso, 'Night and Day' by Fred Astaire, and jazz from the Hotsy Totsy Gang. His luxury item was a mah-jong set, while Richard chose a test-your-strength fairground machine.

It was always difficult for Kenneth to plan a holiday because of his busy schedule, and he hated to turn down any work, but in May he wrote to Richard:

> I mentioned to your secretary this morning that I would like to cancel our 'Music Hall' date on Sunday August 31st owing to the fact that I expect to be on holiday at that particular time.
>
> I have spoken to Miss Lipscombe [the BBC booking manager] about this, and through her tears I rather gathered that she would scrub our names from the list.
>
> As no BBC contract has been issued for that date I feel in no way bound to send you a cheque for 12/6d as I would have done in other circumstances. Please do not let this put an end to a beautiful friendship and kindly give my regards to Mrs Lubbock.
>
> For and on behalf of Inverted Cotton Wool Ashtrays Ltd.

Richard was obviously not too upset because later that month they made a rare television appearance together in the light-hearted quiz show *Know Your Partners*.

After another radio series of *One Minute Please* ended in August, Kenneth managed to get away with Marjorie on holiday. On his return in September, and with no plans for a further series of *Much-Binding*, Kenneth, Richard and Sam Costa agreed to star in *The Forces Show*, a new weekly variety series written by Bob Monkhouse and Denis Goodwin. It eventually ran for six months but it got off to a bad start. Bob Monkhouse recalled what went wrong:

> We couldn't wait to start, gleefully anticipating the pleasure of extending the world of 'Much-Binding' into this one hour musical format. After one working day, Denis and I knew we were in

trouble. The script just would not come out right. First it was a slavish imitation of the 'Much-Binding' style, then it would slide into parody and then into such a feeble pastiche that we felt obliged to gag it up with uncharacteristic one-liners. Never have I marvelled more at the easy, natural humour of Murdoch and Horne's own scripts. Like everything Dickie did, it flowed from a unique and inimitable source.

For the next six months we did our best but our material was like a frantic caricature of an original. Kenneth Horne had a marvellous sniff of disapproval which we came to know all too well in rehearsal. Sam Costa would read a line and then look up at us with the most withering and well-deserved scorn. Only Dickie hid any disappointment he might have felt by chuckling loudly at the least terrible jokes and nodding cheerfully at us now and again as if to say 'Nice try!'

On New Year's Eve 1952 Kenneth and Richard made a nearly disastrous television appearance together as the hosts of a floor show broadcast 'live' from St Thomas's Hospital in London. The programme descended into chaos when it was invaded by a group of students, and afterwards Kenneth was worried that his nascent television career might have been permanently damaged. A few days later he received a letter of apology from Ronnie Waldman, the Head of Television Light Entertainment:

I have not written to you earlier about the sad affair of New Year's Eve because I wanted first to carry out the most careful possible investigation into the cause of the chaos.

I must admit now that my first reaction at the time was a particularly vicious one against members of the Television staff, but I now understand that the hospital authorities have admitted that a small group of students arrived that evening with the deliberate intention of breaking up our show. As you know only too well, they succeeded in doing this, not only by the creation of more noise and interruption than the worst mannered Services audience I ever came across, but also by deliberate interference and tampering with our technical equipment.

On behalf of the Television Service generally then, and of myself in particular, I can only apologise most humbly for something that you will, I am sure, admit was no fault of ours. It was particularly infuriating because this happened on one of your too rare appearances in Television. I hope you will understand my feelings, and that we can arrange to have you back on our screens – in the correct conditions – before very long.

Kenneth replied the next day:

I was extremely relieved to get your letter about the New Year's Eve debacle, because I was a little bit afraid that the position might not have been made clear to those in authority. As you probably know, a good many members of the general public got the opinion that the actual programme that came on the screen was the very one that had been planned by Murdoch and Horne, whereas we had worked out a rather comical ten minute act which under normal circumstances would, I think, have gone over extremely well.

As you know, it is always rather difficult for me to get away to rehearse for a TV show, but in a short talk that we had with Bill Ward after the event we did decide that we would like to have another 'bash' under normal studio conditions.

On 27 February Kenneth marked his forty-sixth birthday with an appearance in the first Royal Command Variety Broadcast, which took place in the Concert Hall at Broadcasting House and featured many of the top radio stars of the day, such as Peter Brough and Archie Andrews, Ted Ray, Bebe Daniels and Ben Lyon, Jimmy Edwards, Joy Nichols and Dick Bentley. To the delight of the audience, Kenneth and Richard finished their act with a special verse of the *Much-Binding* song to celebrate the forthcoming Coronation:

At Much-Binding-in-the-Marsh,
We've got a rather serious confession,
At Much-Binding-in-the-Marsh,
By subterfuge we'll see next June's procession,
We've hired a horse's outfit for the Coronation day,
We've bribed the Royal coachman not to give our game away,
We'll be shouting 'Good old Charlie!'
From inside a Windsor Grey,
At Much-Binding-in-the Marsh,
(I'm the front legs!)
Much-Binding-in-the-Marsh,
(I'm the back legs!)
Much (two, three, four)
Binding-in-the Marsh!

Up until now, Kenneth had done very little work on television. He was simply not able to take the time off work for the lengthy rehearsals that were required on most television programmes. 'Business comes first,' he insisted. 'I like it. Besides, it's likely to last longer!' On radio he could fit in rehearsals at lunchtime or after work, but television was more complicated. 'You simply can't rush from your office desk and throw on a TV variety show with a few evening rehearsals,' he explained. 'It's not fair to anyone – particularly the viewers.'

Another problem with working on television was that he was never able to see himself on the screen. Radio shows were usually recorded at the time of broadcast and repeated a few days later. In the years before videotape, however, almost all television programmes were transmitted live. 'I wish the BBC would film more shows,' he complained at the time, 'so that we could see where we go wrong.'

Marjorie attended almost all of Kenneth's radio broadcasts but she never went to any of his television shows. 'I prefer to watch him on our screen at home,' she admitted, 'it seems much more exciting.'

The solution was a TV panel show which required minimum preparation and allowed him to be his own amiable, good-humoured self, without having to learn a script. In April 1953 he started a six-month run as a panellist on a new television series called *Down You Go*, which was produced by Dicky Leeman, 'with Roy Rich laying the clues and Elizabeth Gray, Kenneth Horne, Paul Jennings and Michael Pertwee finding the letters'. Based on an American format, the fortnightly programme struggled to find its feet at first but gradually gained in popularity. One of the reasons for its success was that Kenneth refused to take it too seriously. 'It didn't break my heart if I couldn't answer any of the problems,' he confessed. 'I went on and enjoyed myself and I hope viewers did, too!'

The only time he admitted to experiencing any difficulty was during the *Down You Go* anagram spot when they had to arrange about twenty-four letters to make a phrase. 'You're up against time,' he said, 'and sometimes there's an awful moment when you see a rude word beginning to loom up on the screen!'

When the series ended in October, Cecil McGivern, the Controller of TV Programmes, wrote to Kenneth: 'The chairman and the team were gay, charming and intelligent and many viewers will miss you. I certainly will.'

After doing a day's work in the office, Kenneth managed to dash down to the BBC's Lime Grove studios on several occasions during 1953, appearing in a television version of *Puzzle Corner* and *The Name's the Same*, in which a team of experts tried to discover the names of contestants who bore the same names as famous people. He also recorded a pilot for *Once Upon A Time*, based on the wartime radio series in which famous stars were granted seven wishes, and took part in a special edition of *This Is Showbusiness* which was televised from the annual Radio Exhibition at Earl's Court.

In October he had 'another bash' at doing a television programme with Richard Murdoch, co-writing and starring in *Free And*

Easy, a half-hour special in which they brought their particular brand of humour to the small screen. One critic commented afterwards: 'This was true TV and true comedy at one and the same time.' The concept of the show was simple: the pair had been given the run of the Lime Grove television studios, where they encountered a number of different stars and programmes. They watched a dance troupe rehearsing in one studio and listened to the singer Mary Miller in another; they tried to work out an anagram on the set of *Down You Go*; while on *Inventor's Club* Richard demonstrated his brilliant idea to speed up the putting of stamps on letters, which turned out to be a piece of damp rag.

A running gag was that they kept coming across famous BBC personalities doing the most unlikely jobs. In the boiler house they found the bandleader Henry Hall shovelling coal and in the *Interlude* studio, where the BBC made the short films shown between the programmes, such as the famous 'Potter's Wheel', the potter was revealed to be the veteran BBC announcer Leslie Mitchell. There were also some filmed newsreel flashes with Kenneth and Richard breaking the world speed record, beating the world champion Joe Davis at snooker, helping the Arsenal football team to victory, and eating their sandwiches on top of Mount Everest.

Television critic Dick Richard reported: 'Lime Grove has rarely seen such an hilarious night as when Kenneth Horne and Richard Murdoch were let loose in the studio with a programme all to themselves. Viewers asked for more, for the whole thing had an air of spontaneity about it so rare in TV humour.'

The BBC tried to persuade them to do another programme together but Kenneth wrote to Ronnie Waldman, the Head of Light Entertainment, Television, turning down his offer. He explained that it was impossible for him to devote enough time to rehearsals, adding, 'In fact I had to take a few days of my official holiday to enable me to do the last show.'

As well as television, Kenneth made guest appearances in more than a dozen different radio series in 1953 from *Ignorance is Bliss* and *Variety Playhouse* to the *Frankie Howerd Show*. In May he was one of the panellists in a celebrity version of *Twenty Questions* in which a team consisting of himself, Brian Johnston, Daphne Padel and Barbara Kelly challenged the regular panel to see who was the quickest at discovering the correct answer; he also filled in twice as the chairman when Gilbert Harding was 'being rested' from the programme. In July he was the Guest of the Week with Marjorie Anderson on *Woman's Hour* and his genial good humour seemed to go down well with the mainly female audience; it would be the first of his many appearances on the programme.

After being off the air for fifteen months, *Much-Binding-in-the-Marsh* returned on 21 July 1953 for a sixth and final BBC series with the new title of *Much Binding* and ran for thirty-five weeks, going out on the Home Service at 9.30 p.m. on Fridays.

For this series Richard Murdoch was said to have inherited a local newspaper called *Sticklecrumpets Weekly*, which had a circulation of just two elderly gentlemen who had forgotten to cancel their subscriptions. He then changed the name of the paper to *The Weekly Bind*. Diana Morrison was replaced by Dora Bryan, as Miss Gladys Plumb, the fashion editor, while Maurice Denham played several new characters such as Mulch the gardener and Mr Bubul the printer, who would say things like: 'I don't know what's come over me – I'm not as rehabubul as I used to beebabubul!'

The *Radio Times* marked the occasion by putting Kenneth and Richard on the cover and they seemed excited by the prospect of their new journalistic profession. 'We'll all have green eyeshields and we'll always be seen in our shirtsleeves,' declared Richard enthusiastically, 'except Miss Bryan, of course.'

'We'll drink cups of tea all day long,' added Kenneth. 'Naturally, we shall smoke incessantly. Cigars for me, cigarettes for the others.' The address of the new enterprise was said to be Jerry Buildings, Fleet Street, with a plaque on the door saying: THE STALE NEWS. 'But don't take any notice of that,' laughed Kenneth. 'Mr Stale was the original owner of the newspaper!'

In another change of style, the musical interludes were supplied by the BBC Men's Chorus led by Leslie Woodgate, who were known as 'The Press Gang', and the BBC Variety Orchestra was conducted by Paul Fenoulhet. In a challenging piece of casting, Sam Costa played the radio critic, Prudence Gush, most of whose excruciating contributions were actually written by Mollie Millest:

COSTA: 'Pleasant Thought for the Day' by Prudence Gush, née Costa. I call it 'I pick the roses but the roses never pick me.'
HORNE: Very nice.
COSTA: How beautiful it is to hear the nightingale in song
How sweet to hear the bleat of lambs as o'er the downs they throng
How glorious to hear the lark a-singing in his flight
Perhaps the loveliest of sounds is this one, 'Frying tonight'!
MURDOCH: What do you think of that, sir?
HORNE: I call it epoch-making.

By the start of the final series Leslie Bridgmont had been the producer of *Much-Binding* for about ten years and he tended to leave the programme to look after itself. Following the recording on a Tuesday evening he would often not visit his office for the rest of the week. Kenneth and Richard were responsible for the scripts and if they wanted to change anything or to book a special guest on the show, Bridgmont's secretary would organize it all. It was quite common for Bridgmont not to see the script until he entered the studio and he often pretended to know more about it than he did.

One day Kenneth and Richard decided to catch him out and gave his secretary about ten extra pages of absolutely filthy material which she duly typed up and added onto the front of the real scripts. On the day of the broadcast Leslie Bridgmont turned up at the Paris Studio as usual for the rehearsal and listened with mounting alarm as the cast performed the additional pages, flipping frantically back and forth through his script to confirm what he had just heard. After nine pages of filth and innuendo he yelled, 'What's going on? We can't do this!' Kenneth and Richard pretended not to understand and made Bridgmont endure a very anxious half-hour before they finally dissolved into laughter.

> MURDOCH: Now Miss Plumb, have you any ideas?
> BRYAN: Oh, the things you say! You're almost as bad as my friend Iris – she's a scream is Iris when she gets going – d'you know she was out with her boyfriend the other day and d'you know what she said?
> MURDOCH: Oh, not now, please.
> BRYAN: That's right!

Two of the best routines in this series featured Maurice Denham. In one famous episode he invited Kenneth and Richard to the first night of his new play *Alone I Done It*, a Mystery Drama in which he played all the parts: Bazeley the butler, Clara the maid, Sir Anthony Dunkels, Lady Dunkels, their daughter Miss Gwen and her boyfriend Michael Daintree, a dashing young pilot officer. He also had to supply all the sound effects, from a Martini cocktail shaker to a horse's hooves and a slamming door. For three minutes he provided an incredible tour de force, switching from one voice to the other, until the play ended with all the characters being shot by a revolver one by one: 'Oooh! THUD!'

In another episode Mr Bubul was typesetting the first edition of the newspaper when he ran out of the letter 'e'. He got round the problem by substituting the letter 'o' which he suggested they could easily correct by 'putting a little line across it'. In a brilliant sequence, the title of the newspaper is printed as 'The Wookly Bind', with Richard named as 'The Oditor'. Sam Costa's sports column is headed 'Crickot' and reads: 'Aftor tho Tost match at Loods, the Onglish toam was agrood by tho soloctors at a committoo mooting'.

> MURDOCH: They'd never stand for this in Floot Stroot!
> HORNE: Not a word to Bossio.

Family Business

IN SEPTEMBER 1948 Kenneth's secretary had announced that she was leaving to get married. After interviewing a number of job applicants for her position, he selected a tall, elegant young woman called Joyce Davis. She was extremely efficient and within a week she had sorted out his chaotic filing system.

Many years later Joyce would recall her first impression of her new boss: 'He was such a nice guy, you wanted to do everything you possibly could to help him. He was never cross or unreasonable and he had such a real appreciation of anything you tried to do.'

One of the first things she noticed about Kenneth was his total lack of pomposity and his ability to put strangers at ease. That did not mean he was unaware of his status within the company. As Sales Director he often had to interview applicants for jobs in his department and Joyce observed that one certain way to lose the job was to treat him with a lack of respect. After one young man had breezed confidently into his office, addressed him as Ken and started to tell him a funny story, Kenneth remarked to Joyce, 'You know, one more crack out of that joker and I'd have told him, "Please don't stand on ceremony; feel free to call me Mr Horne!"'

Kenneth and Joyce shared a lot in common. In particular she enjoyed playing tennis and during the summer of 1949 she used to partner Kenneth at doubles against his cousin Sir Harry Pilkington and his daughter. Pilkington lived in a flat at the top of Selwyn House, the London headquarters of Pilkington Brothers, a beautiful

Regency house overlooking St James's Park. They would meet up at 7.30 a.m. at the tennis courts in Green Park and afterwards they would all go back to Selwyn House where they would change and have breakfast before going to work.

In 1950 Kenneth acquired a new Rolls Royce and soon afterwards he was in Jermyn Street when he recognized Percy Millea, who had been his chauffeur when he was courting Marjorie during the war. Kenneth persuaded Percy to come and work for him permanently and he was to be his chauffeur for the next eight years.

Kenneth's niece Margaret, the daughter of his eldest brother Oliver, also used to play tennis with Kenneth in the early 1950s. She says that Kenneth would arrive grandly in his Rolls being chauffeur-driven by Percy, while Sir Harry Pilkington, who was considerably wealthier, would pedal up on his old bicycle. Margaret was a keen tennis player, who went on to be the women's champion in Basle a few years later, and she confirms that Kenneth was still a very good player himself, even in his mid-forties, although he used to try to distract the others by speaking constantly in French.

Joyce lived with her widowed mother and younger sister at a house in Barnet, north London. After she had been working with Kenneth for a while, she invited him and Marjorie to her home one evening for dinner. This was not exactly Marjorie's idea of an exciting night out. During the meal, Kenneth was embarrassed to see that she was pushing her food around her plate but not eating anything. When he encouraged her to have some more, she replied that she wasn't very hungry. 'I'm so tired,' she sighed. 'I've been standing all day, having fittings for clothes. It's so exhausting, don't you think?'

'I know,' said Kenneth quickly, 'I had a fitting for socks today, absolutely exhausting!'

It was one of the rare occasions when Kenneth openly made fun of his wife. Normally he never spoke out against her, never opposed her or tried to assert his authority. He gave her everything she wanted, showering her with gifts, jewellery and furs, and treating her to expensive holidays.

Her birthday was on Christmas Day and Kenneth used to buy all his presents for the family on Christmas Eve. Percy Millea used to pick him up in the Rolls at 8.30 a.m. and Kenneth would spend the whole day shopping, returning home at about 5.30 p.m., laden with parcels. He enjoyed choosing gifts and apart from his main presents for Marjorie and Susan he could not resist buying little extras such as the latest pen, cigarette lighter or gadget for the kitchen. He would shut himself away in his dressing room for several hours, wrapping up the presents and writing a personal message in each one.

One year he decided to give Marjorie a sheepskin jacket, a popular fashion at the time. She was so petite that the jacket had to be made to order. Kenneth took the measurements from a coat in her wardrobe and went with Susan to the shop, where they selected the skins, the colour and the style, giving thought to every little detail. Nothing was left to chance. On Christmas Day Marjorie was presented with the beautifully wrapped box; she tore off the paper and looked inside. 'Oh, thank you,' she said, without enthusiasm, 'very nice.' She did not even take the jacket out of the box.

For the third time in his life, Kenneth realized his marriage was a failure. As his friends had predicted, he and Marjorie were two different people. They were bored with each other. Marjorie had been widowed at the young age of thirty-two and this was clearly not the life she had envisaged for herself. She was interested in the arts and literature and it is significant that her original invitation to 'come round for a drink' had been intended for the other Kenneth Horne, the playwright, not the workaholic businessman who liked to socialize with his colleagues from the motor trade.

An old friend once asked Kenneth why he had left his second wife Joan and married Marjorie. He thought for a moment and replied, 'Well old boy, I suppose I needed a change. You see, Joan only ever used to laugh at *most* of my jokes. Marjorie never laughs at any of them!'

They shared a bedroom, although the flat was so large that they had separate dressing rooms. However, they slept in twin beds alongside each other, because Kenneth was so much bigger than Marjorie that he would probably have bounced her out of a double bed. One year he put on so much weight that he broke his bed and it had to be repaired.

In spite of their differences, Kenneth was always very considerate towards Marjorie. She had become very attached to an old stuffed koala bear called Marmaduke, which had been given to her by a friend returning from Australia. Eventually the bear became so moth-eaten that she had to get rid of it. Soon afterwards she came home from a game of bridge one evening and noticed a light on in their bedroom. Sitting on her bed was another koala with a note pinned to him saying: 'I hope I can make up a little for your great loss.' Kenneth had hunted high and low until he had found her a replacement. She called him Wiggley.

Marjorie also loved budgerigars and she kept a succession of them in the flat, all called Happy – Happy 1, Happy 2, Happy 3, and so on. They were really hers, but Kenneth grew to like them too, and if they were going to the country for the weekend, they would often take the budgies with them.

Eileen Miller worked for Kenneth and Marjorie for many years and was very fond of her, but even she admits that her employer could be difficult. 'She was wonderful,' she says, 'but she was unusual. She had been brought up differently.'

Marjorie had such airs and graces that everyone believed she came from a very privileged background. She gave Eileen the impression that she considered it almost beneath her to travel in a car smaller than a Rolls. She took obsessive care over her appearance and would never leave the flat unless she was immaculately dressed, often in jewellery and furs. She never went on public transport and always used the chauffeur to drive her everywhere. Yet her grandfather had been a missionary in China and her father was a humble accountant. She certainly knew the value of money. Eileen would often arrive at the flat in the morning to find Marjorie studying the latest share prices in the newspaper. It was also Marjorie who persuaded Kenneth and Richard to give Eileen a long-overdue pay rise.

According to Eileen, Marjorie was 'a little weak thing' and her daughter Susan describes her mother as being 'stick thin' but she was also quite an elegant woman. 'She went out a lot and she liked to dress up,' says Susan. 'She was good at it and looked fantastic.' Kenneth liked Marjorie to look as attractive as possible when she was out with him – after all, he was a public figure and it made him look better.

Kenneth always dressed smartly when he was out in public but at home he preferred to relax in his favourite old clothes, some of which were quite scruffy. It used to fill Marjorie with horror, because she was worried that one of her friends might see him. He had a particular pair of grey flannels which he wore constantly until Marjorie tried to dispose of them in the dustbin. Twice he salvaged them, protesting strongly, but the third time she cut them up into several pieces before throwing them away. When he discovered them later, Kenneth did not make a scene, it was not his style, but he made his disappointment quite plain. When she returned home that evening, Marjorie found a pile of small pieces of grey flannel on the hall table, in the middle of which stood a small cross made of matchsticks, a memorial to his much-loved trousers.

Kenneth liked to give the appearance of being cheerful and contented with life, but he was deeply unhappy in his marriage to Marjorie, and he did not know what to do about it. He knew he had made a mistake. One day he asked Joyce Davis ruefully, 'Why didn't you clock in earlier?' It would appear that she had been asking herself the same question. Years later she confessed, 'If anyone had ever told me that I was going to fall hopelessly in love with a bald-headed man fifteen years older than I was, I'd have told them to go jump in the lake.' Kenneth had become equally infatuated with her and they embarked on a secret affair that would continue for the next ten years.

Kenneth understood how to succeed in business but he seemed

unable to find the same success in his private life. 'He used to put so much effort into making other people happy,' says Susan, 'but I often wonder how happy he was himself.' His religious upbringing and boarding-school education had taught him to keep his feelings to himself and, looking back now, Susan has to admit, 'There were times when I wished he would say more.'

One day he was waiting for a train at Southampton station with Ralph Hewson, his young sales manager at Triplex. They were having a cup of tea in the refreshment room and Kenneth was being unusually quiet and preoccupied. Suddenly he said, 'You know, Hewson, within reason I can have pretty well anything I want; and yet, I'm not happy. Life's jolly difficult, isn't it?'

Hewson was so taken aback, he did not know what to say and stuttered, 'I'm sorry to hear that, sir. Can I help in any way?'

Kenneth quickly realized he had overstepped the mark with his junior colleague and chuckled, 'My dear chap, I don't know what came over me. Yes, of course you can help. Buy me another cup of tea.'

It was never mentioned again.

When Susan finally left home she had no idea how to cook a meal or how to entertain because, unlike most children, she had never seen her mother do it at home. 'Cooking is not one of my accomplishments,' declared Marjorie in an interview, 'and my husband is so good I prefer to leave it to him. Every morning before he goes to work Kenneth brings me my breakfast in bed – tea and toast. If he cannot do the cooking I have a woman who comes in to cook for us.'

Kenneth loved to cook. He found it relaxing. The kitchen at Cottesmore Court was his domain and he always left it spotless, doing the washing up himself. One of his favourite recipes was a pastry pie which for some reason he called Aunt Gladys, and he used to write her name on the top. Most evenings, however, he was either working or simply too busy to cook and he and Marjorie would dine out three or four times a week at establishments such as The Ivy, Wheelers and the Savoy. One evening they were having dinner with

Susan at the Grosvenor House Hotel and Kenneth was so impressed with the béarnaise sauce that he went into the kitchens and persuaded them to teach him how to make it.

Not only did Marjorie not know how to cook but she was not all that keen on motherhood either. Nanny Savage was in charge of the nursery which meant that Marjorie did not have to get involved with Susan on a daily basis. As Eileen Miller observed, 'Some women don't want babies.'

Marjorie seemed to resent her daughter's presence. Susan believes that finances may have had something to do with it. George Thomas's will had stipulated that if Marjorie ever remarried, his money would be left in trust to their daughter, and indeed Susan paid for her own school fees out of the trust. Susan was essentially brought up by Nanny for twelve years and, perhaps not surprisingly, she grew to love her more than she did her mother. In turn, Nanny treated Susan like a member of her own family and would often take her out to meet her relatives.

Susan had never known her real father, who died when she was only a year old, so she always thought of Kenneth as her father and called him 'Daddy'. 'He was lovely,' she says, 'and I doted on him.' In turn, Kenneth was obviously devoted to his stepdaughter but he was also careful to keep his distance emotionally, not wanting to interfere with the authority of Marjorie or Nanny.

Everything changed, however, when Susan was twelve and she was sent away to boarding school at St James's, an exclusive school for girls in West Malvern. As soon as she had gone, Marjorie sacked Nanny without any notice, thus denying Susan a chance to say goodbye to the woman who had cared for her since she was a baby. When she found out, Susan was distraught and recalls, 'It was hard to build bridges with my mother after that.'

This did not help her to settle down at St James's and during her second term Susan went increasingly off the rails. At one point she instigated a sit-in strike which prompted the head-mistress to telephone Marjorie and deliver an ultimatum: either

Susan reformed her behaviour immediately or she would be expelled.

Relations between mother and daughter had broken down to such an extent that Kenneth was despatched to deal with the crisis. He may not have been a hands-on father but he was wise enough to realize that the problem was not a lack of discipline but a lack of affection. After a meeting at the school with the headmistress, he took Susan out for a drive in the Rolls Royce before treating her to a slap-up tea. All through the afternoon they chatted happily to each other without a single word about her disgraceful behaviour. At about six o'clock Kenneth returned her to the school and, saying goodbye, he gave her an enormous hug and whispered: 'Now *try* and behave a bit better, will you?' After that, she was as good as gold.

As Susan grew older and began to appreciate the scale of Kenneth's popularity, she used to love going out with him. When they went to dine at the Savoy Hotel, the orchestra would play the *Much-Binding* theme when he walked into the restaurant. One night they all went to see the Crazy Gang at the Victoria Palace and Kenneth was introduced to the audience, who all applauded.

Susan lapped up all the attention but Kenneth was careful not to spoil her too much. He was quite strict about her not enjoying too many of the trappings of his success. He wanted her to lead as normal a life as possible. When she was about sixteen, he allowed her to use the chauffeur and the Rolls to go to a ball, but it was most unusual. She thinks that it was probably so that Percy could keep an eye on her after the ball, when love-struck teenage boys might be considered to be 'NSIT' – not safe in taxis!

Kenneth had always encouraged Susan not to smoke, but she thought it was cool – after all, she reasoned, Princess Margaret smoked. When she left school Susan was careful never to smoke in the flat, but one day, when she was about eighteen, Kenneth caught her out. He offered her a cigarette and, without thinking, she accepted it. He said triumphantly, 'I *thought* you were smoking!'

Marjorie seemed to enjoy the attention brought by her marriage to Kenneth. When she went shopping with Susan at Harrods and was asked for the name of her account, she would always reply in a loud voice, 'Mrs Kenneth Horne', much to her daughter's embarrassment. Kenneth, by contrast, would often pretend to be someone else. Taxi drivers would recognize him and say, 'You look just like that chap off the radio,' and Kenneth would reply casually, 'Yes, isn't it remarkable!'

Kenneth was becoming more easily recognizable because of his many television appearances and on New Year's Eve 1953 he started a second series of *Down You Go*, which would run until the end of September. After a few weeks he took over from Roy Rich as the chairman and he was replaced on the panel by Richard Murdoch.

One of his co-panellists on the original series of *Down You Go* had been Paul Jennings, who soon afterwards came down with a severe case of tuberculosis. He had been admitted to Midhurst Hospital, where he had an operation to remove one of his lungs. When Kenneth heard about his plight, he organized a group of friends including Daphne Padel, Jerry Desmonde and Joyce Davis, and one Sunday he drove them all down to Midhurst, where Jennings was recuperating. There he put on an improvised panel game called 'Chit for Chat' for all the convalescent patients in the hospital, with Paul Jennings as the chairman. It was hilarious. 'I am sure no patient who was there will ever forget it,' recalled Jennings years later. 'I can see them all now, laughing as they climbed out of that splendid Rolls.'

In June 1954 Kenneth went with Marjorie to Australia for three weeks. *Much Binding* was a big hit in Australia where it was transmitted on the Australian Broadcasting Commission (ABC) network, and Richard Murdoch had signed a four-month contract to star in a weekly variety series called *Much Murdoch*. He tried desperately to persuade Kenneth to go with him but told Australian reporters that extracting a decision from his partner had been 'as hard as wooing a diffident maiden'.

The problem was that Kenneth simply could not take such a long sabbatical from his job at Triplex. The *Much Murdoch* radio series started broadcasting on ABC in mid-May but it was not until five weeks later that Kenneth finally arrived in Australia after catching a last-minute flight on a Qantas Constellation.

It would appear that he had managed to persuade Triplex to grant him permission for the trip by agreeing to carry out business for them while he was in Australia. When his flight touched down at Darwin airport on the way to Sydney on 16 June, he was asked by a reporter if he was the famous Mr Horne and he replied: 'Yes, that's me, of Triplex Safety Glass Company, London. We make the safety glass you've got in your car . . . but excuse me, no commercials!'

Three days after arriving in Sydney, he and Richard were supposed be the guests of honour at a special reception for over 150 guests given by the Royal Empire Society. To the embarrassment of the society and their guests, however, Kenneth announced at the last minute that he had 'an important business matter in Adelaide' that prevented him from going, and Richard had to attend the reception on his own.

Kenneth had consented to do half-a-dozen variety broadcasts with Richard called *Much Murdoch and Horne* and to appear in a Variety Concert in the Sydney Town Hall which would also be broadcast by the ABC. The pair seemed genuinely pleased to be working together again. At the rehearsals for the first radio show they acted like a couple of boys out of school, reading each other's lines and ad-libbing outrageously.

'Watching Richard Murdoch and Kenneth Horne rehearsing together is like seeing the two halves of the same apple reunited,' declared the local Sydney newspaper. 'They go so well together that, when separated, they seem more than a little lost. In fact, they're a team in the full sense of the word.' In the end, they recorded eight shows at the ABC Theatrette in Broadcast House, Sydney, including five in one week.

At the end of June Kenneth sent a telegram to Dicky Leeman, the producer of the *Down You Go* series: 'Working out hangover upside down in Australia. Hope my stand-in not brilliant.'

He flew back home with Marjorie via Honolulu and the United States and soon after his return he was a panellist on a new radio quiz called *What's It All About?*, which also featured Celia Johnson and Dilys Powell and was chaired by Brian Johnston. Listeners sent in cards relating an extraordinary incident which had happened to them and the panel had to guess what it was. Johnston later described it as 'fairly childish', but it became quite popular.

During the summer he also made several guest appearances as compere of the *Show Band Show*, a long-running radio series 'spotlighting the world of popular music', which was a showcase for the BBC Show Band directed by Cyril Stapleton.

Meanwhile the second series of *Down You Go* ended its long run at the end of September, and two days later Kenneth was reunited with Richard and Sam Costa on the television series *Variety Parade*:

MURDOCH: It is good to see you again and if I may say so you look real extra grouse, fair dinkum you do.

HORNE: I beg your pardon.

MURDOCH: I said you look real extra grouse, fair dinkum you do.

HORNE: That's what I thought you said.

MURDOCH: That's a little thing I picked up in Australia. You ought to know that – you flew out there to join me.

HORNE: Do you mean to say that month I wasn't here I was in Australia?

MURDOCH: Of course.

HORNE: Good heavens, those whiskies must have been stronger than I thought.

At the beginning of November Kenneth became a panellist on the new television game show *Find the Link*, which would run for the next seven months. The show featured five pairs of contestants each week and the panel had to discover the link between each pair. Some of the links were 'applause getters', such as people who had been especially brave or had done something outstanding, while other links were designed to be 'unusual' and some 'highly comical'.

He also started a ten-week stint on radio as the compere of *The Forces Show*. One of the highlights each week was a serial sketch called 'Without a Clue' which featured Kenneth as 'The Dean of Detectives, Klaxon Horne'. He was usually in hot pursuit of 'Shishka Bab the Beautiful Spy', played by Joy Nichols, ably assisted by his secretary Miss Nicklejoy, who was also Joy Nichols, with Derek Roy as Boy Roy, and Bob Andrews as Inspector Pillbody of the Yard.

The contract for this programme had caused quite a few problems after Kenneth crossed out the BBC exclusivity clause. He sent the contract back with an explanatory letter to Pat Newman, the Variety Booking Manager:

I am always opposed to any restrictive clauses in any contracts in business. I can well understand the BBC's wish that an artist should not undertake a series for a competitive organisation during the period of a BBC series, but it is I think a little invidious to tie one down by not allowing an artist to undertake an odd recording or broadcast.

Incidentally, it is possible that in about a year's time the situation will become a bit more complicated, and in that connection I am wondering what the BBC's definition of 'broadcast' is. Does this include TV?

The BBC persuaded Kenneth to reinstate the exclusivity clause for the series, but with commercial television due to start in Britain in September 1955, the Corporation was becoming increasingly worried about losing some of its most popular stars to 'the other side'. In November 1954 Michael Standing, now Controller, Entertainment Sound, invited Kenneth to lunch to discuss a long-term contract. He calculated that in the year ending September 1954 Kenneth had earned £3272 from his radio appearances, plus an additional £1798 from overseas repeats, and £958 from television appearances. This made a total BBC income of £6028.

Standing told Kenneth that the BBC would guarantee that his annual income from all BBC sources would not fall below £4000 over a period of three years and would offer him not less than twenty-six radio and twenty-six television engagements in each year if he would sign an exclusive contract with BBC Sound and Television.

Kenneth was tempted by the offer but he had other more pressing considerations on his mind. A week later he wrote to Standing:

> I have one or two other problems to consider at the moment which may have a bearing on your proposal and therefore it may of necessity be a little time before I can give you any decision. The problems . . . are entirely associated with the other side of my business life.

After twenty-seven years, his successful career at Triplex was about to come to a sudden end.

13

British Industries Fair

KENNETH'S COUSIN, Sir Harry Pilkington, as well as being chairman of the family company Pilkington Brothers, was also on the board of Triplex and a member of its sales committee. So he had been able to observe Kenneth at close quarters and he was impressed with his exceptional ability.

Sir Harry was President of the Federation of British Industry which promoted an annual Fair as a shop window for British goods. The Federation had been founded at the outset of the First World War in 1914, to encourage British businesses to manufacture goods that had previously been imported from overseas. Subsequently the emphasis had shifted to concentrate on promoting British exports.

There were actually two Fairs: one for heavy engineering exhibits, which was held in Birmingham and organized by the Birmingham Chamber of Commerce, and the other for light industries, which took place in London and was sponsored by the government through the Board of Trade.

There had been growing dissatisfaction among exhibitors at the way the London Fair was being run by the Board of Trade, where civil service bureaucracy frequently brought decision-making to a standstill. Early in 1954 it was decided to set up a new private company, called British Industries Fair Limited, to run the Fair with financial support from the government.

Sir Harry Pilkington was asked to nominate six honorary directors to sit on an advisory board, representing the top rank of

British Industry. The Chairman was Sir Ernest Goodale, a leading figure in the textile industry, and the other directors included the financier Sir Nutcombe Hume, of Charterhouse Investment Company, and Reginald Whitehouse, Chairman and Managing Director of the Chad Valley Company.

To everyone's surprise, Sir Harry appointed as the sixth director his cousin, Kenneth Horne. When eyebrows were raised, he explained that Kenneth had tremendous drive, business experience, flair and personality and would be invaluable to the new company when it came to publicity. The Chairman of Triplex, Sir Graham Cunningham, was consulted, and he agreed to allow Kenneth to serve on the board of BIF for one year.

The day-to-day running of the company was left in the hands of a permanent civil servant, J. Reading, seconded from the Board of Trade. Mr Reading had no experience of business, and the decision-making process continued to be tied up in Whitehall red tape. The advisory board decided immediate action had to be taken and sought permission from the government to appoint a full-time paid Managing Director and to send the hapless Mr Reading back to the Board of Trade. Permission was granted and the Chairman and the other four directors unanimously nominated Kenneth to fill the new position.

Meanwhile in January 1955 Kenneth and Richard were the guest stars in the first of a new TV variety series called *Face the Music*, introduced by the bandleader Henry Hall. The following day Peter Black, the television critic of the *Daily Mail*, declared: 'Horne and Murdoch were better than anybody. This pair should be seen much more often. They have a high degree of professional competence; an easy, relaxed, friendly manner, and a rarer quality that TV is at present short of – humour that is pleasantly zany in a traditionally English way that owes nothing to American influence.'

Robert Cannell in the *Daily Express* was equally impressed: 'Viewers saw Kenneth Horne and Richard Murdoch actually *doing* the things which made so many millions laugh for so many wartime years. Murdoch and Horne have always been nervous about trying to re-create the lunatic world of 'Much Binding' in vision. They need have no more doubts.'

It was a tremendous compliment but Kenneth's appointment as the Managing Director of BIF was going to demand his full attention and even he could not handle three separate careers – Triplex, BIF and broadcasting – at the same time.

At the end of January he had a meeting with Michael Standing at the BBC and confided that a matter had arisen in his business career which had to be resolved one way or the other before he could be sure whether he would be in any position to even continue as a broadcaster at all. Whatever happened, he assured Standing, he was not interested in commercial television and if he signed up with anyone, it would be the BBC.

On the surface, Kenneth's position at Triplex seemed secure. He had worked there for more than a quarter of a century and had been a huge success as Sales Director in the nine years since the war. When Kenneth joined the company in 1928, turnover was about £400,000. In 1955 it would be £5,000,000, a twelve-fold increase. Profits for 1955 would also be higher than ever before – £611,679 – an increase of more than £230,000 on the previous year. Kenneth was being widely tipped to be next in line to be the Chairman and Managing Director of Triplex, which would have made him one of the most powerful figures in the motor industry, probably leading to a knighthood.

He decided to ask Sir Graham Cunningham at Triplex if he would allow him to be seconded to the British Industries Fair for two years. Sir Graham was as an authoritarian chairman, whose word was regarded as law, and he was said to resent Kenneth's popularity within the company. He put Kenneth's proposal to the Triplex board and the following day he informed Kenneth that his request for a secondment had been comprehensively rejected. Either he stayed on as Sales Director at Triplex or, if he wanted to take up the appointment at BIF, the board would accept his immediate resignation.

Kenneth was stunned and angry. He felt betrayed by his fellow Triplex directors, some of whom he had worked alongside for years. At that point, he had not yet made the decision to become the chief executive at BIF but after the board's decision, he must have realized that if he stayed at Triplex, his authority within the company would be severely compromised.

He handed in his resignation to Triplex after twenty-seven and a half years, losing his company pension in the process. He later described the transitional period that followed as 'months of chaos of handing over and doing three jobs at once'. Over the next few weeks he had to oversee the annual British Industries Fair while at the same time continuing his job at Triplex and appearing on more than a dozen radio programmes.

His face was now so familiar that in March he had to adopt a special disguise to take part in a ground-breaking new radio series called *Let's Go Somewhere* with Brian Johnston. This was one of the first programmes on radio or television to test the reactions of the public at large and was in many ways an early version of *Candid Camera*, which came later on ITV. The fifteen-minute programmes were transmitted 'live' and all the participants were heavily disguised and wore hidden microphones to capture the genuine reactions of the people whom they encountered.

In his first appearance on the programme, Kenneth had to don a false beard and spectacles and stand outside Charing Cross Station singing the old chestnut 'Comrades' non-stop for a quarter of an hour, while Brian Johnston attempted to play 'Underneath the Arches' on an old upright piano in a street near Piccadilly Circus and the sports commentator Raymond Glendenning cranked out 'Knees Up Mother Brown' on a barrel organ in Leicester Square. The idea was to 'test the generosity of Londoners' and see how much money they could raise from the unsuspecting passers-by. None of them seems to have been recognized and after fifteen minutes Kenneth managed to collect one shilling and fourpence and

Glendenning just twopence halfpenny, while Johnston emerged the winner with three shillings.

The series turned out to be a fascinating insight into the British character in the 1950s. People were so afraid of being embarrassed that they would do almost anything not to attract attention. In a later programme Kenneth and Brian Johnston tried to hand out ten shillings (probably worth about five pounds in today's money) to passers-by outside Victoria Station. Using the Victoria Palace as their base, they ventured forth in turn to try to give the money away. Johnston was dressed as a tramp, saying that he had won the football pools and wanted people to share his luck. Almost everyone looked embarrassed or pretended not to hear him, apart from one soldier returning off leave who grabbed the money gratefully.

Kenneth was even less successful. He was dressed as a business-man, with a large black beard and spectacles and a bowler hat, and told people that he was carrying out the wishes of a dead aunt. It was the anniversary of her death and each year she wanted money to be given away in her memory. 'So will you accept ten shillings?' asked Kenneth, proffering the money. Even though he was offering brand-new ten-shilling notes, people just stared at him or brushed him aside. He was unable to give away a single note.

Kenneth made a brief return as the chairman of *Twenty Questions* in April, while Gilbert Harding was away on sick leave in Switzerland. Harding still had a devoted following, but in the audience research Kenneth was welcomed back warmly by many of the listeners who praised his ready wit and above all, his evident realization that it was only a game and intended, first and foremost, as entertainment.

On 1 July 1955 he finally started work as Managing Director of British Industries Fair Limited in their offices at Ingersoll House in Kingsway. Kenneth viewed BIF as a tremendous challenge. After such a long association with the same company he welcomed the change and he was inspired by a feeling of patriotism. At first his appointment attracted some favourable publicity, although it soon became apparent that it would take more than his personal drive and charm to restore industry confidence and enthusiasm in the Fair. Nevertheless he pulled out all the stops to try and make it succeed.

This is the time when Susan believes Kenneth was probably at his happiest. 'He was doing something he knew he was good at,' she explains, 'and he loved going to work.'

During the Fair, visiting trade delegations and buyers were wined and dined and there were evening receptions at Lancaster House, while the Lord Mayor hosted a banquet at the Mansion House for members of the diplomatic corps, as well as the trade delegations and exhibitors. At various times the Queen and the Duke of Edinburgh, the Queen Mother, Princess Margaret and other leading royals all visited the Fair, escorted around the stands by Kenneth along with Sir Ernest Goodale. The royal visitors used to buy a large amount of merchandise during their visits, which made them very popular with the exhibitors who were able to tell prospective overseas buyers that their products had been purchased by royalty.

In keeping with his new status, Kenneth traded in his old Rolls Royce and bought a brand new Silver Cloud with two-tone green coachwork, which he registered in Kingston-upon-Hull so that he could obtain a KH numberplate. He had wanted KH1, but that had been allocated to the Mayor, and the lowest number available was KH6, so he settled for that, and he used it on his cars for the rest of his life. He was once asked why and he explained, 'Swank has a lot to do with it, but in my particular case it is rather friendly and it has enabled other people to start a conversation with me which I might have missed.' His godson, Tim Murdoch, says that the Rolls also had the initials KH embossed on the door. When Tim pointed them out, Kenneth joked that it was pure coincidence, because he had 'bought the car off a chap called Keith Heinz!'

As a condition of his appointment Kenneth had stipulated that Joyce Davis would be employed as his secretary. But Joyce had a change of heart. She was in love with Kenneth but it had become clear that he was never going to divorce Marjorie, and she came to the conclusion that her only option was to make a new life for herself elsewhere. She had friends in Canada and, within days of Kenneth's departure from Triplex, she flew out to stay with them in Vancouver, where she quickly found herself a new job.

Kenneth was desolated. Joyce had become an essential part of his life, both emotionally and professionally. He wrote constantly to her in Canada, telling her about his problems at BIF. At first she did not reply, although finally she wrote back, admitting that she too was unhappy. Kenneth had to acquire a new secretary, Kathleen Haynes, known as Kate, who had worked for the former General Manager at BIF. She proved to be efficient, tactful and charming and would soon become devoted to her new boss.

Kenneth still had to resolve his negotiations with the BBC. After further discussions, he informed the BBC in September that he had decided not to proceed with the exclusive contract. He added that he would 'not at any price' work for commercial television and he was, in fact, precluded from doing so by reason of his position at BIF. But he would make himself available to the BBC as before and he was anxious that they should call upon his services as often as required.

They took him at his word and he would continue to combine his demanding business career with an equally arduous schedule of programmes on radio and television. In the latter half of 1955 he took over as the chairman of the television series *Find the Link* and appeared on a number of other BBC TV programmes such as *Variety Parade*, *This Is Showbusiness* and *Fast and Loose*. He appeared with Richard Murdoch for several weeks on the radio series *Variety Playhouse*, and also made a guest appearance in *Murdoch in Mayfair*, the new radio series in which Richard played the manager of a new nightspot, owned by Michael Trubshawe.

When Gilbert Harding was taken ill in November, Kenneth replaced him for the next few weeks as a panellist on *What's My Line*. Since its debut four years earlier, *What's My Line* had become the most popular show on British television with audiences of over four million, a huge number in the days before a majority of house-holds possessed a television set.

The chairman was Eamonn Andrews, a bluff Irishman with a genial manner who had made his name as a boxing commentator on radio, and the regular panel consisted of Gilbert Harding, the Canadian actress Barbara Kelly, the doctor and magistrate Lady Isobel Barnett, and the magician David Nixon. The challengers would sign in by writing their names on a blackboard and then do a piece of mime to illustrate something they did in connection with their job. The panel of two men and two women would then have to ask them questions to try and guess the job, which could be anything from a hairdresser or a taxi driver to a chicken sexer, a jigsaw puzzle cutter or even a tennis ball inflater. The most famous challenger of all was a Mr Adams from Burslem, who turned out to be a sagger maker's bottom knocker.

It was a simple game but in the early 1950s, with the panel dressed in their dinner jackets and evening gowns, the sparkling wit and banter seemed like the height of sophistication. When it was shown initially mid-week it was said to have been responsible for emptying the pubs, and after it was moved to Sunday evenings, it had a similar effect on church attendances. As with *Twenty Questions*, many people tuned in to see whether Harding would lose his temper and on Monday mornings the main topic of conver-sation on the train or in the office would often be: 'Did you see Gilbert Harding on *What's My Line*?' On one occasion he became so irritated by the answers given by a whisky broker that he snapped, 'I'm tired of looking at you,' and had to apologize on the next programme.

After the end of his appearances on *What's My Line*, Kenneth became the host of a new television talent show, *Camera One*, which was produced by Albert Stephenson. The series began in January 1956 and at first it was transmitted monthly, but the reaction was so positive that from the end of May it became fortnightly. After *Camera One* ended in September, Stephenson wrote to Kenneth:

'Many of the artists who have spoken to me since their appearances have said how much at ease you put them and the confidence you gave them. When you come to look back, we really have started a large number of people on the road to fame.'

Given his family background, it is perhaps surprising that up until now he had stayed away from any religious broadcasting, but at the end of January Kenneth was invited to appear on the BBC television programme *Sunday at Six*. Afterwards the Head of Religious Broadcasting, Reverend R. McKay, wrote to thank him for 'a quite excellent talk, given in such a sincere, friendly way which must have appealed greatly to many viewers'.

Kenneth's income from television had increased substantially but with *Much-Binding* off the air and looking unlikely ever to return, his radio income had more than halved in the previous year. In February he wrote to Pat Hillyard to enquire whether there was any chance of a new series for 'the old firm of Murdoch and Horne'. Hillyard replied that he had discussed the idea with the Controller of the Home Service and his planners but there was very little enthusiasm for a return of *Much-Binding*, which they quite frankly felt to be dated in formula. However they would be open to suggestions for a brand-new vehicle for the pair.

The truth is that by 1956 the comedy landscape had changed. The popular wartime series such as *ITMA*, *Waterlogged Spa* and *Stand Easy* had been replaced by a new generation of comedy shows such as *Take It From Here*, with Jimmy Edwards, Joy Nichols and Dick Bentley; *Ray's A Laugh*, with Ted Ray and Kitty Bluett; *Educating Archie*, with Peter Brough and Archie Andrews; *Hancock's Half Hour* with Tony Hancock, Bill Kerr and Sid James; and of course *The Goon Show*, with Spike Milligan, Harry Secombe, Michael Bentine and Peter Sellers. Wartime austerity and rationing were already becoming a distant memory and young writers like Frank Muir and Dennis Norden (*TIFH*), Ray Galton and Alan Simpson (*Hancock*), Eric Sykes (*Educating Archie* and *The Goons*) and Spike Milligan (*The Goons*) reflected a new feeling of optimism in the country. Their humour had a harder edge to it and the Goons in particular were creating a new style of radio comedy with their outrageous characters, surreal plots and innovative use of sound effects.

The gentle humour of *Much-Binding* now seemed rather old-fashioned, but that did not prevent Kenneth and Richard continuing to be in demand as a double act, and in March they were the stars on *Henry Hall's Guest Night*. The next day the *Glasgow Evening Times* commented: 'The treat of the show was Richard Murdoch and Kenneth Horne, the most intelligent and slick comic pair we have. They put through their script swiftly, accurately and very funnily.'

By early 1956 Kenneth had succeeded in raising the profile of the BIF and had begun to resuscitate the Fair but time, and money, were running out fast. It became clear that the company needed a further £50,000 from the government in order to stay afloat while Kenneth tried to drum up more support. He asked the President of the Board of Trade, Peter Thorneycroft, for help and he promised that he would do what he could to save the Fair, but then the government suddenly announced that it had withdrawn its backing.

Kenneth felt 'terribly disappointed' and badly let down. The BIF staff had to stage the final Fair in March knowing that they would be out of work when it was over. Many of them had given up secure jobs to join the new company, in the belief that it enjoyed the support of the government. They knew that Kenneth had done everything he could to save BIF, but he still felt personally responsible for the welfare of his staff. He used every contact in his book, calling in favours wherever necessary, to ensure that not one member of his staff was left without a job.

Only then did he worry about himself. He had been approached with a number of interesting offers, but after the collapse of BIF he did not know where to turn. At the top of his shortlist was an attractive proposal from the Ford Motor Company, inviting him to become a roving ambassador and public relations officer for the company, travelling the world to promote their British cars. Kenneth considered this proposal very seriously. He even wrote to Joyce in Canada, seeking her advice, and she encouraged him to accept the offer, although it would probably have confirmed the end of their relationship.

One of the less appealing propositions came from a fellow member of the BIF board, Reg Whitehouse, who was also Chairman of The Chad Valley Company, the toy manufacturers. The company was struggling, and Whitehouse was in his late sixties and preparing to retire; he urged Kenneth to take over from him at Chad Valley as Chairman and Managing Director.

While he was still trying to make a decision, Joyce wrote again to say that she was returning to England because her mother was ill. She was looking for a job in public relations. Kenneth immediately contacted Reg Whitehouse and suggested that Chad Valley should employ Joyce as their Public Relations Officer. When Whitehouse agreed, Kenneth accepted the offer to succeed him as Chairman.

He had previously asked Kate Haynes to stay on as his secretary, whichever job he chose; when he announced that they were going to Chad Valley, she looked amazed. He asked her why, and she told him she thought he had made the wrong choice.

At the beginning of July Kenneth escaped on holiday for a week to the Hotel La Baie Dorée at Cap d'Antibes in the South of France, leaving Kate to wind up operations in the one remaining office at Ingersoll House. After his return, he set her up in a temporary office at Cottesmore Court.

The Chad Valley Company Limited was principally based in Birmingham, with its head offices and factories at Harborne, to the west of the city centre. There were also some showrooms at Newgate Street in the City of London, but they were in a poor condition. New showrooms were being prepared in the West End at Chandos Street, off Cavendish Square, and the plan was for Kenneth to spend the first half of his week in London and the second half in Birmingham.

In practice, his radio and television commitments meant that he was often required to be in London during the evenings and he frequently travelled to and from Birmingham three or more times a week. When he had to spend several days at the annual toy fair at Nuremberg in Germany he commuted daily from London by plane so that he did not miss any of his broadcasting dates. By now this non-stop travelling had become second nature for him, but he was no longer working for a major business like Triplex, and his lavish business expenses proved to be rather a shock at the much smaller Chad Valley.

His workload was immense. In the same week that he became Chairman of Chad Valley, he took over as the compere of *Variety Playhouse* for two months; between April and September he was also a guest panellist on *Twenty Questions*, while Richard Dimbleby was busy launching his new *Panorama* current affairs programme; and he began a new four-month series as chairman of *Find the Link* on BBC Television. After the second episode of *Find the Link*, however, he wrote to Ronnie Waldman, the Head of Light Entertainment, to complain about the standard of the contestants:

> I am a little bit worried about 'Find the Link' which, basically, I am sure is a better idea than any of the other panel games. It seems to me that we ought to give a bit more advance thought to each edition. If I can be of the slightest assistance in choosing the links, or interviewing the selected people earlier than I do now, then I will willingly help.
>
> But the fact remains that an hour and a half before the show comes on, I am faced for the first time with a list of links which quite frankly are not always strong ones. I then interview the competitors, and again it is obvious that if someone had really auditioned them all then quite a number would never have come through to the final. We do not want everyone to 'speak posh', but we do want people who can make themselves understood and who are 'interviewable'.

I am still certain that, with more attention from all of us, 'Find the Link' ought to be the 'tops'.

In August the National Radio Show opened at Earls Court in London and Kenneth co-starred with Eric Sykes and Irene Handl in a one-hour television special from the exhibition called *Opening Night*, a 'star-studded comedy spoof' devised and directed by Sykes. BBC Television and Radio were closely involved with this annual event, and this show was typical of the tie-in programming they used to put on at the time. A week later Kenneth returned to the Radio Show, but this time as one of the judges in a bathing beauty contest.

In September Kenneth and Richard starred in their third television special, *Show For the Telly*, a thirty-minute sketch show in which they were given 'carte-blanche to deliver their particular brand of affable humour'.

The programme featured a number of filmed inserts and began with a sequence outside Kenneth's flat at Cottesmore Court, showing his Rolls Royce waiting at the kerb, with the chauffeur holding a rug by the open door. Kenneth and Richard were seen emerging from the front door of the mansion block, followed by a charlady, who was helped into the car by the chauffeur while Kenneth and Richard mounted a pair of bicycles and pedalled away.

Another sketch was set in a Wild West Saloon packed with rough-looking customers drinking and gambling, with an old piano being played in the corner. Suddenly the swing doors were flung open and Kenneth and Richard entered the saloon, sauntering confidently up to the bar.

BARMAID: Name your poison, strangers.
MURDOCH & HORNE: Two small ports, please!

During the year it seemed as if Kenneth was hardly off the television screens, compering another series of *Camera One* and taking part in

other programmes such as *Ask Pickles, This Is Showbusiness,* the
Petula Clark Show, and a new game show from Manchester called
The Laugh's on Us. Sometimes he was on television two or three
times a week.

He was obviously very much in demand but he was also at risk
of becoming over-exposed. Matters came to a head when it was
proposed that he should be the chairman of a television version of
Twenty Questions. Ronnie Waldman turned down the idea and in
November he wrote to Kenneth to explain why:

> I was becoming increasingly disturbed by the increasing number of
> slightly barbed references to the number of times you were
> appearing on the television screen. Whenever this happens the
> artist concerned is in a most dangerous position. If I was going to be
> successful in maintaining your value both in 'Find the Link' and in
> your compering activities it seemed to be essential that I would have
> to break this absolutely regular run of appearances of yours for a
> short while.

Kenneth accepted the decision and admitted that he had not really
expected to be in the television version of *Twenty Questions.*

Meanwhile commercial television had begun in Britain with the
launch in September 1955 of the two London commercial con-
tractors Associated Rediffusion and the Associated Broadcasting
Company. Kenneth had always insisted that he was a BBC man but
in August 1956 he made his debut on ITV when he made a guest
appearance on an RAF show with Richard Murdoch. Although he
was a freelance and not contracted to the BBC, he had written to Pat
Hillyard to seek permission:

> My old sparring partner Murdoch is doing a week of concerts at
> RAF stations (ghastly thought!) and one of these is to be televised by
> Associated Rediffusion for half an hour on August 7th. Dick has
> asked me to help him out and pop on as a surprise guest, and I said

that I would, provided you had no rooted objection. As you know,
I have no BBC contract, but I don't 'stray'.

He had agreed not to appear on other commercial television
programmes but it would seem he had no objection to advertising,
and in November he recorded a thirty-second TV commercial for a
Christmas gift cheque scheme organized by the Midland Bank and
the other four big banks.

On 12 December 1956 Kenneth finally moved into his new
offices at 9–10 Chandos Street and the Chad Valley showrooms were
officially opened a month later. Roger Swinburne-Johnson, who
served as a director at Chad Valley with Kenneth, described him as
'a very enjoyable companion, who had a most stimulating effect on
his colleagues and staff'.

He may have been able to motivate his colleagues but he knew
next to nothing about the toy business. Kenneth had never been a
hands-on father with Susan and he had no idea what were the
current likes or dislikes of children in the 1950s. He soon recognized
that he was out of his depth.

He recalled later, 'Injecting bright ideas is all right if it is a general
company but when you come to a specialised company, making an
article about which you know absolutely nothing, it is not so easy.
When I went to Chad Valley, very soon after I got there I was asked
to decide which of about forty new lines we were going to make and
sell. I pointed to the two that I liked and they were the two, it
subsequently transpired, they could never sell at all. They were too
nice – the children wanted the revolting stuff.'

14

Surviving a Stroke

IN JANUARY 1957 Kenneth was booked to be the compere of *Variety Playhouse,* a popular comedy and music show which had been a feature of Saturday nights on the Home Service for four years. He had appeared on the show many times before, but for this series his scripts would be written by the up-and-coming team of Eric Merriman and Barry Took.

Merriman was a comedy writer with the leading writers' agency Associated London Scripts and his credits included popular radio shows such as *Henry Hall's Guest Night* and the BBC television series *Great Scott – It's Maynard!,* starring Terry Scott and Bill Maynard. He and Took had first met in 1951 when Took, then an aspiring stand-up comedian, paid Merriman five pounds for some gags to use in the final of a BBC radio talent contest. Took had gone on to make regular appearances on radio and in variety, touring the provincial theatres and starring in the West End revues *For Amusement Only* and *For Adults Only.* When he started to write his own material, Merriman suggested that they team up to write for other comedians, although at first Took 'ghosted' for Merriman, as it was called, because his name did not appear in any of the credits. Once they started to write for Kenneth on *Variety Playhouse,* they found the perfect match for their quirky brand of humour, as demonstrated in this typical opening monologue:

Hello, good evening, and welcome once again to our weekly date in Variety Playhouse . . . and first of all, tonight, I have a special word for all French waiters. Garçon. Well now, any visitors to London will find a wide variety of interesting and unusual events. For instance, next month the South Kensington White Hunters and Explorers' Club will be going on their Annual Safari through Hampton Court Maze. When I asked the Secretary and Gun Bearer the origin of this old-established club he said, 'Well, we all met in the maze twenty years ago and we've been going round together ever since . . .'

Kenneth was originally booked for four months but the combination of Merriman, Took and Horne worked so well that the contract was extended until the end of June.

Meanwhile he had also become a critic for the new women's magazine *She*, writing a column every month in which he looked at the content from the male point of view. Joan Werner Laurie, the editor, announced: 'Each month he will examine the final proofs of *She* and give us his uncensored views (with which I certainly won't always agree). I think his blend of lunacy and sound business common sense should cover every aspect of *She*!'

Sometimes he would praise an article or a feature but he was often highly critical, especially when it came to fashion. In his first column in January 1957, he commented:

'All Set For Spring' is the heading, and can you possibly imagine anything more repulsive than that coat? As far as the cloche hat is concerned, well . . . I don't know, do you? I can think of some uses for it. Why don't people try and look like reasonable human beings instead of following these really ghastly fashions?

So they're going to have twelve TV programmes all about having babies, are they? Well, well, what on earth are we coming to? I suppose if it's going to make young married girls feel comfortable about having babies, then it is a good thing. But I don't think it's the sort of programme that I shall watch.

He was encouraged to pass comment on everything from the photograph on the cover to the quality of the recipes, and he was not afraid to disagree with an article or say if he thought a short story was badly written. But not all of his criticisms were quite so outspoken. In a later issue he commented:

> I always feel a bit sad that proofs I see are eventually corrected, because one comes across some fascinating printing and spelling mistakes. For example, Snowy (p.31) is described as 'a splendid white crathorse'! Well you could have knocked me down with a father!

Kenneth enjoyed writing his column for *She* and he would continue to do so, in sickness and in health, for more than a decade. He was immensely popular with its readers, many of whom would read his comments first, and the editorial staff also appreciated his frank and often humorous observations. After Kenneth died, the editor of *She* said he would be greatly missed and described him as 'a wonderful colleague, a loyal friend, a much-loved contributor and the cruel-kindest critic'.

During the spring Kenneth appeared on a variety of television programmes such as *The Benny Hill Show* and *It's Magic*, and in May he made another guest appearance with Richard Murdoch on the long-running series *This Is Showbusiness*. The show was hosted by the veteran comedian Vic Oliver and highlighted the different aspects of entertainment, being divided into different segments: Music, Drama, Opera, Recording, Music Hall, Cabaret, Musical Comedy, Ballet and Radio.

Kenneth and Richard starred in the radio segment and took part in a comedy sketch set in a doctor's surgery, which featured a nurse played by a pretty twenty-one-year-old actress called Sheree

Winton, better known nowadays as the mother of the radio and television star Dale Winton. Kenneth was Dr Kenworthy and Richard was the patient: 'Well, Doctor, when I wake up in the morning I just can't sleep. Often I'm awake all day!'

> HORNE: I'll test your reflexes, sit down.
>
> (MURDOCH AND NURSE BOTH SIT DOWN. HORNE HITS MURDOCH'S KNEE AND THE NURSE'S LEG REACTS.)
>
> HORNE: Strange!
>
> (HORNE TRIES IT FROM THE OTHER SIDE, WATCHING MURDOCH. NURSE'S LEG REACTS AGAIN AND KICKS HORNE IN THE PANTS.)
>
> HORNE: Oooh!
>
> (HORNE SITS IN CHAIR. MURDOCH HITS HORNE'S KNEE, WATCHING NURSE, AND HIS OWN LEG KICKS.)
>
> MURDOCH: Oh, well, one of us is all right!
>
> HORNE: Now then, Nurse, take off his shirt.
>
> (NURSE APPROACHES AND MURDOCH GOES SHY.)
>
> HORNE: Murdoch, don't be silly. You don't imagine she's never . . .
>
> MURDOCH: I bet she has!

One of Kenneth's more enjoyable tasks during the summer of 1957 was a fortnightly series called *Pleasure Boat* in which he travelled by a variety of pleasure boats, along the River Thames at Maidenhead, on the Oulton Broads in Suffolk, across the Solent to the Isle of Wight, and up the Mersey and the Clyde.

In May he filled in as the chairman of *Twenty Questions* for three weeks while Gilbert Harding was absent owing to ill health, and this was followed by a trial recording for a new radio panel game called *Off the Cuff*. The theme of the game was serious music and sounds, although it was to be played 'strictly for laughs'. Kenneth was a member of the panel, alongside the Australian comedian Dick Bentley from *Take It From Here*, Gerald Moore and Carole Carr, and the show was later turned into a short series.

After his six-month stint on *Variety Playhouse* ended in June, Eric Merriman and Barry Took found that Kenneth had been so 'easy and delightful to write for' that Jacques Brown, the producer of the series, suggested they try to devise a new thirty-minute show for him.

Kenneth said later, 'We thought the same way, and from the first, Merriman seemed to have the knack of writing the kind of things I found it easy to say. We felt it would be a pity to break up a promising partnership; and when the twenty-six *Variety Playhouse* programmes were over, Jacques said we should stick together and try to hit upon an idea of a series for me.'

At the end of June Kenneth wrote to Pat Hillyard, the Head of Variety:

'Variety Playhouse' finished last Sunday and a good time has been had by all (I hope!) for 26 weeks. Our script-writer, Eric Merriman, did a wonderful job for me, and really got in the Horne style, and so he and I put together, with Jacques Brown's connivance, a suggested framework for a future series which we believe would be successful. It has a degree of originality both in construction and ideas.

The working title for the new series was *Don't Look Now* and Eric Merriman sent an outline of the proposed format for the show to the BBC producer Jacques Brown:

As you know, since I have been working on 'Variety Playhouse' for and with Kenneth Horne, I have felt that his potentialities for a solo comedy series are very strong, with a particular emphasis on the style of humour we have built up on 'Playhouse' and I see the basic pattern of the new show being largely an extension of this. Namely that the formula is based on a week in the life of Kenneth Horne, broken into three actual spots, one to vary and the other two constant. In support we will be able to remain fairly flexible, going for either character actors with a wide range of voices or revue artistes. Musically there will be two spots to break the sketches. However I have listed a rough synopsis of content for discussion as follows:

<u>Suggested title</u>: 'Don't Look Now'.

<u>Opening spot</u>: Kenneth Horne to open with a brief patter routine on 'my week' and after a few gags to fade into one particular happening, these being in the vein of what we've already successfully done, such as the opening of a wine festival in Chalfont St Giles, the Kensington and District Working Man's Hunt Ball, the adjudication of a festival of amateur dramatics.

<u>Second spot</u>: This is to be the day in the week when Kenneth presides as chairman over a discussion group with a set of characters, some regular, others not, who answer questions (cod) on topics of the moment.

<u>Final spot</u>: A regular spot. A day in the week where Kenneth collates the material for his weekly documentary feature 'Hornerama'. This is where we present, in comedy documentary technique, the facts on various subjects, either straightforward topics such as steel, transport, which are given a humorous treatment, or questions of the day such as 'wine gum addiction in the United Kingdom'. This particular framework, I feel, does attempt to break away from the routine pattern of sketches and I think we can get a lot of fun, in the Kenneth Horne manner, from the apparently important trivialities which Kenneth does so well.

Pat Hillyard replied to Kenneth that he had seen the proposal and thought it was promising, but there were no openings for a new series in the immediate future. He suggested that they might go ahead and make a pilot programme.

The next task was to establish a budget. A few days later Jacques Brown wrote to Jim Davidson, the Assistant Head of Variety:

Further to my memorandum of June 25th, I envisage a programme as individual and distinctive in its own way as the Eric Barker or Braden shows. Like them, it would not depend on star guests or big names apart from the principal but employ very solid character people.

A first rough breakdown would be:

Kenneth Horne £52.10.0

Five character people say £150

Singers £59.17.0

Script say £70

Total £332.7.0

There could be music charges varying from nothing to £40 per programme.

Merriman asked Barry Took to join him as his co-scriptwriter on the new show and by mid-August they had completed a pilot script. Kenneth wrote to Pat Hillyard:

Jacques Brown and I have now seen and discussed the script which you were good enough to commission for a possible new show for me. I really believe that Eric M. and Barry T. have done a first class job, and I hope you will be able personally to spare a few moments to read through the script.

The whole format (BBC word!) is a little out of the ordinary, there are several original ideas and, apart from anything else, the show appears to be an economical one to produce. I hope we may be allowed to proceed.

Others did not agree. Two days later Jim Davidson, the Assistant Head of Variety, wrote to his superior, Pat Hillyard:

I do not think this will stand up to a successful series. As a show entitled 'Don't Look Now' the basic idea does not emerge and it has little to say in that direction. Therefore it seems to me the title is nothing but an excuse to string together a couple of flimsy situations. I think it is not good enough for the following reasons:

a. Weak format

b. Comedy writing not strong enough.

c. Changes of scene and entries too abrupt.

d. Eric Merriman could do better.

In the end, both sides won the argument. The script was kept essentially the same but it was decided to change the title and Took was given the task of coming up with some new ideas. Merriman wanted to call it *Hornerama* but Took preferred *Round the Horne*. In the end he put forward about six alternatives out of which the BBC chose *Beyond Our Ken*.

When it came to casting *Beyond Our Ken* they wanted strong comedy actors who could play a variety of different characters, and they recruited Ron Moody, Hugh Paddick and the singer Pat Lancaster from *For Adults Only*. They also chose Betty Marsden, for whom Merriman had been writing on television, and Kenneth Williams, who was making a name for himself in the popular *Hancock's Half Hour*.

Everything was ready and at the beginning of September Kenneth was finally able to go on holiday for a month. As soon as he returned, the trial recording took place and on 2 October Kenneth Williams wrote in his diary: 'Did the Kenneth Horne radio show in morning and fluffed a line!! The script was by Eric Merriman and Barry Took. V. good.'

After the pilot show, Peter Dion Titheridge, the Script Editor, wrote to Jim Davidson:

Just to say that I was at the trial recording of [*Beyond Our Ken*] this morning and thoroughly enjoyed it. The fact that the audience around me seemed to be enjoying it too is perhaps more important. I think we have a pretty good potential here. Some witty, offbeat writing (I have always thought Merriman had possibilities) and a very happy cast with Horne's warm, relaxed personality to weld it all together. I do hope this is accepted as a series.

At the end of October Jim Davidson wrote to Kenneth to inform him that the trial programme had been liked sufficiently to warrant the BBC to pencil in a series of *Beyond Our Ken* to start in April 1958. He recommended that he advise the writers of the BBC's intentions.

Although he was about to embark on his first series under his own name, Kenneth still enjoyed performing his double act with Richard Murdoch, and in November they teamed up for a live broadcast of *Saturday Night on the Light* from the VHF Exhibition in Southampton:

MURDOCH: Oh sir, it is good to see you.

HORNE: Thank you, Murdoch – I'm going to reciprocate.

MURDOCH: Are you sir – it's probably the Southampton beer.

HORNE: More than likely – by the way, Murdoch, what brought you to Southampton?

MURDOCH: Well, sir, it's a long story – pull up a chair.

HORNE: Thank you.

MURDOCH: Well, do you remember last Sunday?

HORNE: Last Sunday – now what was I doing last Sunday? (Laugh) Yes, I remember. I had a couple of tickets for a charity concert, so I went.

MURDOCH: Splendid – by the way, how is Bessie?

HORNE: Fine, thank you, but not a word to her about last Sunday.

By January 1958 the scripts for the first series of *Beyond Our Ken* were well under way, but then there came an unexpected hitch. It occurred to the programme planners at the BBC that Kenneth Williams was booked to appear in the new series of *Hancock's Half Hour* and – if *Beyond Our Ken* started as scheduled in April – he would be in two radio series simultaneously. Pat Hillyard wrote to

Kenneth to say that he felt Williams had a very distinctive voice and a limited number of characters upon which to draw. He did not feel that he should be heard in two shows at once and, as Williams had been in *Hancock's Half Hour* first, they had decided to look for a replacement. Kenneth sent an immediate reply: 'May I put in one plea and that is to be allowed to retain Kenneth Williams notwithstanding your decision? He would help the show immensely – lots of others appear in two or more shows at the same time.'

Before the series started, however, Kenneth had a hectic schedule to complete. On 12 February he was the chairman for the pilot recording of a new BBC television series called *Be Your Own Boss* at Wembley Town Hall. The next day he was in Birmingham to take part in the radio show *Personality Top Ten*. On 14 and 19 February he recorded the first two programmes in a new radio panel game called *Sound Idea*, 'in which Peter West encourages Richard Murdoch and Kenneth Horne to vie with Johnny Morris and John Slater in giving fairly reasonable explanations of varied noises'. The show was divided into several sections, with sequences such as unrelated sounds, one-sided telephone conversations, and noises representing popular phrases. On 20 February he was at the BBC Maida Vale studios in London for the second *Be Your Own Boss* television programme. All this was at the same time as being Chairman and Managing Director of Chad Valley, and on the board of Ronuk Floor Polish, which meant commuting from London to Birmingham and back almost every day.

On 25 February Kenneth drove in his Rolls up to Birmingham for a board meeting at the Chad Valley head office. The weather forecast was not very good, so after the meeting Roger Swinburne-Johnson, one of the directors of the company, invited him to stay the night at his house at Broad Camden in Gloucestershire. When another director, Eric Sutton, mentioned that his actress daughter Pauline was appearing that evening in a play at Oxford, Kenneth suggested that they all drive over to see her in the play, after which he would take them out to supper.

It snowed quite heavily during the night. When Kenneth came down to breakfast at Broad Camden next morning, Swinburne-Johnson noticed that he was not looking at all well. Kenneth admitted that he did feel 'a bit poorly' and had slept badly. He had woken up with terrible pins-and-needles in his left leg and he could not get rid of them.

He claimed that he was well enough to drive Swinburne-Johnson in the Rolls to the Chad Valley office, as they had previously arranged, but as they travelled towards Birmingham, a distance of about twenty-five miles, he was clearly in great distress. Swinburne-Johnson offered to drive, but Kenneth would not allow him. Once they got to the office Swinburne-Johnson insisted that he see a doctor immediately and arranged for a company chauffeur to drive him there.

The doctor informed Kenneth that he had suffered a minor stroke and advised him to go directly to a hospital in Birmingham, but Kenneth was determined to go home. The following day was his birthday and he was due to fly to New York. He asked the chauffeur to drive him to the station and somehow he got himself onto the next train to London.

His condition was gradually getting worse and he must have been in great pain. When the train arrived at Euston, a porter found him alone, slumped in the corner of his first-class compartment, completely unable to move. He was still conscious and the porter helped him into a taxi, which Kenneth managed to direct to his own doctor, Dr John Gordon, at Wilton Crescent in Knightsbridge. Dr Gordon promptly diagnosed the cause of the stroke as a coronary thrombosis and arranged for him to be taken home to Cottesmore Court.

That evening Susan arrived back from her work at Marks and Spencer to find the flat unusually quiet and in semi-darkness. Marjorie told her that Kenneth was 'poorly' and was in bed, and she had to be as silent as possible. Next morning Kenneth was admitted to a nursing home in Queen's Gate. By now he was totally paralysed

Kenneth's father, Rev. Charles Silvester Horne, MP. (Horne family)

Kenneth 'Curly' Horne, in his white tie and tails, 1928. (Horne family)

Kenneth aged about seven, after his father's death in 1914. (Horne family)

Kenneth with his first wife, Lady Mary, 1930. (Horne family)

With his second wife, Joan, and their golden cocker spaniel 'Snip', 1936. (Horne family)

With Richard 'Dickie' Murdoch: 'Good morning, sir, it is good to see you!' (Murdoch family)

Wing Commander Horne with Squadron Leader Richard Murdoch (left) and Joyce Grenfell, 1944. (Murdoch family)

The cast of the first series of *Much-Binding-in-the-Marsh*: (Left to right) Maurice Denham, Richard Murdoch, Marilyn Williams, Kenneth, and Sam Costa, 28 January 1947. (BBC)

With Marjorie Thomas,
after the announcement of
their engagement, 1945.
(Horne family)

With his step-daughter
Susan, Marjorie and the
second Rolls, outside their
flat in Cottesmore Court,
1955. (Central Office of Information)

In disguise with Brian Johnston (left), trying to give away money outside Victoria Station on *Let's Go Somewhere*, 3 December 1955. (Johnston family)

Kenneth welcomes Her Majesty the Queen to the British Industries Fair, 1956. (Horne family)

The cast and writers of the first series of *Beyond Our Ken*, 1958. (Back row, left to right) Kenneth Williams, Ron Moody, Hugh Paddick; (middle row) Betty Marsden, Kenneth, Pat Lancaster; (front row) Barry Took, Eric Merriman. (BBC)

The cast of the second series of *Beyond Our Ken*, 1959. (Left to right) Kenneth Williams, Hugh Paddick, Betty Marsden, Kenneth, Pat Lancaster, Bill Pertwee. (BBC)

Joyce Davis, c.1960: 'Why didn't you clock in earlier?'
(Horne family)

The cast of the final series of *Round the Horne*, 1968:
(Left to right) Hugh Paddick, Kenneth Williams, Kenneth,
Betty Marsden, Douglas Smith. (BBC)

Kenneth looking anxious, with his step-daughter Susan on her wedding day, 2 September 1961. His stroke had left him with a permanent limp, but he was determined to escort her up the aisle. (Horne family)

on his left side and unable to speak. He lay there 'like a log', the muscles on his face had slipped, and his skin was a pallid grey colour.

It was his fifty-first birthday. He had been due to fly to New York that day to meet American television executives, and Ronnie Waldman had written a letter of introduction to Mark Goodson, the producer of the original US version of *What's My Line*. The flight was cancelled and so were all his other business and broadcasting commitments. Jacques Brown, the producer of *Beyond Our Ken*, informed the Assistant Head of Light Entertainment that he had suspended all activities concerning the trial programme.

Joyce Davis had to deal with all his correspondence, signing his letters as his 'acting secretary'. After two weeks he was finally well enough to leave the nursing home and return to Cottesmore Court. His physiotherapist, Joe Friel, who became a close friend, described it as 'one of the worst strokes he had ever seen' but Kenneth was determined to recover as soon as possible. The muscles in his face had been badly affected by the stroke, making it difficult for him to speak, and he had to learn how to talk again. Friel used to massage the muscles of his face and neck, and also mouth words, making Kenneth mime their shape.

Later Kenneth would resort to a course of treatment known as 'proprioceptive neuromuscular facilitation technique' administered by a Canadian female speech therapist. She taught him to suck up cigarette papers or peas by using a straw, over and over again, in order to get the muscles around his mouth working again.

After one fairly heavy session of face exercises, Joe Friel was giving Kenneth a general massage when he applied some considerable pressure on his left thigh. Kenneth let out a yelp of pain and managed to squeeze out the words, 'You bugger!'

He was on the road to recovery.

His left leg had become so weakened that at first he was unable to walk, but after a month of regular treatment he was able to get around the flat using two walking sticks. A month later he was using one stick and eventually he could walk unaided, although he was left with a permanent limp.

As Kenneth's physical recovery progressed, Dr Gordon became more concerned about his mental well-being. He was worried that if Kenneth ceased all his business and broadcasting activities he would succumb to depression. Kenneth was so used to being busy that he hated being unable to work. The solution came from an unexpected source. The programme planners at the Home Service had decided to move the recording of *Twenty Questions* to Monday nights, at the same time as *Panorama* was being transmitted on television. This meant that Richard Dimbleby, the presenter of *Panorama*, would be unavailable as a panellist for the next series of *Twenty Questions*.

Dimbleby was furious. He had not been consulted about the changes and was incensed by the BBC's cavalier attitude towards him, even threatening to accept offers of work from ITV. Having been on the panel of *Twenty Questions* for nearly twelve years, he believed that without him the programme would have to be taken off the air, but the BBC refused to reverse their decision. Instead, they offered Dimbleby's place on the panel to Kenneth, who accepted it gratefully.

Although Kenneth was desperate to get back to work, Dr Gordon felt he still needed a few more weeks to recuperate. The BBC were surprisingly considerate and agreed to 'keep the seat warm for him' on the panel, engaging Brian Johnston as a replacement until he was fit to return. Kenneth was still having difficulty in walking, but the BBC assured him that he could dispense with the warm-up before the programme if necessary, and could be seated at the table before the studio audience arrived. Marjorie Horne thanked Pat Newman, telling him that the decision has been an invaluable help and she was more grateful than she could say.

In early April, only six weeks after the stroke, Kenneth notified the BBC that he was well enough to return to work and he was booked to appear on the fourth *Twenty Questions* in the new series on 21 April. He was extremely worried about making a come-back so soon after his illness. He asked Joyce Davis to accompany him to the first programme, but on the day of the broadcast she was laid up in bed with a heavy cold. On his way to the studio, Kenneth called round to see her at the flat she shared with her mother in Hays Mews, off Berkeley Square in Mayfair. He was limping badly and could only walk with the help of a stick but he made it up the stairs to her flat and sat for a while beside her bed. Later Joyce would reveal that it was the only time she had ever known Kenneth in an acute state of nerves.

Joyce was the only person in whom he felt able to confide his true feelings. He told her he was embarrassed about his limp. He had always walked onto the stage at the Paris Studio before a programme but he did not want his colleagues or the audience to see that he could no longer walk properly. She tried to reassure him that it did not matter and, on the contrary, everybody would be overjoyed to see him back again.

Kenneth managed to fool everyone. Norman Hackforth, who was the 'Mystery Voice' on the show, confessed later that he had no idea what a challenge Kenneth had found this first programme to be. When he arrived at the Paris, according to Hackforth, Kenneth 'practically galloped down the stairs' with his walking stick, as if to prove there was nothing wrong with him. Hackforth had also used a stick for many years, so Kenneth waved his cheerily in the air and shouted, 'Snap!' before joking, 'I shan't need mine much longer.'

When it was time to introduce the members of the panel to the audience, the producer announced, 'We are pleased to welcome back Kenneth Horne!' Waiting in the wings, Kenneth dropped his stick, put on his bravest face, and loped onto the stage with an exaggerated stride as if he was trying to be funny. Recalled Hackforth later: 'The audience rose to their feet and cheered.'

The series ran for three months and when it returned later in the year the schedules were rearranged, with the programme being moved to Tuesdays so that Richard Dimbleby could rejoin the panel. But it had served its purpose and reintroduced Kenneth to broadcasting.

It also confirmed that he had recovered sufficently from his illness, and the BBC gave the green light for the first series of *Beyond Our Ken* to start recording on 18 June. After hearing the good news, Kenneth wrote to Pat Hillyard: 'Thanks for your hospitality, your encouragement and your faith – we shall try to make the show the best ever.'

13

Beyond Our Ken

AFTER RETURNING TO work on *Twenty Questions* in April 1958 Kenneth had some critical decisions to make about his future. Dr Gordon told him that he was lucky to be alive: he had been juggling two separate careers for more than twelve years and the stress had nearly killed him. He had to cut down. He could either pursue a business career, but at a less powerful level than before, or he could carry on broadcasting. But he could not do both.

For Kenneth it was a bitter blow. He had followed two careers because he enjoyed them both, but he had always said that if he had to choose, he would give up broadcasting. He was just fifty-one years old. As a younger man he had been athletic and a sportsman. Now he had to face the reality that he was never going to be one hundred per cent fit again. It was a humbling moment.

Later Kenneth claimed that it was the mental strain caused by his business problems that had led to his stroke rather than the physical hardship of trying to sustain two careers. He had been unable to cope with the pressure of two demanding jobs when he was fit. Now he did not have the physical or the mental strength required to continue in business at the executive level that he had known before. It would not be practical to do such a job on a part-time basis and he was not interested in taking on a less important position.

That left only broadcasting. It was less demanding mentally and more flexible in its working hours. When it came down to it, he had no choice. In early May he wrote to Roger Swinburne-Johnson, tendering his resignation as the Chairman and Managing Director of Chad Valley.

Without his business salary, he needed to make some serious economies. He had always lived beyond his means but now he was forced to change his lifestyle drastically. The first thing to go was the Rolls Royce Silver Cloud. Kenneth sold the car, gave his devoted chauffeur Percy Millea a generous golden handshake and found him another job. He was serious about saving money. He replaced the Rolls with a second-hand Morris 1000.

He also needed more time to recuperate. Kenneth had returned to work earlier than expected but he was still suffering the after-effects of the stroke. Dr Gordon advised him to get as much fresh air and rest as possible, so Kenneth rented a small apartment near the sea at Flat 113, Furze Croft, in Hove. His plan was to live in Hove for the next two months and travel up to London every Tuesday morning for the recordings of *Beyond Our Ken*, staying the night with Marjorie at Cottesmore Court and returning to Hove after lunch each Wednesday.

He was still having difficulty talking after the stroke, so Joyce Davis used to stay with him regularly while he was in Hove, helping him to read scripts and practise his vocal exercises. After a few weeks he had recovered his speech almost completely.

While he was recuperating, he wrote a proposal for a new television series called *Talk of the Town*, which was co-devised by Eric Merriman. The fifteen-minute programmes were to include a hotchpotch of features such as new talent, secret recordings, sketches, interviews, spoof inventions and even antiques.

He also came up with an idea for a thirty-minute series to be called *Birthday Wishes*, based on his old 'Monday Birthday Party' radio slot, in which he would: 'give a TV birthday party to someone and ask them to fulfil five wishes – two or three involve music – one might be to meet a famous person or see a famous place or do something new. Guests would be famous, infamous or ordinary.'

He sent the proposals to Kenneth Adam, the controller of BBC television, saying, 'I am being pestered by the "rival camps" to produce something for them . . . I am at the moment (for the first time in my life) in the position of having to rely on radio and TV work for my income, so naturally I am anxious to have your reactions as soon as possible.' Unfortunately, six months later he heard that both proposals had been turned down.

Meanwhile the long-awaited series of *Beyond Our Ken* finally got under way with the recording of the first show at the Paris on 18 June 1958. It was broadcast on the Light Programme two weeks later, on Tuesday 1 July at 8 p.m., with the *Radio Times* describing it as 'a sort of radio show'. The cast included Kenneth Horne, Kenneth Williams, Hugh Paddick, Betty Marsden, Ron Moody, Patricia Lancaster and Stanley Unwin, with music by the Malcolm Mitchell Trio and, later in the series, the Fraser Hayes Four.

According to the Audience Research Report, the first edition of *Beyond Our Ken* was not particularly well received by the sample audience. One of the problems was the script, which some of the listeners complained had contained some painfully corny gags, was juvenile and 'neither clever nor amusing'. On the other hand others regarded it as a promising start and felt that the script was 'refreshing and delightfully new'.

Most of the cast worked very well together, swapping characters and voices with remarkable ease. The exception was Stanley Unwin who had only one real character, as 'Professor' Unwin with his own gobbledegook language, and he was quietly dropped after the first show.

The producer, Jacques Brown, was a rather eccentric character who came from a Portuguese background and was always seen wearing a beret on his head. He was also a great connoisseur of food and wine. Bill Pertwee recalls that he would often be giving instructions to the cast when he would stop suddenly and say, 'By the way, have you tried Le Caprice?' and then forget completely what he had been trying to tell them.

After Kenneth, the best-known member of the cast was Kenneth Williams. He had made his name on the West End stage as the Dauphin in George Bernard Shaw's *St Joan* and then in the radio series *Hancock's Half Hour* which he had joined in 1955 as the all-purpose voice man. His most popular character was known as Snide, an ingratiating bore with a simpering voice, whose expressions, 'Good evenin'' and 'No, stop messing about!' became national catchphrases. They used to irritate Tony Hancock so much that he insisted that the writers Ray Galton and Alan Simpson drop the character from the show.

At first Williams was not sure what to make of Kenneth: 'Here was this strange establishment figure in a neat dark suit, more like somebody from the Foreign Office rather than a pro.' Soon he came to appreciate that Kenneth Horne, unlike Tony Hancock, was a team player. 'It doesn't matter who gets the laughs,' Kenneth told him once, 'as long as the show gets them.'

Kenneth had been writing and broadcasting comedy for more than fifteen years and he was used to bringing out the best in his fellow performers. According to Williams, Kenneth had a 'card-index' mind, in which there seemed to be stored every funny voice, every comedy trick, which he knew each member of the cast was capable of doing. Sometimes at the first script read-through, if the lines did not sound very funny, Jacques Brown would come through on the talk-back from the control room, saying, 'It's not coming off the paper, dears! Lift it off the paper!'

Then Kenneth would suggest, 'Try that bit Irish', or 'Do your Noël Coward', or whatever voice he thought would make the line work better, and he was almost never wrong.

Kenneth Williams had such an outrageous personality that Hugh Paddick was rather left in his shadow. But Paddick played an equally important role in *Beyond Our Ken*, providing a wonderful variety of voices and characters. He was essentially a stage performer who had appeared in the West End musical *The Boy Friend* and revues such as *For Amusement Only* and *For Adults Only*. Later he would take over the role of Colonel Pickering in *My Fair Lady*. Barry Took described him as 'courteous, amusing, talented and kind'.

Betty Marsden was equally at home on stage, television or radio. Born in Liverpool, she had trained at the Italia Conti Stage School and had performed with ENSA – the Entertainments National Service Association – during the war. She had a strong personality and a 'certain highly strung brilliance' that made her characters come to life with an added sparkle. As the only woman in the cast she had to play everything from a sexpot to a slag and never failed.

The final member of the original cast, Ron Moody, admits that he was not particularly excited when Barry Took invited him to join *Beyond Our Ken*. He was starring in *For Adults Only* at the Strand, with his name in lights above the title. He had performed his solo act on shows such as *Workers' Playtime* and had made guest appearances on other radio programmes. To him, *Beyond Our Ken* was just another radio show. He was in for a shock.

'When I got into it,' he recalls, 'I suddenly discovered that I'd moved into another world entirely and this was the world of virtuoso performers. I was no longer "above the title", I was very much a learner. These people were so expert; they were masters of the craft and I was very green.'

The opening of the show was different to every other comedy series at the time because it dispensed with the customary signature tune. Instead, *Beyond Our Ken* always started with a short sketch, usually a play on words tied in with a film title. Then the announcer, Douglas Smith, would welcome listeners to the show and introduce the 'guests' appearing that week:

SMITH: Among those taking part are General Sir Gertrude Fanshawe, Marion Haste, The House of Lords Banjo Octet, Miss Claudine Caterpillar –
WILLIAMS: She's got a nice pair of legs, pair of legs, pair of legs . . .
SMITH: – To continue, Dizzy Barbirolli, Nina and Fred

Winterbottom, and of course Mr Kenneth Horne, who prefers to remain anonymous. Ladies and gentlemen, Kenneth Horne!

Kenneth would begin by going through his diary of the last week, with comments such as: 'On Monday I bumped into a friend of mine who was looking utterly miserable. Apparently his wife had refused to speak to him for a month . . . and this was the last day!'

This would lead into one of the most popular segments of the show, 'Hornerama', a parody of BBC TV's current affairs programme *Panorama*, which featured a discussion on: 'Topics of our time, in which we take a closer look at people and events in the news'. The subject could be anything, from insurance to the state of the British film industry. This was the only part of the show which included stock characters, a regular panel of experts, who appeared each week to discuss 'this week's searching question', and always uttered the same catchphrases.

Kenneth Williams was Arthur Fallowfield, a rustic Somerset farmer with an eye for the ladies, particularly his neighbour, Mrs Forrester – 'I make no bones about it, I'm looking for someone to love.' Fallowfield's response to everything was: 'The answer lies in the soil.' Williams was also the doddery old gentleman who had always been doing something for 'thirty-five years'.

Hugh Paddick played Stanley Birkinshaw, whose ill-fitting dentures caused him to splutter and spray his answers over everyone in sight. One of his funniest moments was when he recited 'To Be or Not to Be' to celebrate the 400th anniversary of the birth of Shakespeare. He was also the hopeless pop star Ricky Livid, based on 1950s pop idols such as Tommy Steele and Marty Wilde, who often ended his answer with the comment, 'I like the backing.' When the topic was foreign holidays, he revealed, 'I like the packing!'

Another of Paddick's characters, actually written by Kenneth Horne, was Cecil Snaith, an accident-prone BBC reporter who never managed to complete his commentary and would gasp, 'And with that, I return you to the studio!'

Betty Marsden played Fanny Haddock, a perfect take-off of the ghastly TV cook Fanny Craddock, whose husband Johnny was always trying to get his hands on her dumplings:

MARSDEN: Hullo there, my darling people! I'm delighted to be back after a long spell in the kitchen. I've also been busy writing a book which is published this month and it's called '101 things to do with a cucumber'.

HORNE: Yes, well we won't ask what the odd one is, will we?

Two of the best-loved characters were Rodney and Charles, played by Williams and Paddick, a pair of effete young men who always greeted each other with an excitable 'Hello, Rodney! Hello, Charles!' – even down a coal mine:

WILLIAMS: Hello, Rodney!

PADDICK: Hello, Charles!

WILLIAMS: Shan't be a minute. There . . . are my seams straight?

PADDICK: Absolutely dolly, Rodders. You make a first class coal miner.

WILLIAMS: Thank you, Charles. I wish the others thought so too. They keep giving me such black looks.

PADDICK: Oh, take no notice, Roddy. They're jealous. Just because you've got a special lamp.

WILLIAMS: It is rather swish, isn't it. Don't you just adore the way the light keeps changing colour?

PADDICK: Yes. What a novel idea to have it set in a Chianti bottle. I say, what do you think of my new trousers?

WILLIAMS: Oh, rather! They're lovely. They're such a dinky shade of walnut brown.

PADDICK: Mmmm. I call them my nutty slacks!

The initial contract for *Beyond Our Ken* was for just six weeks but it was such an immediate success that it was extended to twenty-one weeks, running until mid-November.

Kenneth was supposed to be taking things easier but in July Richard Murdoch approached him with an offer from Radio Luxembourg for the pair of them to do a forty-week series of half-hour comedy and music programmes, to be sponsored by Curry Bicycles. Kenneth wrote to Pat Newman, the Variety Booking Manager, to seek permission from the BBC, saying that his recent illness had forced him – temporarily he hoped – to give up his interests in the business world. He added that he thought of himself as a BBC man, but Richard wanted him to do it. The BBC gave the series its blessing, although nothing seems to have come of the idea.

Kenneth was keen to get back onto television but he was worried about whether he was fit enough to cope with the stress. In June he told a colleague, 'I'm better, though one hundred per cent recovery will take a few more months.' He was being bombarded with offers from commercial television – 'being ITV-ized from all directions', as he put it – but for the moment he decided to stick with the BBC. On 24 July he made a guest appearance on the *Jack Payne Show* and, to his relief, it went well. Afterwards he wrote to the producer, Ernest Maxin: 'A thousand thanks for re-introducing me to television so quietly and sympathetically. It was great fun.'

Now that he felt more confident, Kenneth gave in to the pressure from commercial television and accepted an offer from Tyne Tees TV to present a weekly advertising magazine called *Trader Horne*. The fifteen-minute programme was transmitted on Sunday afternoons at 4.25 p.m. and also featured the actress Ann Croft and a character called Stallibrass, played by Graham Tennant, a part-time radio actor and the managing director of a local office equipment company, who was hired by Kenneth to provide a regional accent.

In the early days of ITV each region had its own local advertising magazine, which was designed to look like an ordinary programme but was simply an excuse to promote an assortment of products and services. Each advertiser paid to have their product mentioned on the programme for a specific amount of time, which could be from 30 seconds up to three minutes. Kenneth tried to make the programmes as entertaining as possible, with the emphasis on humour, and enlisted Joyce Davis to liaise with the advertising agencies and to help him write the scripts.

Every Friday Kenneth would take the train up to Newcastle with Joyce and Ann Croft to record the programme for the following Sunday. They used to while away the time by playing 'Consequences', which Kenneth made more difficult, and much funnier, by insisting that each consecutive line had to rhyme. One week there was a strike by railway buffet staff which meant there was no food available on the train. After travelling to Newcastle without a meal, they were not looking forward to the journey home after the programme, but when they arrived at Newcastle station they were greeted by three white-coated waiters from the Royal Station Hotel. Kenneth had ordered three hampers containing champagne, whisky and other drinks, cold chicken, bread rolls and butter, plus an assortment of sandwiches for any other hungry passengers. The hampers were delivered to the dining car, where about twenty people joined Kenneth, Joyce and Ann for a riotous party all the way back to London.

The advertisers would often supply Kenneth with free samples of their various products, such as ties, socks and bars of chocolate, which he would take back to London to share with the cast of *Beyond Our Ken*. They were suitably grateful but at one rehearsal a hopeful member of the cast suggested, 'Try advertising Rolls Royce next week!'

Kenneth still had many important business contacts and they came in useful in September when he had to conduct the first in a series of interviews for the BBC World Service programme *Calling East Africa*. These were essentially publicity programmes for British industry and involved talking to leading businessmen about their connections with East Africa. Among his subjects were the

Chairman of Walls Group, who were exporting ice cream to East Africa; De Havilland, who had sold two Comet airliners to the region; and Lord Halsbury, Managing Director of Research and Development Corporation, who had developed the new wonder drug Cortisone from sisal juice in East Africa.

It was clear that *Beyond Our Ken* was a major hit and at the end of September the BBC commissioned a second series to start in March 1959. They offered Kenneth his usual fee of 50 guineas per programme which prompted the following plea to Pat Newman:

I am delighted at the confidence that the BBC are showing in 'B.O.K.' I am hoping that you will be able to consider a revision of my fee in the near future (upwards if poss:!)

As you know I am now relying on the BBC to pay my rent for me, so every penny is important. It may of course be that you consider my fee is adequate compared with performers of similar standing – if so, then you must say so please.

The BBC increased his fee to fifty-five guineas, which meant that after fifteen years he was finally being paid the same amount as Richard Murdoch. It was also, one should point out, much more than the rest of the cast of *Beyond Our Ken*.

The first series ended on 19 November and Kenneth invited the whole cast of *Beyond Our Ken* to lunch at Cottesmore Court where they discussed plans for the following year. Afterwards Kenneth told Pat Hillyard, now Head of Light Entertainment (Sound), that the cast were 'tickled to death' at the confidence the BBC had shown in the series. He had just one request – for some new music for the orchestra. The BBC had been saving money by using old musical arrangements from other programmes for the songs by Pat Lancaster and also recycling musical links from former radio series such as *Bedtime with Braden*.

The cast went their separate ways, with Kenneth Williams returning to *Hancock's Half Hour*, which he found a depressing experience after the friendly atmosphere on *Beyond Our Ken*. 'Did the Hancock show from the Piccadilly,' Williams wrote in his diary. 'It was a general disaster. Really terrible. This team is so dreary to me now! – how different to the jolly warmth of "B.O.K."'

Kenneth needed a rest and in December he rented the flat in Hove for a further three months, telling Pat Newman, 'by which time I expect to be 100 per cent fit.' Susan used to visit Hove at the weekends but unfortunately relations between Marjorie and her daughter had not improved. Susan had left school and, after doing a course at Queen's Secretarial College, she had started a job at Marks and Spencer in London. Now that she was older – she turned twenty in January – she refused to submit to her mother, and by Saturday morning she would often have reduced Marjorie to tears, much to Kenneth's distress. On one occasion, he told Susan, 'If you can't behave better than that, I don't think you should come any more.'

While he was staying in Hove, Kenneth made regular journeys up to London as before, to record editions of *Variety Playhouse* and *London Lights* with Richard Murdoch, and to appear every Wednesday on *Roundabout*, reading six short stories which he had been specially commissioned to write for the programme. Since resigning from his business interests, he had been without a regular secretary, although Joyce worked with him occasionally on his television programmes. Richard Murdoch offered to help by sharing the services of his own secretary, Eileen Miller, known affectionately as 'Mick', after the champion greyhound Mick the Miller. Richard kept a flat in Chelsea Cloisters, a luxury block of flats in Sloane Avenue, which Eileen used as her office.

From now on she would also do secretarial work for Kenneth, dealing with his correspondence and his radio and television contracts. It was the start of a happy working relationship which would continue for the rest of his life.

16

Arrivals and Departures

THE SECOND SERIES of *Beyond Our Ken* started on 19 March 1959 and ran for twenty weeks until the end of July. While it was off the air there had been one or two important changes. Ron Moody had left the cast, to be replaced by Bill Pertwee, and the Fraser Hayes Four had taken over as the regular musical act, with incidental music by Edwin Braden.

Some people thought Moody had quit the programme because he did not like being a team player and wanted to be a star. 'That's not true,' he says:

> I left because I wasn't very good at it. When it came to performing in these sketches and these very witty routines that Barry and Eric had written, I found that I couldn't make it work. Either I was playing to the radio audience, the distant millions who were listening, although I wasn't really aware of them, in which case I couldn't get the studio audience, or I would play to the studio audience and find I was off mike.
>
> When it was played back, there were all these wonderful rich, multi-resonant voices coming in and my thin little voice somewhere over to the side. I never felt that I was good enough in the company of such fine performers. It was good fun, but I wasn't really a member of the cast.

Another significant change was that the programme was given a repeat broadcast each week. The first series had been broadcast only on Tuesday evenings but the second series was repeated the following Sunday at 2.15 p.m., at a time when most families were gathered together for Sunday lunch, and it helped the programme to reach an enormous new audience.

After the first recording, Kenneth Williams noted: 'Did the broadcast from the Paris OK. It was indifferent well. Ron Moody is dropped! and replaced by Bill Pertwee. Negative. Pity to break up a team in this way.'

Despite Williams's misgivings, Bill Pertwee was a valuable addition to the cast. Apart from anything else, he played all the parts that nobody else wanted to do. He had originally met Kenneth through his friendship with Joyce Davis; they were both members of the Olympic Club in Gerrard Street, Soho, in the area now known as Chinatown. Joyce had another friend who was a pianist and they used to perform together as members of The Star Timers' Amateur Dramatic Society in village halls in the Barnet area. She invited Pertwee to join them and he was doing his comedy act one evening when Kenneth came along to see Joyce and was introduced to him.

A few years later, now a professional, he performed a four-minute comedy spot, doing a number of different voices, in an edition of *Variety Playhouse* starring Jack Hulbert and Cicely Courtneidge, which had been compered by Kenneth, written by Eric Merriman and produced by Jacques Brown. Then during the summer of 1958 he was appearing in the Fol-de-Rols revue at the Winter Gardens Theatre in Eastbourne when Kenneth, Kenneth Williams and Jacques Brown were in town for the weekend and popped in to see the show. A few months later Brown contacted him to explain that they were slimming down the cast after the first series and he wanted Pertwee to be the new utility man.

At first Pertwee was booked for only six shows. He was moving into a new flat and needed some extra money to pay for carpets and fittings so he went to see his bank manager to ask for an overdraft. When the bank manager asked him whether he had any work,

Pertwee carefully showed him his BBC contract for *Beyond Our Ken*, covering up the words 'six weeks' with his fingers, and he got his overdraft. Soon afterwards his contract was extended and he was to work with Kenneth and the rest of the team for the next eight years.

PADDICK: Roll up! Roll up! Get your tickets now. It's the greatest little show on earth. Performing fleas that will astound you. Roll up! roll up!

PERTWEE: Well, blow me down, it's Alfred Nuthatch.

PADDICK: Do you mind, the great Alfredo.

PERTWEE: 'Ere, don't you recognise me? Herbert Fitch.

PADDICK: Of course, Herbert, it's ages since we've last seen each other.

PERTWEE: I'll say. You were a travelling salesman then. What's all this?

PADDICK: Well, since 1956 I've been running a flea circus.

WILLIAMS: That was an excerpt from *The Seven Year Itch* – another in our series, 'A Film Worth Remembering', which is more than can be said for the next half hour!

'It was a glorious time for me,' relates Pertwee. 'I was living in Brighton and I used to get off the train at Victoria and walk through St James's Park with a smile on my face every Wednesday morning. We used to get to the Paris Studios in Lower Regent Street around about ten o'clock. Then we'd have a chat about Kenneth Williams' latest exploits, or whatever it might be, and a cup of coffee, and then somebody would say, "Are we ready to have a read-through?"'

Williams would delight in discussing his latest medical ailments, of which there were many, in colourful detail. One week he was describing the condition of a large boil on his bottom when Kenneth enquired politely, 'Is that the same boil as last week or a different one?'

The cast made Pertwee feel very welcome, with the possible exception of Williams who would joke to the others in front of him, 'Why have we got *him* in the show? We can do all the voices!'

Pertwee used his skill at doing comic impressions to introduce some regular new characters to the show, such as the drunken Irish poet Seamus O'Toole, who was always on the lookout for some booze, and Hanky Flowerd, a wickedly accurate send-up of the comedian Frankie Howerd. My favourite was the television reporter Ryfe Hobertson, a brilliant parody of Fyfe Robertson, the eccentric Scottish reporter on the *Tonight* programme, who was always outside at some distant location, saying, 'I'm standing now . . .'

Kenneth would often help him develop his characters. 'He was a very kind man,' recalls Pertwee. 'I was a raw recruit, but he would say, "Why not try this?" He was a terrific feed, with a natural sense of timing. Somebody once pointed out to him that he had not been on for four pages but he didn't mind. He knew it was his show.'

Apart from his limp, Kenneth showed few outward signs of having suffered a stroke. He found it difficult to stand for any length of time and sometimes he would lean heavily on Kenneth Williams' shoulder when they were together at the microphone, but his voice sounded as strong as ever and he always seemed to be cheerful. His godson, Tim Murdoch, believes that it was all part of maintaining his public image. 'Stoicism ruled the day,' says Murdoch. 'He was putting on an act the whole time.' Occasionally he would have to drop the pretence and one day he asked Bill Pertwee if he would fetch him a small brandy from the Captain's Cabin, the pub around the corner from the studio, to steady himself before a show.

For several months Kenneth had been travelling to Newcastle each week to record the advertising magazine *Trader Horne,* and in April, he wrote to Barrie Edgar, a television producer in the BBC Midland Region:

I do a T.V. Ad Mag each week from Newcastle and one of my clients is desperately keen on getting into Ad Mags as an actor! It is, as you can imagine, difficult for me to tell him not to be a twerp because he's no good anyhow!

Do you ever audition optimistic types? And if so, can you audition him and tell him to forget any ambition as far as TV is concerned? He's quite a nice type – somewhat Mongolian and about 50!

Barrie Edgar sent a swift reply:

I, personally, cannot offer your client an audition as I do very little drama these days. However, if he lives in the Midland Region our drama producer, Peter Dews, may be able to help. In any case I feel that our call on middle aged Mongolians may be somewhat limited.

In April Kenneth gave a talk on *Woman's Hour* about what he had 'Learned from Life'. Afterwards he sent a note to the producer of the programme, Antony Derville:

I enjoyed the experience immensely and am always available for other tasks should I be able to assist in any way. How about a 5 minute per day sort of Dornford Yates type of serial – told as a monologue (expense!)? Author available.

Derville politely declined his offer but the letter was typical of Kenneth. He almost always sent a thank-you letter to producers immediately after doing a programme and he was always trying to drum up more work. Not that he had much spare time. In a typical week at the beginning of May 1959 he was filming a television show in Southampton all Monday and Tuesday morning; on Wednesday he was rehearsing and recording *Beyond Our Ken*; and at 7.50 a.m. on Thursday he was off on the train to Newcastle to present *Trader Horne*, returning home on Saturday morning.

Among other programmes that month, he recorded an appearance on the panel game *Does the Team Think?* and deputized for Richard Dimbleby on the panel of *Twenty Questions* while

Dimbleby was in Canada to commentate on the official opening by the Queen of the St Lawrence Seaway. He was also the celebrity guest on the children's television series *A Dog's Chance* with Brian Johnston and TV animal expert Stanley Dangerfield, where, despite knowing nothing about dogs, he had to help them choose the 'Personality Dog'.

Meanwhile the second series of *Beyond Our Ken* had reached the end of its run and after the recording of the final show at the Paris on 22 July Kenneth took the whole cast, as well as the production staff and the sound effects boys, out to lunch.

The next day he was at the BBC Television Theatre in Shepherd's Bush, where he was the chairman of the judges and compere of the GPO Personality Girl Contest, a task which he must have enjoyed because he continued to introduce the annual contest for several years.

Then the following morning he departed with Marjorie on a six-week holiday to Porto d'Ischia on the Isle of Ischia, off the coast of Naples. Before he left, he wrote to Pat Newman, the Variety Booking Manager:

> Just a reminder that I'm off for a (?) well earned holiday on Friday July 24th (9 a.m.). In order that I may not be entirely forgotten during my sojourn abroad, please 'phone Miss Miller ('Mick') at KNIghtsbridge 2195 from time to time.
>
> I intend once again to burst upon an unsuspecting England on Monday, September 7th, broke and eager for work however lowly. Mick knows my itinerary; she has my diary (the good one) and will deal with the recipients of this letter much more courteously than they deserve!

Pat Newman replied:

> I am convinced your holiday is extremely well earned and it will probably have to be well paid for too I guess. We will keep a special

night staff so that Miss Miller is 'phoned ceaselessly, thus assuring
you of our interest.

It was less than eighteen months since his stroke and Kenneth was
in need of a long break. He once described his perfect holiday as
'reasonable comfort, really warm swimming, and something to
occupy my time in the event of lousy weather'. After four weeks at
the Hotel Ischia he sent a note to a colleague: 'This is a nice joint,
and sun and food and drink are doing me a power of good.' Even on
holiday, however, he could not stop thinking about work, and he
wrote from the hotel to Pat Hillyard:

> I have mentioned to Jacques [Brown] that I am well through
> writing a Christmas B.O.K. (we did one last year) – hope you'll be
> able to find room for it. The scribes will be doing T.I.F.E. so I
> thought I'd take it on. Eric Merriman will be livid!

The second series of *Beyond Our Ken* had been such a hit that when
Frank Muir and Denis Norden announced they were leaving the
immensely popular radio series *Take It From Here* to work in
television, Eric Merriman and Barry Took were asked to take over
from them. A special Christmas version of *Beyond Our Ken* was
indeed broadcast on 21 December, so, with Merriman and Took
otherwise engaged writing the new series of *Take It From Here,* it
would appear that most of the script for it was written by Kenneth
himself.

After returning from Italy, he was reunited with Richard
Murdoch in October for a TV Ad Mag called *Top Gear*, which was
recorded at the ATV studios in Wembley but transmitted in the
Midland region. It is a perfect example of how advertising was passed
off as entertainment in the early days of commercial television. In a
fifteen-minute programme they would mention about nine different
motoring products or businesses, ranging from antifreeze and
radiator additives to car magazines, scooters and caravan centres:

(GARAGE. RICHARD HUMMING TO HIMSELF AND CLANKING TOOLS AS IF BUSY ON AN ENGINEERING JOB. A GOOD SECOND-HAND BARKER AND SHENTON CAR STANDS NEARBY; ON A RAMP IS A MODERN ONE; ALSO SOMEWHERE AROUND IS AN OLD WRECK CALLED AGNES WITH A NUDE NYMPH ON THE RADIATOR CAP.

KENNETH, RESPLENDENT IN BLACK JACKET, PINSTRIPES, HOMBURG, CARNATION, ENTERS CARRYING BROWN PAPER CARRIER BAG CONTAINING ASSORTED GROCERIES, A CAN OF BOOTS ANTIFREEZE UNSEEN, AND A COUPLE OF STICKS OF CELERY.)

HORNE: (COUGHS)

MURDOCH: (NOT LOOKING) Ah – good morning. Mr Staveley?

HORNE: No.

MURDOCH: Oh. Mr Hamfrith?

HORNE: No.

MURDOCH: Gordon Stolgiton?

HORNE: Murdoch!

MURDOCH: Oh sir – it is good to see you. I'm so sorry – I'm expecting a Mr Polsworth-Gleach, a customer.

(KENNETH MOVES TO HANG UP HAT)

HORNE: Haven't you finished that job yet?

MURDOCH: (WITH BATTERED TIN OF SARDINES AND A CHISEL) No sir. It's no good – I'll just have to get a tin opener. (THROWS TIN AWAY)

(KENNETH TURNS AND SEES THE BARKER & SHENTON CAR)

HORNE: Good Heavens! What's this?

MURDOCH: It's a car, sir – I think – yes, it's a car.

HORNE: I can see that. It's a beauty. But where did it come from?

MURDOCH: Barker and Shenton of Uttoxeter, sir.

HORNE: What-sitter?

MURDOCH: Tox. Itter. Actually they're at a place nearby called Checkley.

HORNE: (FEELING FOR CHEQUE BOOK) That reminds me – could you possibly – ?

MURDOCH: No, sir. They've got over 400 cars on show there and they're holding a Great Autumn Sale next Ss –

HORNE: Next Spring?

MURDOCH: No, sir – next Saturday. The 31st. And there are some real bargain offers in high quality second-hand cars. For instance, this one is only £175.

HORNE: That's £174.17.4d more than I can lay out at the moment.

MURDOCH: Don't worry about that. Barker and Shenton can give you very easy confidential H.P. terms.

HORNE: Confidential, eh? You mean not a word to Bessie?

MURDOCH: That's right, sir.

HORNE: What <u>are</u> their confidential terms?

MURDOCH: Well, sir – they're so confidential they haven't even let me know. But I'm sure they'll be delighted to tell anyone who asks.

HORNE: (PRODUCING OLD ENVELOPE, READY TO WRITE ON THE BACK) I must make a note of that. What's the name?

MURDOCH: Barker and Shenton Limited, Checkley, Near Uttoxeter.

By the end of the second series of *Beyond Our Ken*, Eric Merriman and Barry Took had written forty-one editions of the show together, but the challenge of succeeding Muir and Norden on *Take It From Here* would lead to the end of their writing partnership. It soon became apparent that they had very different ideas about what to write for the programme.

One of the problems was that Merriman liked to use joke books, in particular a series of compilations by the American Robert Orben. If Merriman was stuck for a joke he would often pass some Orben books to Took and tell him to look up a joke about girlfriends, or whatever subject they needed. Took would protest, saying it was quicker to invent something new. As the deadline approached for the start of the new series of *Take It From Here*, their working relationship deteriorated to the point where they found it impossible to write together and would sit and stare at each other in resentful silence.

The Assistant Head of Variety, Jim Davidson, a no-nonsense Australian, suggested that Merriman and Took should step into the back alley behind the BBC offices in Bond Street and sort the matter out with a fist fight. This was not thought to be terribly practical and a compromise was reached whereby Eric Merriman would write the middle sketch for each edition of *Take It From Here*, generally a film parody, and Barry Took would the write the first and the last sketches with his new writing partner, Marty Feldman.

It signalled the end of Merriman and Took's working relationship. On 22 November Merriman asked for a meeting with Kenneth at his flat and informed him that he refused to write the next series of *Beyond Our Ken* with Barry Took. A few days later Kenneth wrote to Merriman:

> First of all let me say I appreciate immensely the fact that you came to see me on Sunday. Secondly I shall, of course, respect those aspects of our discussion which you would expect me so to do.
>
> On the other hand you were anxious to assure me that I might describe your visit as 'official' and, in that interpretation, communicate your views to our mutual friends at the BBC. It is with that concurrence, therefore, that I am sending copies of this letter to Pat Hillyard, Jim Davidson and Jacques Brown – the three people, other than myself, yourself and one other, most basically involved.
>
> May I summarise our discussion?
>
> 1. For personal reasons, which should not be the subject of record, you do not wish (notwithstanding any supplications that either I or the BBC may make) to be associated, script-wise, with Barry Took, after your 'Take It From Here' and Christmas 'B.O.K.' commitments have been discharged.
>
> 2. Naturally my prime interest is in 'B.O.K.', a show in which I

firmly believe the BBC have great faith and for which they foresee a great future.

What, therefore, are the alternatives for the scripting of the show?

(a) Eric Merriman.

(b) Eric Merriman and A.N. Other (even K. Horne).

(c) Barry Took.

(d) Barry Took and A.N. Other (even K. Horne).

(e) Another scriptwriter or combination of scriptwriters (even including K. Horne).

3. There must be no question of 'B.O.K.' going off the air. Let us, therefore, dissect the foregoing alternatives, as we did on Sunday:

(a) Writing a complete show on one's own is a laborious and very often unsuccessful job; this is something that you and I know and recognise. It is quite pointless to recall (nor did you) the comparative success that you and I had as Writer and Performer in 'Variety Playhouse', as a result of which, thanks to the enthusiasm of Jacques Brown, 'B.O.K.' was born. For one thing, the co-operation so essential between Writer, Performer and Producer, was always there – we willingly took advice from each other; even though every now and then you and I used to get into a corner and revile Jacques (in a most pleasant way) for not letting us 'get away' with something!

(b) You say, and I have no reason to doubt it, that you have worked with other scriptwriters before and could do so successfully again. That the bulk of the 'B.O.K.' scriptwriting was yours I think more than likely, but you did say that Barry, especially in the early days of your association, was invaluable in submitting and in 'sparking off' ideas. No doubt you could find, or maybe already have in mind, someone to assume that task.

Frankly, what worries me is whether any association might not have similar results to those which have brought about this present impasse. You told me that the reason for the difficulties that exist between you and Barry were due (you thought) to the fact that he is 'temperamental'. I suggested when you said that, that if a poll were taken among those at the BBC and those artists who had worked with you, the mantle of temperamentality might fall on someone else! My one desire is to ensure the future of 'B.O.K.' but I am not prepared to act for another season as permanent peacemaker. I know that, as a top-grade scriptwriter, you are, as you put it, a 'perfectionist' and as such like to guard jealously your work. But both Jacques and I have <u>infinitely</u> greater experience of scripts than you have, and even have occasional good ideas. Good humoured discussion is one thing – refusal to listen is another.

> (c) and (d) The qualifications of Barry as a 'Number One' in a scriptwriting team cannot be assessed. But he might be able to 'spark off' someone else and, thereby, create a successful team. I have already said, however, that I believe you to have been the brains behind the pair (no disrespect to Barry) and, therefore, I am not over-optimistic.
>
> (e) This again is anybody's guess. I have various people who have written comparatively successfully for me before (including myself!). I would hate to depart, for the moment at any rate, from the 'B.O.K.' accepted formula and I gathered that you might consider that you had some moral right to certain of the current characters and ideas in 'B.O.K.' scripts.

Well, there we are! I hope that even though I have been outspoken, I have also been scrupulously fair in what I've said. You know me well enough to know that I would not have it otherwise.

That the break between you and Barry should be necessary is tragic. On the other hand I must stress again that 'B.O.K.' has the reputation of being the happiest show on the air. For one reason and one reason only I had my job cut out to keep it so during the last series! And indeed it was only because of the importance that I attached to that particular aspect, that I refrained latterly in making suggested script amendments which I <u>knew</u> to be improvements (a shocking confession to make). Luckily I also knew that such a course would be, in another sense, disastrous!

I expect that Pat, Jim or Jacques will contact me when they have digested this and, no doubt, will wish to discuss as a matter of urgency the future scripting of 'B.O.K.'

Please let me know if there is anything in this letter with which you disagree, or which you believe to be a misrepresentation of facts.

And if, for some reason, there has been a change of heart since last Sunday, no-one will be more pleased than I. To have 'B.O.K.' back on the air with the same cast, scriptwriters and producer, but without the 'feelings off', would be my idea of a really good wish for 1960.

His wish was not to be granted. Merriman adamantly refused to back down and a month later, Kenneth wrote to Jim Davidson:

What with telephone calls from all interested parties, my life has been tricky, and my loyalties severely tested!

It would, I believe, sweeten the pill a little if Barry were allowed to write a very small section of B.O.K. script – just enough to warrant the magic phrase 'additional material by Barry Took'. My opening piece comes immediately to mind, and I would be delighted if affairs could be arranged to allow Barry to write it.

Surely Eric is not so bitter as to refuse such a request?

Unfortunately, Merriman *was* so bitter and Kenneth had to write reluctantly to Barry Took:

I am so very sorry to hear that you and Eric have split. I see that we can't possibly continue to use both of you. At the same time we can't afford to *lose* both of you. I do feel it is only fair that Eric, as the senior writer, should be asked to continue. I do hope you will understand that, as far as I am concerned, there are no hard feelings, and I am sure we shall work together again.

Of course, neither of them was to know that five years later they would be working together again to create one of the most popular comedy series in radio history.

17

End of the Affair

KENNETH WAS OFTEN being called on by the BBC to take part in trial recordings for new radio or television game shows, many of which never saw the light of day. In 1960 he acted as the chairman or panellist on a number of projected TV shows such as *Meet Yourself, Live a Borrowed Life* and *Ace High*.

He was also a member of the panel with Iris Ashley and Charmian Innes in a new radio series on the Light Programme called *Play the Game*, 'a medley of games and puzzles' which was devised by John P. Wynn and chaired by Wynford Vaughan-Thomas. The show included musical contests with Robin Richmond at the electronic organ, panel games, mystery guests and a sound quiz for the listeners at home, and the series ran for three months.

At the end of January he acted as the chairman for the pilot of another new game show, *Laugh Line*, which was produced by Harry Carlisle. The idea was for members of the panel to rearrange five cartoons and to supply a new 'laugh line' for each of them. The pilot was accepted but when the BBC commissioned a series Carlisle had other commitments and an up-and-coming young producer called Ned Sherrin was brought in to replace him. Kenneth wrote to him, saying, 'I very much hope you will decide to call on me as chairman', but at the end of March he learned he was being dropped in favour of the disc-jockey Pete Murray. When a second edition of the series was transmitted later that year, Murray himself was replaced by Peter Haigh and Albert Stephenson took over as producer, and Kenneth was booked to appear a couple of times as a panellist.

Now that the dispute over the scriptwriting had been settled in favour of Eric Merriman, the BBC gave the go-ahead for a new series of *Beyond Our Ken*, although not everyone was enthusiastic. On 4 February Kenneth Williams wrote in his diary: 'The BBC have come thro' with the April offer of "B.O.K." – I'm not really very keen on doing it. Must make sure that it doesn't conflict with filming.'

The third series started on 15 April and ran for fourteen weeks, going out at 7.30 p.m. on Fridays, with a repeat the following Sunday lunchtime. The cast remained the same, although the music was now provided by the BBC Variety Orchestra conducted by Paul Fenoulhet.

After the first recording, Williams noted: 'Did the first "B.O.K." in the 3rd series – at the Paris. It went very well, and several friends told me I was splendid. Peter Reeves said it was my show.'

His friends may have tempted Williams to believe that it was 'his' show, but *Beyond Our Ken* was undoubtedly a success because the cast worked so perfectly together as a team. Bill Pertwee believes this was because they were all performers who knew how to use the microphone well. They respected each other's talents and, although they might not have admitted it, they gradually developed a close friendship which made them more like a family, and that same across in the broadcasts.

The series was now so popular that audiences for the lunchtime recordings every Wednesday used to queue halfway up Lower Regent Street. Tickets were free on application to the BBC ticket unit but they were so much in demand that people would offer to buy tickets from those standing in the queue.

With *Beyond Our Ken* now safely back on the air Kenneth became one of the judges on a new BBC TV series called *Top Town* – 'a friendly battle of entertainment for the Top Town Television Trophy of 1960' – in which different towns competed with each other to find out which had the best entertainers. The eight-week series was introduced by David Jacobs, and Kenneth was one of a resident panel of judges who included the singer Vera Lynn, bandleader Eric Robinson, and theatre impresario Leslie Macdonnell.

At the same time his long-running series *Trader Horne* finally ended after what Kenneth described as 'two years hard'. On the morning of the last recording at Tyne Tees Television, he hosted a breakfast party, complete with champagne and oysters, as a farewell to all the artists and production staff on the series. The programme had topped the local television ratings but he was glad it was over. For one thing, without the constant travelling to Newcastle, it meant that he would be much freer to accept other work.

It was only two years since Kenneth had been forced to give up all his business interests because of his stroke, yet he had now earned enough money from broadcasting to sell the Morris 1000 and buy a black Bentley, to which he restored the KH6 number plate. It was a remarkable achievement. He had become so successful as a broadcaster that at one point he even received a letter from an overseas listener addressed to 'The BBC c/o Kenneth Horne'!

Joyce Davis continued to work for Kenneth as his PA on various radio and television shows and in particular a series called *Snakes and Ladders* on Southern Television. This was an audience participation show and she was responsible for interviewing and selecting contestants from a large number of applicants.

The programmes were outside broadcasts from different locations in the Southern region, and during the summer of 1960 they were visiting Eastbourne when Joyce noticed an advertisement in the local newspaper. It was for a period, flint-built, thatched cottage called 'Sturtles' in the village of Alciston, about eight miles from Eastbourne. She pointed it out to Kenneth, who liked it immediately, and at the first opportunity they went together to the estate agents, picked up a key and drove out to look at the cottage. Kenneth fell in love with it at first sight. Ever since his stroke he had been thinking about buying somewhere in the country where he could relax, away from the stresses of London, and from Marjorie.

He had not owned any property since before the war and, quite possibly, not even then: his first wife Mary had paid for their home in Solihull, and the house at Burcot during his second marriage to Joan was probably rented. When he married Marjorie, he had moved into her Kensington flat. Most of the furnishings were hers and so were all the pictures and ornaments. Even after fifteen years of marriage, there seemed to be very few of his own possessions in the flat. This was an opportunity for him to have a house of his own. It would also be somewhere that he and Joyce could spend some time together – 'a love nest', as one of his friends coyly described it.

'The flat was Marjorie's,' confirms Susan. 'Kenneth was not really a flat person, but he didn't have a house of his own until he bought Sturtles. It was his dream cottage.' The dream was nearly shattered, however, when the estate agent rang Kenneth at home to confirm the details and Marjorie answered the phone. It was the first she had heard about the cottage.

Somehow Kenneth talked his way out of trouble. He went ahead with the purchase of Sturtles and for the rest of that summer he went down to the cottage whenever he could. Joyce would often stay there with him, and Jean Merriman remembers dropping in to see them both for tea when she and Eric were visiting Eastbourne.

Meanwhile the third series of *Beyond Our Ken* was coming to an end and one of the cast had mixed feelings. On 22 June Kenneth Williams noted: 'Radio show, Paris. It went off OK. These radio shows leave me feeling quite dead. I feel as though I'm moving in a soporific dream. There is a curious feeling of apathy about all radio entertainment. A negative feeling. The result I suppose of the bifurcated medium – not theatre and not complete sound.'

It was a problem familiar to most radio comedians, as Ron Moody had discovered earlier: how to perform to the audience in the theatre and to a radio audience simultaneously. In July the Head of the Light Programme wrote to Jacques Brown praising the production of *Beyond Our Ken* but complaining that 'the sheer exuberance of the show is obviously causing some of the artists, and I should suspect particularly Kenneth Williams, to play to the audience in the hall, so that the laughter occasionally gets between the listener at home and the show.'

One member of the audience who seemed impervious to the antics on the stage was Eric Merriman's wife, Jean, who never missed a single performance of the show but would sit silently in the audience smiling inwardly, and proudly, but never laugh. It used to irritate Merriman, who would have words with her about it, because, as his son Andy points out, 'Obviously it was not perfect for a radio audience!'

At one of the script readings Jacques Brown said, 'The cast are so marvellous, they don't really need scripts. They could make the telephone directory funny!' Merriman, who had sweated all week to produce his half-hour script, was not amused. At the next recording, instead of giving them scripts, he handed out telephone directories to all the cast, saying, 'Go on, make me laugh.' This was the only encouragement Kenneth Williams needed. He proceeded to stand up and read a selection of names from the telephone directory in a succession of hilarious voices that had the whole room falling about with laughter. Merriman had to concede that Williams really could make the telephone directory funny.

After the series ended in July, Kenneth went on holiday for two weeks starting with an overnight stay at the Grand Hotel in Eastbourne. This prompted him to write to Eric Maschwitz, the Head of Light Entertainment at the BBC, with a proposal for a *Sunday Night at the Grand* television series with himself as the compere. 'It could not fail to be a riotous success,' he declared enthusiastically. The idea was quickly rejected with the comment: 'One has to remember that cosy "Grand Hotel" old-fashioned stuff is of limited appeal and depends largely on the personality of the players and not the compere. Sorry, no enthusiasm.'

During August Kenneth made several guest appearances as the chairman of *Does the Team Think?* on radio, and he was also the chairman of a new BBC television series called *What's It All About?* which was based on an old radio show from the mid-1950s. The panel had to find a logical explanation for the odd situations in which viewers had found themselves, such as 'Why should a man be walking down the street wearing a kilt and a top hat?' At the end of September Kenneth received a note from Tom Sloan, the Assistant Head of Light Entertainment, Television: 'How pleased I am with your usual polished performance as the chairman of a programme which still barely does you credit!!'

It is unclear when Marjorie realized the full extent of the relationship between Kenneth and Joyce. She must have known that they travelled around the country together because Joyce worked as Kenneth's PA on so many of his programmes. But Eileen Miller believes that Marjorie always thought – or chose to think – that it was simply a working relationship. Nevertheless, Jean Merriman recalls a recording of *Beyond Our Ken* at the Paris Studio when Marjorie and Joyce were both there at the same time. There was great speculation amongst the cast as to what might happen, but the pair avoided each other and the afternoon passed off without incident.

The purchase of Sturtles, however, seems to have brought the affair more into the open. One day Eileen went down to Eastbourne to see Richard Murdoch appearing in a play at the local theatre. Afterwards it was pouring with rain so Richard offered to give her a lift back to London in his Rolls. They were driving up the A22, about halfway between Eastbourne and the Ashdown Forest, when Eileen saw a car parked at the side of the road. She recognized it immediately as Kenneth's Bentley by his personal numberplate KH6 and called out to Richard to stop. She was worried that Kenneth might have fainted or have had a heart attack. She made Richard get out in the heavy rain and go over to investigate. The windows of the Bentley were misted up, so he knocked on the window and peered inside, where to his shock and embarrassment, he saw Kenneth and Joyce together. Richard ran straight back to his car and drove off as quickly as he could.

Later that year Kenneth went on a short break to a hotel in Le Touquet, ostensibly to work on some scripts. Somebody informed Marjorie that Joyce had gone with him and she finally became suspicious about what was going on.

Eileen rang Kenneth in Le Touquet to warn him and he invited her to come out and join them at the hotel for a few days. He booked her into the room next to his, with Joyce in the room on the other side of him. Eileen waited until she could speak to him on his own and then she told him that he could not carry on leading a double life with Joyce. He had to make up his mind whether he was going to stay with Marjorie or not, otherwise his health would suffer.

Under different circumstances Kenneth would probably have divorced Marjorie and married Joyce, but he had already been through two divorces and he did not want to experience the trauma of a third. 'I told him he wasn't well,' relates Eileen, 'and a divorce would kill him.' Neither was separation an option, because Marjorie had threatened to commit suicide if he even thought about leaving her. Theirs may not have been the perfect marriage but she enjoyed being Mrs Kenneth Horne and she was not prepared to let him go so easily.

There was also his family to consider. When his brothers and sisters heard about the situation they were dismayed: they believed the scandal of a third divorce or even a separation would bring shame on the Horne family. Kenneth was also worried that publicity about a divorce would harm his career. 'He thought it wouldn't do his image any good,' says Bill Pertwee.

'I wish I could have had a chat with Joyce to advise her,' says Eileen. 'She didn't seem to realise that it was all too much for him. She used to pester him. She thought that he would leave Marjorie, but if he'd wanted a third divorce, his sisters would have killed him. Joyce could have stayed with him, though. He liked her so much. It was more acceptable in those days for a man to have a mistress, but she was getting older and she wanted Kenneth to marry her. He should never have led her on, but he was too nice a man and he didn't want to hurt her.'

Kenneth made a decision. He packed his bags and told Joyce that he was going home. She and Eileen drove him to the airport in the Bentley and as he walked up the steps and onto the plane, Eileen thought to herself, that's the end of that. And it was. Kenneth left the Bentley with Joyce, and for the next couple of days she and Eileen went shopping in Le Touquet and then they drove back home.

According to Jean Merriman, Kenneth gave Joyce two weeks' notice as his secretary and their affair was finally over. Joyce was heartbroken. She had worked with Kenneth for twelve years. In November she suffered a nervous breakdown. The following year she found a job in Germany but later returned to London where she worked as a PA for the bandleader Eric Robinson. Eventually she retired to a cottage in Putney, where she was a member of the Putney Players. She never married and she never forgot Kenneth. Bill Pertwee used to visit her at her cottage until she died in her mid-seventies. 'Joyce loved him,' says Pertwee. 'I don't think there was any question about that.'

Eileen took over as Kenneth's full-time secretary and she was aware that some people blamed her for Joyce's sudden departure, although she insists that it was entirely Kenneth's decision. When he was going out he always wore a red carnation, and on her way to the flat every day she used to buy one for him from a florist opposite the Brompton Oratory. Kenneth was never the kind of person to discuss his health, but one day he was walking with Eileen down the street and he confided, 'You don't know what an effort it is to make every step, mentally.'

'He called me his rock,' says Eileen. He even told her once that he loved her. 'No, you don't really,' she replied.

The fourth series of *Beyond Our Ken* was due to start at the end of October but a few weeks beforehand Kenneth was stunned to hear that the BBC was planning to drop Pat Lancaster as the regular singer on the show. He sent a furious letter to the show's producer, Jacques Brown:

> The news that you gave me today that Pat Lancaster is not to be the regular singer in the new series of 'B.O.K.' comes as a very unpleasant shock. Time and again we have been told how unwise it would be to 'disturb a successful show' – (and, that 'B.O.K.' is a success, I trust is not in doubt.)
>
> Pat, with unsuitable numbers and orchestrations foist upon her, has given of her best and has been a first-class member of the team. I have never suggested that it would not be possible to find a better singer, but a better singer would not by any means ensure a better show.
>
> I can only assume that this is one of those prejudiced decisions influenced by some wretched 'listener research' – and judging by the hundreds of letters that I receive, the scapegoat might just as easily have been myself, Kenneth Williams, or even the script-writer.
>
> What appals me most is that such a decision (and I suppose it is final?) should have been made without anyone thinking 'I wonder if out of common courtesy we might have a word with Horne before we do anything'.
>
> Many a time I have said (and meant it very sincerely) that even though my name happens to appear at the top of the list, that is incidental, as it is a team show. Now it is abundantly clear that any thoughts that I may have in the choice of a singer couldn't have any importance anyhow.

The BBC decision *was* final. When the fourth series of *Beyond Our Ken* started on 20 October 1960, Pat Lancaster had to alternate as the singer with Janet Waters, and additional music was supplied by the Hornets. This time the series was broadcast on Thursdays at 7.30 p.m. with the repeat being moved to Sunday evenings at 6.30 p.m., and it ran for twenty weeks until February 1961.

During the autumn Kenneth found himself in the middle of another family crisis. A few months earlier his stepdaughter Susan had been on holiday in Majorca and had met and fallen in love with a young man called Andrew Montague. On their return to England the couple had continued to see each other and decided that they wanted to get married. Andy Montague came from a very well-respected family, with connections to the *Guardian* newspaper. He had been educated at Rugby and Magdalen College, Oxford, and worked as a sales manager at Dexion, an industrial shelving company, but he was not wealthy, although he had inherited some money from his parents, who had died when he was a child.

Susan was now twenty-one and was legally entitled to marry without the consent of her parents but she wanted to receive their blessing. She asked her mother for her permission to marry Andrew but to her utter amazement, Marjorie refused, declaring that he was not good enough for her. Andrew went to see Kenneth, who offered no objection to the marriage but declined to get involved, saying, 'Nothing to do with me, dear boy. You'll have to ask her mother.'

But Marjorie was not to be dissuaded. She was adamant that she did not approve of Andrew and she would not change her mind. She insisted that they must wait for at least a year, but after several bitter arguments a compromise was reached and they agreed to an engagement of nine months.

On the evening of 16 November Gilbert Harding presented two editions of *Round Britain Quiz* in the BBC studios at 5 Portland Place, opposite Broadcasting House. During the recordings he was perspiring profusely and complained of feeling 'absolutely awful', having to resort to an oxygen mask and a bottle of whisky in equal measures. As he left the main entrance of the building afterwards he collapsed on the steps, falling back into the arms of his friend Christopher Saltmarshe, a BBC current affairs producer, and died instantly. His body was carried back into the building and laid out on two tables in the canteen while they waited for an ambulance. He was just fifty-three.

Two weeks later, Kenneth wrote to Lindsay Wellington, Director of Sound Broadcasting:

> A respectable time having now elapsed, I feel that I can write and put a plea in for being allowed once again to take over the Chairmanship of 'Twenty Questions' when it returns.
>
> As you may know, I occupied the Chair for two years, and have also appeared many dozens of times on the panel; obviously to succeed to the Chair is my ambition, as it was my favourite task of all.
>
> Incidentally (such is fame) I was voted the most popular Chairman by a national newspaper! I believe also that the panel which I controlled, and which is still the same, were very happy under my guardianship.

His letter was passed to Pat Hillyard who replied that, because of the popularity of *Beyond Our Ken*, the chairmanship of *Twenty Questions* had been offered instead to the Conservative politician and broadcaster Lord Boothby. Kenneth was bitterly disappointed but after two months he received another letter from Hillyard stating that Robert Boothby had accepted the offer, but had subsequently taken on some appointments which would require him to travel overseas, and in view of that they had agreed to cancel the engagement. 'Now the circumstances have changed,' declared Hillyard, 'we should be delighted to offer the long coveted chair to your good self.'

Kenneth took over as the new Chairman of *Twenty Questions* in April 1961 and he would continue to host it until he died nearly eight years later. He brought a new vitality and a much-needed sense of humour to the programme and it seemed to take on a new lease of life. Norman Hackforth, the 'Mystery Voice', who would later join the panel after Richard Dimbleby retired, said that he had never enjoyed any broadcasts as much as those while Kenneth was chairman. He brought 'a glorious sense of the ridiculous to the whole proceedings', with remarks such as:

'No, the object is an "electric tooth-brush"; which of course is something with which you clean your electric teeth.'

'It's a "metronome". And for the benefit of those who don't know, let me tell you that a metronome is a very small dwarf who lives in the Paris Underground.'

At the end of his first series as the regular chairman of *Twenty Questions* in September, Kenneth was informed that the audience figures were 'well up' for the programme. Audience research showed that he was a very popular chairman, with many listeners commenting appreciatively on his 'genial good humour' and fairness in dealing with the panel, although some felt that he was much too lenient in dealing with them. They complained that he allowed them all to talk, and frequently shout, at once and he was often far too helpful with his answers. One listener lamented: 'Gilbert Harding would have put a stop to this!'

18

Outside Assistance

IN JANUARY 1961 Kenneth became the 526th castaway to be interviewed by Roy Plomley on *Desert Island Discs*, nine years after he had first appeared on the programme with Richard Murdoch. He also took over as the compere of *Variety Playhouse* for four weeks while Vic Oliver was away.

He was always trying to come up with new ideas for radio or television shows and he had developed a radio panel game with Daphne Padel called *Tell the Tale*. In early 1961 he carried out two 'dry runs' with audiences to iron out any unforeseen problems and then he paid for a trial recording with himself as the chairman and two teams consisting of Daphne Padel, Brian Johnston and Richard Murdoch against Eleanor Summerfield, Eric Sykes and Harold Berens. A few weeks later, however, he heard that the programme had been rejected by those present at the BBC Light Entertainment Meeting with the comments: 'Too confused, too many contributors; needed a break in the middle. Very complicated for the listener at home. Not suitable in its present form.'

In April Kenneth received a surprise letter. It was from Mollie Sharp, the schoolgirl who had contributed script ideas to the last two series of *Much-Binding-in-the-Marsh*, but had given up writing to devote her life to the work of the Salvation Army. At the age of twenty she had married a young captain in the Salvation Army called Daniel Millest but two years later her husband injured his spine in an accident which left him totally incapacitated and unable to work.

Dan Millest had to resign his full-time position with 'The Army' and Mollie also had to give up her job to take care of him. With no income, they were existing on National Assistance (social security benefits) with their three children, Christopher, Andy and Mark, in a small house with no electricity in Derby. Mollie used to listen to *Beyond Our Ken* on her transistor radio and one day she decided to write to Kenneth, telling him what had happened to her during the last six years. On 29 April he wrote straight back to her:

> I am indeed sorry to hear of your husband's accident and illness. I have tremendous sympathy with him because three years ago I had a stroke which means I shall never again be able to get the normal enjoyment out of life. However, we're lucky to be alive. One thing that <u>you</u>, of all people, need <u>not</u> worry about is the financial future. With your talent for writing, I would take a bet that it won't be very long before you are earning very good money.
>
> Now then – as far as 'B.O.K.' goes the position is rather delicate! Eric Merriman, who writes the script, is very temperamental and (a) doesn't like his 'masterpieces' altered and (b) often fails to clock in with a script in time, with the result that K.H. has to do a last minute job!
>
> I would love you to submit a few jottings, because I have a feeling that in the next series (starting September) I shall be increasingly called upon to help. In that case, we'll put the whole thing on a proper financial basis. Meanwhile, there will be lots of other script-writing opportunities, and you have my assurance that I'll see you get one of them.
>
> I look forward to hearing from you again.

Kenneth was so confident in Mollie's potential as a comedy writer that on the same day he wrote to Jacques Brown, saying: 'I shall suggest officially, that I write the first six scripts [of *Beyond Our Ken*]

<u>now</u>. I have the perfect colleague with whom to write them.' Two weeks later, he wrote again to Mollie Millest:

> I think the best thing is for you to tackle a 'spot' in a BOK programme – i.e. my opening piece (which is probably the easiest) and which sometimes leads into the second part of the show, broken into by the singer – or have a bash at a 'Hornerama' which can be on any subject.
>
> If you feel that any of this is too formidable, then just odd Mollie-isms which I could fit in anywhere. For instance I've got three TV Agricultural Show Advertising Magazines to do. Most of the content is 'hard advertising', but I'm allowed about two and a half minutes out of the fifteen as 'linking-material'. Any agricultural whimsicalities?

Kenneth did all he could to encourage his young protégée, giving her hints and advice; he wrote her more than a hundred letters over the next seven years and he was not afraid to criticize her when she got it wrong. He enjoyed writing scripts with a partner and he liked to spark ideas off someone else. In one letter he pointed out:

> There's a lot of useful stuff in the script you submitted and here's a 'little something' to encourage you. The snags are:
> (a) Too many puns
> (b) Too many old gags (maybe you <u>think</u> you've invented them!!)
> (c) Too many situations that have already been used. There is no disgrace in this, especially when one gets characters such as Stanley Birkinshaw whose tag line must always imply spraying or splashing, and Cecil Snaith, who I am sorry to say fell down the funnel of the 'Queen Mary' from an aeroplane in a recent edition!
> I shall be thinking and talking about scripts the week after next and I'll drop you another line. Meanwhile let's get the Millest brain to work on something else – I have promised to appear in a Children's

Programme (once only) in a regular feature called 'How not to . . .'
I thought I'd do 'How not to appear on Television'. Any ideas?
Maybe not necessarily funny lines, but comic situations.

On 8 June Kenneth had a meeting with Eric Merriman and told him
about Mollie Millest. He enquired discreetly whether he might be
prepared to accept a little 'outside assistance' when writing the next
series and Merriman agreed to consider it. Kenneth sent him the
two sample scripts that Mollie had written and a few weeks later he
wrote to her:

> Eric Merriman has now seen your second 'epic' and says that there
> are a number of very good ideas there. He would like to come to
> some 'working arrangement' with you, either on a regular weekly
> basis, or accepting anything from you as you do it.
>
> He does suggest however that final details should not be
> arranged until after a meeting of the cast which we are holding on
> August 18th – it is probable for instance that there will be several
> changes in Hornerama and it would be a waste of time for you to
> work on something that would not be used.

Mollie sent him some new material, which he liked, and for the next
seven years she would contribute jokes, sketches and other script
ideas which Kenneth used on dozens of different radio and
television programmes. Apart from *Beyond Our Ken*, he was
involved with so many different programmes that he was constantly
in need of new material. Her contributions were almost always
uncredited but Kenneth paid her well for them. In fact, she became
so adept at reproducing his style of humour that sometimes she
would write a whole piece which would subsequently appear in a
magazine under Kenneth's name with almost no alterations, but she
was the first to acknowledge that without his name it would never
have been published at all.

It is impossible to establish which jokes and sketches on *Beyond*

Our Ken credited to Eric Merriman were in fact written by Mollie Millest. In some cases he took her original idea and improved on it, but in many others he accepted her scripts as they were written. Merriman told his wife Jean that Mollie was very good, although Jean disputes how much of a contribution she made to each programme. Moreover, she was not the only 'ghost' writer on the series. Patricia Newman also used to submit ideas and short sketches to Merriman, which he would include in the scripts under his name.

Some years later, in a letter about Mollie to his friend Doreen Forsyth, a producer on *Woman's Hour*, Kenneth revealed: 'During the last three seasons of "Beyond Our Ken" she provided about one-third of each programme, though Eric Merriman got the credit (and, presumably, paid her). This is quite a story, and what is more interesting is that some of her stuff is fractionally "near the knuckle"!'

It is true that some of Mollie's material sounded remarkably risqué for a member of the Salvation Army, but she claims it was all in the performance. 'If you see the script, it doesn't look saucy,' she explains, 'but I knew what the cast could do with it.' Among her contributions used in the programme were parodies of The Mikado, Carmen, and Svengali, and sketches about the Willow Pattern, Tutankhamun, and Sir Francis Drake, or 'Oh dear, what can Armada be?':

WILLIAMS (Bosun): Excuse me, sir, permission to speak.

HORNE (Drake): Permission granted, bos'n.

WILLIAMS: I was just wondering, sir. Where has your sword gone?

HORNE: I do not possess one.

WILLIAMS: No, then what was that cutlass I saw you with last night?

HORNE: That was no cutlass, that was my knife.

WILLIAMS: I don't wish to know that, kindly leave the bridge!

HORNE: Silence, you scurvy knave.

WILLIAMS: I know, sir, that medicated shampoo works wonders.

HORNE: Bos'n?

WILLIAMS: Yes, sir.

HORNE: The sixteenth century equivalent of 'belt up'.

WILLIAMS: Sorry, sir.

HORNE: Yes, you do well to go red of face.

WILLIAMS: Oh, that's not me, sir, it's the storm. The rain's washed the red dye out of my hat. I'm marooned!

In July Kenneth presented a special tribute to his late father called *Quest and Conquest*, 'a radio portrait of the Reverend Silvester Horne'. After the broadcast on the Home Service he received dozens of letters from listeners who had been very moved by the programme. One listener from Yorkshire wrote: 'I want to thank you for your beautiful broadcast on Sunday night. With the world in its present state, it was indeed heartening to hear the sentiments of a man like your father, expressed in your beautiful voice . . . I don't think anything has ever touched me more than this account of your father's life, which you were able to amplify so well.'

On 2 September he attended the marriage of his stepdaughter Susan to Andrew Montague at Christ Church, Kensington, around the corner from Cottesmore Court. Marjorie also went to the wedding, although somewhat reluctantly. Kenneth had agreed to give the bride away but he was worried about whether he would be able to walk with her up the aisle. He was still having great difficulty with his left leg and he was unable to stand unaided for any length of time. A chair was placed at the back of the church in case he should need to sit down, but with grim determination he managed to walk all the way up the aisle with Susan, limping only slightly.

Afterwards, the reception was held at the Hyde Park Hotel and to Susan's amazement, among the guests was Happy the budgerigar, whom Kenneth had brought along in his cage to keep Marjorie happy. Even though they were now married, the bride and groom were kept apart on separate floors while they changed for their honeymoon, and later the Maître d'Hôtel, Ron Massara, told Susan that her mother was going around the guests downstairs telling everyone that she did not give it a year.

After the wedding, Kenneth went off to the South of France for a brief holiday, and on his return he teamed up with Richard for a guest appearance on *Variety Playhouse*:

> MURDOCH: Tell me, when you were in St Tropez did you see Brigitte Bardot?
> HORNE: I <u>think</u> so. A girl who was terribly like her came up and spoke to me.
> MURDOCH: What did she say?
> HORNE: She asked me if I knew what time the Barnsley coach party was leaving.

On the back of Richard's script for this edition of *Variety Playhouse* is a perfect example of one of Kenneth's favourite jokes, which he used to try out on his friends and colleagues. He would draw a triangle on a piece of paper with the top sides two inches long and the base side about one inch. Then he would ask them to write along the right side of the triangle, 'What did Mary', and on the left side, 'say on the first'. Finally he would ask them to write along the base of the triangle, 'night of her honeymoon.'

On the back of his script Richard had tried to fill in the last line but, like everyone else who tried it, he ran out of space. This used to provoke an exasperated comment such as, 'I can't squeeze it in!' or 'It's too big!' at which Kenneth would roar with laughter before adding it to the collection in his diary. He told a friend once at Triplex, 'I've got some beauties!'

The fifth series of *Beyond Our Ken* started on 12 October 1961 and ran for twenty weeks until February 1962. By now Pat Lancaster had been dropped from the show altogether and she was replaced as the singer by Jill Day. The repeats were restored to 2 p.m. on Sundays.

Mollie Millest had started to contribute to the scripts and wondered whether she was entitled to a credit at the end of each programme. In November, Kenneth told her:

The answer to your query is a simple one – it all depends for whom you are writing. Under the present circumstances, with the scripts being 'hand to mouth' instead of a fortnight in advance (to me that is, not as far as recording is concerned) I can't see how you can be officially recognised. The BBC certainly wouldn't alter the credits from week to week according to whether you'd contributed or not.

If however the time were to come when someone gave you say three months notice of a series, I don't see why you couldn't prepare enough material in that time to justify at least an 'additional material by' caption. If I were the principal writer and had confidence in you (which I have) that is the way I'd work. Meanwhile let's get this series over, and let's make it a real success, then we can talk.

Of course one of the hardest things to do is to alter someone else's script – the ideal way is to write a script jointly, in every sense of the word, throwing ideas across the table. I know that's not possible as things are.

Anyhow you're doing a splendid job. I'll write again, because I intend to chat to E.M. at a suitable moment (and there are not many of those!)

On 3 November Kenneth had acted as the anchorman for a new half-hour BBC television programme called *Let's Imagine*. The first topic under discussion was 'Taking a Pub' and the series proved to be very popular. Over the next eighteen months he would chair more than twenty discussions on subjects such as 'A Fresh Start in Life', 'A World without Advertising', 'A Life of Luxury' and 'Meeting your Ancestors'. My favourite, for reasons which will become clear, was *Let's Imagine: Christ Came Back* – for which

Kenneth's contract stipulated: 'Pre-recording in lieu of live appearance'!

After the programme Kenneth wrote to Mollie Millest:

> Although the producer thought it was just so-so, I thought it was quite good. Anyhow, I enjoyed it, and those taking part played their pieces well. But of course, half an hour is, to say the least of it, somewhat economical for that subject.

Kenneth had never done much religious broadcasting before but at the end of 1961, possibly prompted by the radio programme about his father in the summer, he was invited to tell three five-minute stories about Moses from the Bible on the BBC television programme *Sunday Story*. The first episode was transmitted at 6.15 p.m. on New Year's Eve and it received such a positive reaction that he was asked to record a total of seven Bible stories. They were a huge success. His religious background and his warm, comforting voice made him the perfect storyteller. The audience figures for children and adults went up to about five million and the final programme in February was watched by more people than ITV's expensive and highly publicized *Journey of a Lifetime*. John Elphinstone-Fyffe, the series' producer, informed Kenneth he had received 'loads of fan letters' and after the series ended in February Kenneth Adam wrote to Kenneth thanking him for 'the real enthusiasm, allied with a matchless technique, which you have brought to this storytelling'.

Kenneth was delighted, replying: 'Having been broadcasting now for a long time, this is the first occasion on which I have ever received a "thank-you" letter from a V.I.P.' After he referred to his producer one day as 'John Elphinstone-Hyphen-Fyffe', he became known by all the television crews at the BBC as 'Hyphen'.

At the beginning of 1962 Eric Merriman was at his office writing another episode of *Beyond Our Ken* when he heard by telephone that his eight-month-old son Christopher had died from cot death at home. Merriman was in the middle of writing a sketch about seaside concert party shows, called 'The Twinkle Dolls'. After such terrible news he was not able to carry on with the sketch and he put it aside, but later in the series he completed it as a tribute to his son, and it became one of his all-time favourite sketches. There was tremendous pressure on Merriman to come up with a script every week and he often finished them so close to the recording date that there was no time to spare. As Andy Merriman reflects, 'It is unbelievable to think that he had to carry on writing and get the script in by the end of the week under such circumstances.'

Mollie Millest was also continuing to write sketches for the programme. She insists that it did not bother her that she never received any credit for them because she was a mother, with three children, and she considered that to be her full-time job. She would often go to the rehearsals where she would always stay in the background, but she believes that the cast 'sort of knew' about her. She was told that John Simmonds, the producer, had joked that Merriman must have someone helping him out in the background because some of the scripts were rather good! Kenneth also confided to Kenneth Williams that parts of the script were written by a woman in the Salvation Army, but Williams thought it was a joke.

On 18 February Kenneth wrote to her:

> I've just listened to 'Svengali' and it was excellent – congratulations. Glad you enjoyed your visit. The show you saw was much better in the studio, and came over very poorly – badly balanced and badly cut. However we finished the series with a good one last Wednesday, so all is well and the VIPs are pleased.

The VIPs were certainly pleased, with Denis Morris, the Chief of the Light Programme, acclaiming *Beyond Our Ken* as 'the most successful radio production of its kind'.

The following day Kenneth was caught by Eamonn Andrews with his famous red book when he was the subject of *This Is Your*

Life. Among the guests on the BBC TV show were Richard Murdoch and Sam Costa, Kenneth Williams, Bunny Austin, 'Bo' Aylward, Sir Miles Thomas of BOAC, the bandleader Ted Heath with his sax section, and Susan, who had to walk on carrying Happy the budgerigar in his cage.

Kenneth also took part in a special feature that month on *Woman's Hour* called 'Simple Sums for Shopkeepers', in which he had to test a grocer, a greengrocer, a butcher and a draper. Listeners had complained that shop assistants were slow with their mental arithmetic – in the days before adding machines and calculators – and Kenneth had to challenge them by giving them sums, interrupting himself and having second thoughts, like the average shopper. The first shopkeeper to get the correct answer, and call it out, was the winner. The feature went down well with the *Woman's Hour* listeners and he was invited back several times during the year, hosting quizzes on music and holidays and chairing discussions about ideas and food.

On 27 February Kenneth celebrated his fifty-fifth birthday and he was interviewed at home by Brian Johnston for the weekly feature 'Many Happy Returns' on the *Today* programme, chatting about how he was going to spend his birthday and what sort of presents he would like to be given.

In April he started a second series as chairman of *Twenty Questions*, which would run for four months until the end of August. There were big celebrations on 1 August when the BBC broadcast its 500th edition of the programme, and Kenneth calculated that he had taken part as chairman or panellist in about a hundred of them.

On 24 April he wrote to Mollie Millest:

Any news in your script-writing life? I ask because I know that Jacques Brown mentioned you to one of the 'powers that be' at the BBC. Don't get too tied up with E.M., who is becoming more swollen-headed and difficult each day. I really don't know whether

I can face another series with him at the helm. The date was fixed for Sept 18th and now E.M. has said that he's not prepared to produce anything till at least December!

RM and I are to do 4 consecutive 'Variety Playhouses' starting May 20th. We have no ideas as yet, but I think some fractional continuity would be a good idea. Would you like to help on a professional basis?

Kenneth and Richard had been booked to appear on the radio variety series *Holiday Music Hall*. Mollie submitted a script for the first recording and Kenneth replied:

A splendid script for which many thanks. I shall be sending a copy of the final 'epic' so you'll be able to see how much we are using. It's difficult to know how to recompense you! Please accept the enclosed as a start, until we've sorted out the BOK situation.

And please can we have the next script? Dick and I are due to get together again next Saturday and Sunday and your efforts by then would be a great help.

Now re BOK – I've talked to Jacques and the whole thing is all very indefinite. I'm quite certain that it will come back, if I am prepared to do it. But I've been so mucked about by E.M. that I've a jolly good mind to say 'no'.

If only we could persuade the BBC to accept another show with KH, RM, K. Williams and Hugh Paddick, script by KH, RM and MM, all would be well. I don't want to pry too much into what EM pays you, but do be careful before committing. I think you should have some advice. Drop me a line if I can help.

Now that Susan was married, Kenneth and Marjorie were finding that their flat at Cottesmore Court was simply too big for them. It was also very expensive to maintain. After seventeen years, they moved out on 16 May to a smaller flat a few minutes away at 11c Albert Hall Mansions. As its name suggests, the flat was right next door to the Royal Albert Hall, which was handy for concerts but not so good if they were hoping for a quiet night in. Kenneth used to joke, 'When Sir Malcolm Sargent conducts the mass brass bands, everything on the mantelpiece rattles!'

During the summer of 1962 Kenneth did his usual assortment of radio and television programmes, such as compering Miss Interflora GPO 1962 and presenting an edition of the BBC series *Outlook* from the Norfolk Broads Yacht Club at Wroxham. On 28 August he proposed the health of the Bride and Groom at Belinda Murdoch's wedding. He got a big laugh when he said, 'I can't pretend that I ever dangled Belinda on my knee – her mother, yes!'

At the end of September he went on holiday with Marjorie to the Caribbean. After a fortnight in Grenada they were lying on the beach one day when Marjorie asked, 'If you could have anyone here, sharing this holiday, whom would you most like?'

After a moment's thought, Kenneth replied, 'Susan. It would be nice for us all to be together again.'

Marjorie must have been thinking the same thing, because she immediately suggested that Kenneth invite Susan to join them for the rest of their holiday in Barbados. He went straight back to the hotel and later that day he rang Susan in London to tell her that he had booked an air-ticket and they would love her to join them for ten days.

By now, Susan and Andy Montague had been married for just over a year but Kenneth neither invited her husband nor even mentioned him. Andy was working and probably could not have gone anyway, but it was as if he did not exist. When Susan told Andy about the telephone call, he insisted that she must go: ten days on holiday in the Caribbean, all expenses paid, was too good an offer to turn down. So she went, and enjoyed herself, but she never forgot the way that Kenneth and Marjorie had deliberately excluded her husband.

On 12 November the BBC marked its fortieth anniversary and Kenneth was booked to introduce the recordings in a special documentary produced by BBC Radio Newsreel called *Forty Laughing Years,* a celebration of comedians past and present. This led to an almighty row in the corridors of Broadcasting House.

As this was different from his usual type of programme, Pat Newman, the Booking Manager, had telephoned Kenneth personally and offered him a special fee of 30 guineas, which he had accepted without question. After the programme was broadcast, the Editor of Radio Newsreel, Brian Bliss, complained to the Chief of the Light Programme that he felt the fee was 'rather on the austere side' for such an experienced broadcaster and suggested that Kenneth should be paid a further 20 guineas. The Chief of the Light Programme agreed and sent a memo to Newman instructing him to arrange it. Newman replied that, in his opinion, it would be 'the wrong move' to increase the fee: the contract had been signed by Kenneth and processed for payment and it was too late to do anything about it, adding, 'These types of programmes are inclined to get a bit excited on the rare occasions that they use "personality" artists.'

The Chief of the Light Programme sent a second, rather more terse, memo informing Newman that the previous memo had not been a suggestion but a directive and would he please get on with it. Newman responded that he did not consider he had the authority to do so and passed all the correspondence on to his superior, the Head of Programme Contracts.

By now it was the end of January and Newman rang Kenneth to explain the impasse over the extra fee, reporting back that Kenneth was faintly embarrassed about the whole affair but felt there was nothing he could do other than give a sort of mumbled 'thank you'. He assured Newman he was perfectly happy with the original fee, although he would no doubt find something to buy with the extra 20 guineas should they send it, and he would not worry in the least if he never received it.

Memos continued to fly back and forth between the various offices until finally the Head of Programme Contracts upheld Pat

Newman's position and insisted that the contract must stand. Newman felt responsible for the whole embarrassing shambles and rang Kenneth to apologize, offering to take him out to lunch at Le Caprice to make up for it. As the Booking Manager, Newman was allowed to claim hospitality expenses from the BBC on the rare occasions when he had to entertain an important artist. A week later he met Kenneth as arranged at Le Caprice and, after the waiter handed them two menus, Newman announced, 'Have a good look at the best from the à la carte dishes, because you're not getting up from this table until you've eaten twenty quid's worth of lunch!'

It's Ken Again

THE SIXTH SERIES of *Beyond Our Ken* was due to start after Christmas but there were more changes in the air. Once again, Kenneth had not been consulted and on 2 December 1962 he wrote to Mollie Millest:

> Nobody has told me anything about BOK! I don't know who the singer/singers is/are, what time we rehearse etc etc. Exactly what EM has told the new producer (if anything) I don't know, but we'll have to clear the air before you meet him.

On Boxing Day he took part in a ninety-minute BBC radio production of *Three Men in a Boat* by Jerome K. Jerome, which had been adapted for radio with additional songs by the actor and composer Hubert Gregg. Kenneth starred as Harris, with Hubert Gregg as J and Leslie Phillips as George.

The sixth series of *Beyond Our Ken* finally started on 27 December and ran for thirteen weeks until March 1963, with Eileen Gourlay taking over as the new singer, and Douglas Smith now being billed as 'a sort of announcer'. Jacques Brown had also left the programme and the new producer was John Simmonds. It was broadcast on Thursdays at 8 p.m., with a repeat at 2 p.m. on Sundays.

After the recording on 2 January, Kenneth Williams wrote: 'Did "B.O.K." from the Paris. I was ragging Betty M[arsden] a lot, and felt v. guilty after, because she was v. ill and husband came (Dr) with medicine. I apologised. She was v. nice. We got through the show OK. It was a rehash of an old script. Certainly went over OK.'

The new series had got off to a promising start, although three weeks later Williams commented: '"B.O.K." The radio show went very well. Eric M[erriman] said I was "outrageous" – I think I will never know what people mean by this. One spends a deal of energy, time and vulnerability, trying to raise a laugh and one is accused of being outrageous. The critics are exactly the same. They simply don't understand the very thing they're supposed to be watching.'

In January Kenneth started a six-month series on Anglia Television as the compere of a quiz game called *I Packed My Bag*. It meant travelling to Norwich every Thursday and Friday to record the programme, but he complained, 'I can't afford to refuse.'

The truth is that he was driven by the need to earn money to maintain his lavish lifestyle, but he also wanted to keep himself as busy as possible. 'He was a slave to work,' says Eileen Miller. 'He wasn't happy. He was afraid to be alone. He once told me, "I don't want to stop and think."'

The *I Packed My Bag* series was shown only in the Anglia region but it must have been popular because Bill Boorne, the television critic of the *Liverpool Echo*, reported: 'Friends who have seen it regard it as a weekly must. Several have written to me to say how good it is and to express surprise that it has not come into the wider world of Channel Nine [ITV].'

In between his other commitments, Kenneth managed to find time to speak at a Salvation Army rally in Derby, as a special favour to Mollie Millest. On 14 March he wrote to her confirming the arrangements:

One thing I meant to ask you. Is the 'do' a very serious affair? Is it in a place in which laughter is frowned upon? It would be bad if I were to paralyse everyone with clean witticisms, and then have to say: 'And now we will sing four choruses of "Fight the Good Fight"'. Or is the whole affair a pleasant un-religious (as opposed to irreligious!) concert?

By the way, if absolutely necessary I shall have to come up on the train reaching Derby at 4.35. My point yesterday was that, in the normal way, an artist hates getting to a show a minute before he has to – indeed they arrive about 5 minutes before they're on (unless they have music to rehearse).

You see, one is much better and fresher without having to meet a lot of people beforehand! That is the dread of entertainers, and the most tiring part of all! But if I'm not really wanted till the show starts, then I can reach Derby at 6.42 – marvellous.

With his upbringing, Kenneth was comfortable in such religious surroundings and he seems to have had a good time. Mollie Millest recalled later, 'He was a riotous success, of course. He told us dozens of unlikely but funny stories; he told us about his work; he told us about his father, and he sang, and joined in with us. His presence was a joy to us, and he told us that he enjoyed every second as much as we did.'

In June Kenneth was booked to make three appearances with Richard Murdoch on *Holiday Music Hall* and he asked Mollie for some script ideas. He suggested that the pair of them might be in a 'kitchen sink' drama in which 'we say we're going to use rude words – and we actually do! Words like "crushed grapes" and "kneecaps"!'

After the *I Packed My Bag* series ended in June Kenneth began his own fifteen-minute one-man series for Anglia Television called *Ken's Column*. It was transmitted in the Anglia region at 11 p.m. on Saturday nights and the programme was billed as: 'Kenneth Horne looks at life'. It got off to a rocky start and after the second show he wrote to Mollie:

The producer, the controller of programmes and Horne were especially pleased with the first 'KC' and we spent a happy half hour congratulating ourselves. The TV critic of the Eastern Daily Press wasn't entirely in agreement with us, as next day he said: 'Ken's Column is shapeless, pointless and boring'! However, I dealt with him in the second show last night! I'm asking Peter Joy the producer to send you copies of the first two scripts (such as they are) in the hope you may have some ideas.

A month later the scripts for *Ken's Column* had still not improved and he told her:

I think the crying need is for a few 1½ or 2 minute very funny monologues for me, on any subject topical or otherwise. The Anglia boys do me quite well on local stuff and funny headlines, but the whole show comes to life when a little Horne/Millest humour is injected.

In July Kenneth presented a ten-minute radio quiz on *Woman's Hour* called 'For Amusement Only'. It had such a good reaction from the listeners that he was invited back in October to be chairman of a special 'Kenneth Horne Quiz' which featured 'questions with a catch'. Many of these were old chestnuts going back to his days as the host of the Comedy Quiz on *Ack-Ack Beer-Beer*, such as: 'How many months have twenty-eight days? Answer: All of them' and 'Who killed Cain? Answer: Cain killed Abel. Nobody killed Cain.' But the *Woman's Hour* office received more than two hundred letters from listeners saying 'what a splendid quiz' and later that year they invited him back again to present another 'Kenneth Horne Quiz' on New Year's Eve.

In September he and Richard co-hosted an edition of *Star Parade*, a radio series in which the star guest each week was allowed to choose the artists he or she wanted to hear on the programme, budget permitting. Kenneth was told by the producer that the series had been 'somewhat lamentable' up to that point and they wanted him and Richard to present an edition with the possibility of them taking over the whole series the following year. They chose 'Professor' Stanley Unwin, the comedy actress Athene Seyler, and 'a Chinese girl who took the lead in "The World of Suzie Wong" called Tsai Chin', who he said could sing very well and read lines competently. Kenneth and Richard struggled to complete the script – 'By the time we'd got to the sketch, we were getting a bit flogged out, but just went on writing!' – and sent their script to Mollie with the plea: 'If you have any ideas for improvement anywhere, please let me know.'

Meanwhile Marjorie Horne had not been feeling well for several months and after seeing a specialist she discovered that she had cancer of the mouth. She had always been a heavy smoker and her breakfast usually consisted of two cups of tea and two cigarettes, with possibly a piece of toast. She was admitted to hospital, where she underwent a course of treatment which made it painful for her to eat. For the next few weeks, when Kenneth was not working, he used to make her a special broth in the kitchen at home and take it in a thermos flask to her at the hospital, where he would sit by the bed and read to her. Eventually Marjorie recovered fully and was allowed home. She was even permitted to carry on smoking and her cancer would stay in remission for another ten years.

The seventh series of *Beyond Our Ken* started on 24 November 1963 and ran for thirteen weeks until February 1964. It had become such a feature of Sunday lunchtimes that the original broadcast was now at 2 p.m. on Sundays with the repeat the following Wednesday at 7.30 p.m.

Eric Merriman had become the first writer to be given top billing in the *Radio Times* above the cast. At the same time he was also writing material for Norman Vaughan who was the compere of the top-rated ITV show *Sunday Night at the London Palladium*. Merriman used to drive in to the rehearsals on Sunday afternoons while *Beyond Our Ken* was on the radio. At the traffic lights he would often look over at the other drivers and see them all roaring with laughter at his own show. When the seventh series of *Beyond Our Ken* came to an end on 16 February it had achieved an average audience of ten million for each programme. It is perhaps not surprising if Merriman became a bit swollen-headed.

In January 1964 Kenneth made his debut as the presenter of *Housewives' Choice*. This immensely popular record-request show had been running since 1946 and possessed an annoyingly catchy signature tune called 'In Party Mood'. The programme was broadcast at 9 a.m. each weekday, with a regular audience of eight million, and attracted thousands of postcard requests every week.

In those days the presenters were given a box full of postcards to take home with them and they had to write a script to link the requests. Mollie Millest recalls sitting with a pile of cards on the floor of her new home in Gillingham, Kent, trying to think up some witty remarks for Kenneth to include in the programme. As its title suggests, the series was aimed specifically at women at home, and the presenters were almost always men – among them Richard Murdoch, Sam Costa, Gilbert Harding and Eamonn Andrews. Kenneth would present the series on several other occasions before it ended with the launch of Radio One in August 1967.

He continued to make regular guest appearances on *Woman's Hour* and in February he recorded two editions of a 'Driving Quiz' for the programme. On 14 April he was on again as the 'Man in the Kitchen' and a few days later he wrote to the Editor of *Woman's Hour,* Joanne Scott-Moncrieff:

> Just to let you know I haven't forgotten the cliché epic – but alas, it
> has been impossible to strike while the iron is hot; however I'm now
> putting my shoulder to the wheel. After all, time and tide wait for
> no man, and where there's a will there's a way.

Later in the year he would take part in other features on *Woman's Hour* such as 'The Way I Dress', 'Myself and Gardening' and another of his quizzes called 'How Good a Listener Are You?'

During May Kenneth had a very busy month, with the start of a new five-month series of *Twenty Questions*; an appearance with Richard Murdoch on *Music Hall*; a return visit to *Sunday Story* on BBC television for a three-week series about the character and beliefs of his father Silvester Horne; and another week as the presenter of *Housewives' Choice*. After which he wrote a typical thank-you note to the producer, Michael Bell:

> Yes I really <u>did</u> enjoy it, thanks to the kind administrations of Lilian Duff who was quite 'unflap-able'. I hope one day to be asked again for H.C., and I'm always just across the park should you want me in an emergency.

At the end of the month he was also a member of the team on the long-running radio series *Any Questions* presented by Freddie Grisewood. It was unusual for Kenneth to take part in a programme of a political nature. He never expressed any interest in politics, although with his social and business background it is fair to assume that his loyalties would have leaned towards the Conservatives. One of the questions from the audience was about pirate radio ships, which had started broadcasting with Radio Caroline in the North Sea two months earlier. Kenneth was all in favour of them and declared, 'I believe commercial radio will come and these boys should be given a licence. I've heard it in America and enjoyed it.'

In August he went on holiday with Marjorie to Cavalière, near St Tropez in the South of France, but he had to fly back to London to record the first of a new thirteen week comedy and music series called *Starlight Hour*. The programme had started originally in 1948, featuring Geraldo and his Concert Orchestra and Singers, with Edwin Styles as the compere, and had enjoyed several successful series in the early 1950s. In the autumn of 1964 the BBC decided to revive it with Kenneth as the new compere but he had already booked his holiday at the time of the first recording in September.

He did not want to let the BBC down, so he interrupted his holiday and flew back for the day. To the horror of the BBC contracts department, he charged them £90 expenses for his first-class return air fare from Nice to London but, after a flurry of memos, they reluctantly paid up in full. The first show featured the

'Singing Star' Kenneth MacDonald, 'World of Comedy' with Kenneth Connor, June Whitfield and Ronnie Barker, and 'Special Guest' Moira Lister, and the series ran until Christmas.

When Kenneth got back from his holiday in mid-September he walked straight into a major crisis. He had been booked to take part in an edition of the radio series *Comedy Parade*, to be called *Down with Women*, which was scheduled to be broadcast on the Light Programme in October.

Eric Merriman objected. He felt that he had made Kenneth Horne into a star and therefore no other comedy series should be allowed to use him. He also believed that part of *Down with Women* was similar to *Beyond Our Ken* and he accused the BBC of 'passing off' – in other words, stealing his idea. Merriman threatened to quit *Beyond Our Ken* if the other programme was not withdrawn, but the BBC stood its ground.

Merriman had probably been thinking of leaving the programme anyway. He had been writing the series for seven years and it made sense to finish while it was still at the top. He could also make considerably more money writing for television. But he was not prepared to let anyone else take over his creation. On 24 September, he wrote to the Head of Light Entertainment, Pat Hillyard: 'I note that you have decided to continue with your plans to broadcast "Down with Women". Regretfully therefore I confirm that you must now consider that "Beyond Our Ken" is at an end.'

Five days later, Kenneth Williams wrote in his diary: 'Hugh Paddick came at 7. We went to Biagi for dinner. He said that Merriman had incurred the wrath of the BBC, and that consequently the series ("B.O.K.") was off. So that is that. That's the end of that little annual source of income, and prestige and everything.'

It may have spelled the end of *Beyond Our Ken* but Kenneth was determined not to break up such a successful team. He suggested to the BBC that he could create a new series for the same cast, and he knew just the person to write it with him. On 4 October Kenneth wrote to Mollie:

EM is going through one of his phases! Having said BOK can return in December, he then said next Spring and now next Summer, if ever! And if they broadcast a show in which I appear called 'Down with Women', never. Because he thinks there is some slight similarity with BOK in one spot – entirely untrue.

Anyhow I have written to Pat Hillyard (the Boss) and said that all this must be sorted out. I have also said that if he wants to scrub BOK, then you and I will write an entirely new series for the BOK cast. I am assuming that I have just called on your services should that arise?

Next day Kenneth had a meeting with Kenneth Williams, Hugh Paddick and Betty Marsden at which they all agreed to do everything they could to keep the team together. Meanwhile Roy Rich had taken over as the Head of Light Entertainment from Pat Hillyard.

On 23 November Kenneth Williams noted: 'To the Aeolian [Hall] to attend this conference with Roy Rich who is now in charge of Entertainment on the Light Programme. The upshot of it all is that we're to have a new series entitled "It's Ken Again" around Mar-April of '65. They're approaching Barry Took about the actual writing.'

At first Took was reluctant to get involved. He and Marty Feldman attended a meeting at the BBC with Kenneth, Roy Rich, John Simmonds, the producer, and Edward Taylor, the Light Entertainment Script Editor. However Took and Feldman turned down the BBC's offer to write a successor to *Beyond Our Ken* because they believed it would be difficult to find anything new for such a long-established cast to perform.

After the meeting they returned to Took's flat for lunch and, over a cheese pudding cooked especially by Lyn Took for the vegetarian Marty Feldman, they started speculating about what sort of programme *could* be put together around the cast of *Beyond Our Ken*. By the end of the lunch they had come up with so many ideas that they rang Roy Rich and, somewhat embarrassed, informed him they had changed their minds and would like to have a shot at writing the new series.

According to Lyn Took, afterwards Feldman told Took, 'I knew we were going to do it somehow when Roy Rich's carnation fell out of his buttonhole and rolled across the office in Broadcasting House. It was so much a thing of you and me that we've got to do it!' Edward Taylor always referred to it as 'the moment when the Head of Light Entertainment was deflowered'.

Kenneth was delighted with news, but he was still hoping that Mollie would also be involved and he wrote to her:

> Script by Barry Took (very nice) and Marty Feldman (I don't know him) and (I hope) Mollie Millest. I have mentioned all the work you did and I am having another meeting on Friday at 11.30 a.m. to sort out details. Could you drop me a PC before then giving me the names of about a dozen of the sketches you wrote – the more recent the better.

Eric Merriman had been waiting outside the BBC offices in Bond Street while the cast held their meeting. When he heard about the plans for the new series he was furious. On 27 November Kenneth Williams wrote: 'Morning began with irate and bitter telephone call from Eric Merriman saying I was disloyal to take part in a radio show which was written by other people after seven yrs. etc. etc. but that he should have expected it because "I know you're only in the business for what you can get out of it . . ." I said that's right and eventually he rang off with the threat of court action against the new show.'

Bill Pertwee had been a friend of Eric Merriman's for many years and had been a godfather to his late son Christopher. He even used to play cricket with his other son Andy in the Merriman's back garden. But he received an equally enraged letter from Merriman, saying, 'How can you do this . . . a Godfather to our son?' 'He just turned on me,' recalls Pertwee. 'I didn't even reply to it. We didn't speak for years after that.'

Andy Merriman admits that his father saw the world in black and white. 'You were either with him or against him,' he says. 'He even fell out with the neighbours and I never knew which ones I was supposed to talk to.'

Merriman fired off another angry letter to Roy Rich: 'I consider the piratical action you propose to take . . . highly unethical . . . in that you intend to reproduce the whole essence of an established show which I created and originally cast.' This was not exactly true. Merriman had created the format of *Beyond Our Ken* but the original cast of the show had included Hugh Paddick, Ron Moody and Pat Lancaster, all colleagues of Barry Took in the West End revue *For Adults Only*, while Kenneth Williams had joined at the suggestion of Pat Hillyard.

Eric Merriman never forgave Barry Took for writing *Round the Horne*, particularly after it was so successful, and he became the *bête noire* of the Merriman family. Andy Merriman says that every time Took appeared on the radio or television in programmes such as the *News Quiz* and *Points of View*, his father would exclaim, 'It's Took again!' He blamed Took for all his misfortunes and if anything went wrong in his life, he would complain bitterly, 'I bet Took's behind it!'

Kenneth had taken Mollie Millest to meet Took to see whether she could contribute to the new series, but on 28 November Kenneth told her:

Bad news I'm afraid. The two new scriptwriters have said that in the first instance they feel they must 'go it alone' – whether or not they will be successful in this way, or whether they are going to need assistance later I cannot say.

Personally I think they are making a mistake, but there is nothing I can do at this stage. I hope I haven't wrecked your chances with the Dick Emery Show by all this stalling. Please put me in the picture.

Meanwhile John Simmonds tells me he is going to write to you

to see if you'd like to submit material for the Des O'Connor Show
(whatever that is.) I think eventually you'll be 'one of us' but I've
jumped the gun a bit. Sorry – it was over-eagerness.

Eric Merriman had also objected strongly to the proposed title of *It's
Ken Again*, claiming that the use of 'Ken' and more particularly
'Again' implied a sequel to the original title. The BBC lawyers
disagreed. On 10 December Roy Rich wrote to him:

> I have only one comment to make about the structure of the new
> programme and that is to reiterate my intention, and it is to use the
> same actors in a new context and that it will not be a replica of the
> whole essence of an established show as you appear to fear. Finally,
> as to the title 'It's Ken Again', it is our considered opinion that this
> clearly refers to the actor Kenneth Horne and not to the old formula
> of 'Beyond Our Ken'.

Having been given the go-ahead, Took and Feldman drew up some
ideas for the format of the new series. They included a section called
'Trends' in which characters would discuss ideas on fashion and
music; TV from around the world; a history of London theatres by
a couple based on the American actors Alfred Lunt and his wife
Lynn Fontanne; Reminiscences of An Old Bag, about 'an aged,
wealthy crone'; answers to last week's puzzle; and a tramp character
to be played by Kenneth Williams.

Many of these ideas found their way into the actual series: The
answers to last week's quiz became a regular feature, while the Lunt-
Fontanne couple evolved into Dame Celia Molestrangler and ageing
juvenile Binkie Huckaback; Reminiscences of An Old Bag turned
into the Clissold Saga; and the Kenneth Williams old tramp became
J. Peasmold Gruntfuttock.

On 18 January 1965 Kenneth and the rest of the cast assembled
at the BBC for a read-through of the pilot script. Afterwards
Kenneth Williams commented: 'Hurried to a meeting of the radio

team at Aeolian Hall. Barry Took and Marty Feldman now writing the series. We read a sample script and I think it will provide a good sound show. I'm written in very thinly, but doubtless the weight will shift from week to week.'

The BBC had a cast and a script but they still had to resolve the dispute over the name of the series. Eventually they settled for a title originally suggested by Barry Took. On 5 February the BBC's Assistant Solicitor sent a memo to the Light Entertainment Booking Manager:

Following the advice given by counsel last evening, Mr Roy Rich decided to adopt the name 'Round the Horne' for the pilot programme which is to be performed before an invited audience at the Paris Cinema on the 18th February.

20

Round the Horne

IF KENNETH HORNE had retired from broadcasting after the final episode of *Beyond Our Ken*, he would still have been remembered as the star of two of the most successful radio comedy series ever. His place as one of the all-time greats of British comedy, however, is due to the extraordinary popularity of *Round the Horne*.

It was very much a series of its time. It tuned in to the popular culture of the Swinging Sixties – the clothes, the music, theatre and films – and the growing permissiveness in society, in a way that pushed back the barriers of radio comedy. The enormous success of the satirical West End revue *Beyond the Fringe*, starring Peter Cook, Dudley Moore, Jonathan Miller and Alan Bennett, and the groundbreaking BBC television series *That Was The Week That Was*, had made it acceptable to poke fun at figures in authority such as politicians and royalty, and even the BBC itself, and allowed the writers to tackle hitherto taboo subjects such as sex and religion. The show was unashamedly vulgar, provoking a furious backlash from the self-appointed guardians of public morals, but Took and Feldman believed in writing 'down-market material in an up-market way'. Most importantly it was very funny:

WILLIAMS: Scream as much as you like, my dear. No one can hear you here.

MARSDEN: But why have you strapped me to this operating table?

WILLIAMS: Call it an old man's whim.

MARSDEN: All right, why have you strapped me to this old man's whim, and what are you doing with that little black box?

WILLIAMS: Don't worry, my dear, you won't feel a thing. I just attach a wire here, a wire there, then I turn this knob and . . .

SMITH: This is the BBC. Ladies and gentlemen, it's *Round the Horne*.

MARSDEN: No, no. Anything but that!

Barry Took saw Kenneth as the 'maypole' around which the brilliant cast would dance – a 'master of the revels'. His natural authority provided a solid core which held the various elements of the programme together. His avuncular presence also served to reassure the audience, who reasoned that if Kenneth Horne was involved, the programme couldn't be that dirty – could it? Bill Pertwee describes it as 'a classic bit of casting, to put these lunatics around this pillar of English society'.

The first episode of *Round the Horne* was broadcast on Sunday 7 March 1965 at 2.30 p.m. and was described by the *Radio Times* as 'five characters in search of the authors'. The series ran for sixteen weeks until the end of June, but it took a while to find its feet. After the recording of the second show, Kenneth Williams commented: '"Round the Horne" went drearily. No house. I suppose they're all waiting for a regular routine. The material is not v. good, I'm afraid.'

The BBC Audience Research Report revealed that the radio listeners were equally unsure about the new programme. A typical comment came from a railway clerk, who said, 'Nothing out-standing in the way of regular sketches but once a pattern is established it should prove most entertaining.' Many thought that its format was too similar to *Beyond Our Ken*, with 'the same silly voices telling the same old jokes', and a considerable number objected strongly to the vulgarity of the script.

The level of the humour was already causing some concern and after the second programme, the Chief of the Light Programme wrote to Roy Rich to complain about the 'dirt':

> I understand from Henry that both he and Con were pretty shocked by the lavatory humour in the recording of RTH and in fact one member of the audience subsequently telephoned to this effect. Would you stress to producers that it is entirely wrong and indefensible to have two standards of humour, one for the studio audience and one for the air. It could be most embarrassing to take young people or people with a clean mind to a show which is going to subsequently have a lot of editing done to it to meet broadcasting standards.

Barry Took believed that it took him and Feldman about six episodes to really get on top of *Round the Horne*, by which time they had invented the folk singer Rambling Syd Rumpo; the ham actors Fiona and Charles; and the immortal Julian and Sandy.

The original idea had been to write a sketch about two elderly Shakespearean actors who turned up to do Kenneth's housework. Took and Feldman sent the script to John Simmonds and were surprised when he told them he hated the idea. 'These poor old men are not funny, they're sad,' he complained. 'Can't you make them chorus boys?' So they did, and Julian and his friend Sandy were born. They were named after Julian Slade, the composer of *Salad Days*, and Sandy Wilson, who wrote *The Boyfriend*:

HORNE: Hello – is anybody there?
PADDICK: Hello – I'm Julian and this is my friend Sandy.
WILLIAMS: How bona to vada your dolly old eek again, Mr Horne. What brings you trolling in here?
HORNE: Well, I felt that I was badly in need of some Public Relations.
WILLIAMS: Well, chacun à son goût – that's your actual French, you know.

Julian and Sandy spoke in a camp slang known as 'Polari' – a mixture of fairground, romany and backslang – commonly used in the 1960s by dancers and choreographers and others connected with musicals and revue. For instance, in the sentence above, 'Bona' meant good, 'vada' was see, and 'dolly' was nice, whilst 'eek' meant face; other words used backslang, such as 'riah', which was hair backwards.

Most listeners had never encountered such overtly gay characters before; homosexual acts between men remained illegal in Britain until the Sexual Offences Bill became law in July 1967. This led to the following classic exchange when Kenneth visited a firm of solicitors called 'Bona Law':

HORNE: Will you take my case?

PADDICK: Well, it depends on what it is. We've got a criminal practice which takes up most of our time.

HORNE: Yes, but apart from that, I need some legal advice.

WILLIAMS: Ooh, isn't he bold?

Sometimes it was the most innocuous of scripts which caused the most offence. On Easter Day 1965 Kenneth delivered a monologue to mark 'the centenary of the birth of the crumpet', which he claimed had been invented by a Master Baker from Nuneaton, Tammany Wilkinshaft, hailed as the Father of the Modern Crumpet. Unusually, he had written the piece himself and, according to Lyn Took, it was his sole script contribution to *Round the Horne*. 'In fact,' Lyn recalls, 'neither Barry nor Marty were keen on it, but as Kenneth seemed so tickled by it, they put it in.' It was a decision they would quickly regret.

The first crumpet, said Kenneth, was square in shape and had no holes, so the butter ran off it and Wilkinshaft became known as the man with the greasy lap. However he persisted until he perfected the crumpet as we know it today. Soon he was asked to make triangular crumpets for the YWCA, circular crumpets for the Round Table, and, on one occasion a crumpet shaped like a carpet slipper for his Masonic Lodge. His great moment came when he was asked by Parliament to make a giant crumpet to celebrate Queen Victoria's Diamond Jubilee:

> HORNE: In honour of the occasion he built a crumpet that was fifteen feet across and six feet high. As an added novelty he hollowed out the centre and a Gaiety Girl was secreted inside. When the Loyal Toast was drunk, she leapt out, wearing pink combs and waving a Union Jack – either that or the other way round, I don't remember. In any event the whole affair was a great success and, as many people commented afterwards, 'It was a smashing bit of crumpet.'

This provoked an outraged letter from a well-known member of parliament and a memo from the BBC's Director of Sound Broadcasting, Frank Gillard, to the Chief of the Light Programme, Denis Morris:

> Sir Cyril Black, M.P. has complained about the programme broadcast on Easter Day. In reply I have told him that this is a series which is given a certain amount of latitude and that it operates in the broader belt of permitted broadcast humour.
>
> He may stir up some trouble for us, and I think it would be a good thing if 'Round The Horne' could watch its step, particularly over the next few weeks and keep itself within reasonable bounds.

Kenneth responded with a closing speech written by Took and Feldman at the end of the following week's programme, in which he answered the criticism 'levelled at us by a minority of killjoys':

> HORNE: Let me say to them that our scripts are whiter than white, as is the face of the producer when he reads them. You see, evil is in the eye of the beholder – and we believe that you can make anything

sound as if it has a double meaning – if you know how. So, cheerio, see you next week.

Later Kenneth was heard to remark, 'I'm all for censorship. If ever I see a *double entendre*, I whip it out!'

In May the Chief of the Light Programme was still concerned about the language on *Round the Horne* and he wrote to the Head of Light Entertainment:

> It seems to me that we must take positive and perhaps drastic steps to clean this show up. It will either shortly be one of the very best Light Entertainment programmes we do – the characterisations improve with every number – or else it will give such offence to a vociferous minority that we shall find it difficult to sustain it and I personally don't think we should at this time on a Sunday.
>
> There was no doubt on Sunday that the artists were 'hamming it up' and on one occasion the length of the sustained laughter before a single word was said, showed without any doubt at all, either unintelligent editing or else that members of the cast were playing for laughs with the studio audience.
>
> My affection for this group of artists is proven and well known so I would have no objection at all to you showing them this note of mine and indeed A.D.S.B.'s as well. The Ball is at their feet – I hope they don't put it through their own goal.

When further complaints were received, the Director General of the BBC, Hugh Greene, asked to see the offending scripts and he would always return them to the Chief of the Light Programme with the note, 'I see nothing to object to in this.' Some years later Took asked Sir Hugh why he had defended the show so robustly. He replied, 'Well, I like dirty shows!'

Andy Merriman has suggested that many of the characters in *Round the Horne* were based on his father Eric's original creations in *Beyond Our Ken*. This is undeniably true when it comes to Hugh

Paddick's sibilant 'Dentures', who is a direct descendant of *Beyond Our Ken*'s 'Stanley Birkinshaw', and also Betty Marsden's 'Daphne Whitethigh', an equally close relation of 'Fanny Haddock'. But it is not surprising when the roles were voiced by the same actors.

There were many wonderful new characters, however, such as the dirty old tramp J. Peasmold Gruntfuttock, Japanese mastermind Chou En Ginsberg M.A. (Failed), and Spasm the butler, all played by Kenneth Williams. Hugh Paddick portrayed Colonel Brown-Horrocks of MI5, the palmist and seer Madame Osiris Gnomeclencher, and the cockney concubine Lotus Blossom; while Betty Marsden was the elderly ex-Gaiety Girl Lady Beatrice Counterblast (née Clissold), 'the pure brass of the Music Hall', who had done everything 'many, many times!'

My personal favourites were the terrible ham actors Dame Celia Molestrangler and 'ageing juvenile' Binkie Huckaback, played to lip-trembling perfection by Betty Marsden and Hugh Paddick:

> MARSDEN: Excited, Charles?
> PADDICK: Yes, Fiona, intoxicatingly, flutteringly, heart-thumpingly, passionately excited. And yet somehow – calm. And you, Fiona?
> MARSDEN: Yes, I'm calm too. Resignedly, tranquilly, stoically, placidly calm. And yet – somehow – excited.
> PADDICK: I know.
> MARSDEN: I know you know.
> PADDICK: I know you know I know.
> MARSDEN: Yes, I know.

An honourable mention should also be given to the announcer Douglas Smith, a regular Radio Three announcer more used to introducing Beethoven and Mozart. As the series progressed he was given more and more silly things to say. The writers even invented a spoof product for him to advertise on the programme, Dobbiroids, the Magic Horse Rejuvenator, 'guaranteed to ease tired hooves and take the flock off the wallpaper'; not to mention Dobbimist, 'the Horse Deodorant that nine out of ten Hollywood stars prefer'. Smith was often called upon to supply human sound effects and in his time he impersonated a drophead Bentley, a telephone box, a smouldering volcano, a semi-detached house and, most memorably, a cow:

SMITH: Moo Moo – Splosh!
HORNE: Splosh, Smith?
SMITH: Yes, sir. I kicked over the milk pail.

The musical interlude in the middle of each programme was provided by the Fraser Hayes Four, a highly talented but rather old-fashioned close harmony group, once introduced by Kenneth as: 'The Fraser Hayes Four – three voices in perfect harmony.' And, after the first six episodes, the resident house band was the excellent Edwin Braden and the Hornblowers, led by the luxuriantly mustachioed Eddie Braden, often referred to by Williams in the scripts as 'that great hairy fool'.

Kenneth Horne, of course, always played himself, even when his characters were given such exotic names as Ebenezer Kukpowder, Lord Tantamount Horseposture, Ramsden Gnomefumbler, or Arbuthnot Nydle – known to his friends as Dean Nydle. The first series of *Round the Horne* came to an end on 10 June 1965 and Kenneth wrote to Barry Took: 'It's been a marvellous series, thanks to all of you and, personally, I'm agog at the thought of starting again next March. Mind how you go – there aren't many of us left.'

Kenneth had become a grandfather in March 1965 when Susan gave birth to a daughter, Sarah, at the Middlesex Hospital in London. He went with Marjorie to see the new baby in the hospital, although they both seemed rather ill at ease. When Sarah was christened three months later at Christ Church in Kensington, where they had been married, neither Kenneth nor Marjorie attended the ceremony, even though the church was just around the corner from their flat. Susan felt sad and disappointed. 'I've no idea why they didn't come,' she says. 'In those days you did what your family told you and it took a lot of guts to confront my mother about things.'

In April Kenneth started another week as the host of *Housewives' Choice*. During his previous stint on the programme in January he had received hundreds of record requests. One had been from a widow in her mid-forties called Christine Bennett and he had sent a standard reply thanking her for her charming letter. After he had played her request for a piece by Schubert on the programme, she wrote again to thank him. For some reason her letter struck a chord with Kenneth. He wrote back and it was the start of a remarkable correspondence that would total more than sixty letters over the next four years.

The letters were informal and friendly, but never romantic. She would write chattily about her day-to-day life, commuting to work in an office and living in a flat on her own, and he would describe his own experiences, travelling from one radio or television studio to another. Most of his letters were written on long train journeys, when he was probably feeling tired and alone. He seems to have derived some comfort from reading the ordinary details of her daily life and, in turn, he gradually began to confide in her about his work and the true state of his health.

In one letter she described her flat and he responded with the following poem:

I find it a time-passing dodge
To try and imagine Park Lodge,
Of course it's especially fun
To conjure up Flat Number One.

Does the sitting-room glisten like new?
And has it a fabulous view?
And is the settee

As a settee *should* be,
To seat (rather close) only two?

Is the kitchen of modern design
With a table at which one can dine?
Do the cupboards conceal
Everything for a meal
Plus those neat little racks for the wine?

And now for the bedroom – oh dear!
I mustn't be too nosey here!
Silken sheets – and between –
Lies the owner Christine –
Close your eyes, Horne, and then disappear!

I find for a poet like I'm
Christine is quite easy to rhyme,
But as for that other name, Bennett,
Well, that's quite impossible, 'ennit?

Eventually they met, when Christine went to see one of his broadcasts, and one Saturday morning he even visited her flat, where they sat drinking Dubonnet Blonde and talking, quite innocently, until it was time for him to go. As she walked with him out to the black Bentley, Christine asked him, 'What's it like to be a celebrity?' He grinned and replied, 'Do you know, it's really rather fun!'

As well as *Round the Horne* he was also involved in several other long-running series. In April he had embarked on a twenty-three-week series of *Twenty Questions* which would continue until the end of September, and in May he started an eighteen-week series on BBC TV as the chairman of *First Impressions*.

Then in July he started a thirteen-week series of Sunday morning record programmes on the Light Programme. After the first show Kenneth was asked by the BBC if he could include 'a bit more comic chat' and he contacted Mollie Millest to see if she could come up with a few ideas, while pointing out, 'As you know the fee for doing a record programme is notoriously low – in fact if I were to present you with 50 shillings [£2.50] each week for comic ideas it would be 10% of the total.' For the next few weeks Mollie supplied him with dozens of witticisms, most of which he used in the programmes.

During July Kenneth also presented a feature on *Woman's Hour* called 'Books for the Beach' and a few weeks later he received a letter from Mrs Doreen Forsyth, a producer on *Woman's Hour*, suggesting that he might like to present a whole edition of the programme, selecting all the features and interviews. He was intrigued by the idea and invited Doreen to discuss it over lunch in the Grill Room at the Hyde Park Hotel.

They seem to have got on very well together and their correspondence reveals a growing attraction between them. Before the lunch Doreen had written to him as 'Dear Kenneth', signing herself 'Yours sincerely'. A month later she was writing 'My dear Kenneth', and signing off 'Love . . .' By November that had changed to 'My dear Kenneth' and 'My love as always'.

Kenneth had enormous charm, combined with an irrepressible sense of humour, and many women were attracted to him. Having grown up with his mother and four elder sisters, he liked to be with women, and he was flattered by their attention. He fell in love quite easily but he also had a roving eye, which is one of the reasons why his three marriages were such failures. If he had divorced Marjorie and married Joyce Davis, it is quite probable that within a year or two he would have acquired another mistress. 'He didn't want just one girlfriend,' says Eileen Miller. 'He enjoyed the company of women and he gathered them like a moth to a flame.'

When *Twenty Questions* finished in September, Kenneth joined John Ellison as the second question master in the popular radio schools quiz *Top of the Form*. The shows were recorded every Tuesday and for the next three months he undertook an exhausting schedule which took him to towns and villages all over the country, leaving London at midday on Monday, and often not arriving back home until Wednesday afternoon.

Towards the end of October he was suddenly taken ill and was in so much pain that he had to pull out of that week's recording of *Top of the Form*. He went down to Sturtles to recover and on 29 October he wrote to Christine Bennett:

> For the first time in my life, I've had to cancel a broadcast. Something happened to my inside a few days ago, which absolutely doubled me up. The medicos think it's probably something to do with the kidneys, maybe a stone, but we await the result of an X-ray, which hasn't been taken yet!

The X-rays turned out to be clear, although, he informed Christine later, 'they showed that something has recently been wandering over the kidney!'

At the beginning of November he wrote to Doreen Forsyth: 'This coming week is hectic – two TV shows and five radio, varying from Tottenham to Falkirk and Newcastle!'

One of those TV shows was the pilot recording of a new BBC quiz series called *Top Firm* on which he was the question master. The pilot was successful and the series was commissioned, starting a month later on 10 December.

The other TV show was a new weekly series called *Home and Around* on Tyne Tees Television. It was one of the first afternoon programmes designed specifically for the female viewer and was described as 'a half-hour programme for the woman of the mid-60s . . . the woman with an enquiring mind, an independent outlook and wide interests, both in the home and the world outside. *Home and Around* is a lively meeting point for the exchange of ideas and views on every topic affecting women today, in which viewers have a special place.' The programme was presented by Sheila McCormack, with Kenneth alternating as co-host every other week with Colin Reid. In a similar fashion to his monthly column in *She* magazine, Kenneth provided an 'amusing and provocative' male point of view to the various topics of the week.

In an interview to promote the programme, he said proudly that he was taking things easy and was now 'down to a 60-hour week'. 'I did much more than that at one time,' he admitted. 'Indeed, I was doing so much work of one kind and another that I finally collapsed. All in a heap. That was the danger signal and I had enough sense of self-preservation to take notice of it.'

He rather defeated that argument when he revealed that his idea of taking things easy was to travel by train instead of plane to Newcastle so that he could continue to work on his scripts during the journey. Bill Pertwee recalls that Kenneth would often return to London on the overnight train but would not sleep. Instead he spent the time going over his scripts and would arrive at the Paris Studio in London to record *Round the Horne* without having slept at all.

He was now doing five television shows for different companies around the country and sometimes he found it difficult to remember where he was. On one occasion he introduced a television game show by saying, 'Welcome to *Twenty Questions*!' but fortunately nobody, not even the producer, appeared to notice.

He seemed incapable of turning down any offer of work. If he could physically do it, he would, even if it meant travelling hundreds of miles. He used to say, 'If I don't like doing something, I don't bloody well do it!' But privately he would complain that he could not afford to slow down. That was probably true but he also told Richard Murdoch that he never felt happy unless he was working.

For his edition of *Woman's Hour,* Kenneth had suggested that he should interview Mollie Millest about how she combined her comedy scriptwriting with working for the Salvation Army, and on 5 November he wrote to Doreen Forsyth from the Royal Station Hotel, Newcastle:

You ought to come here for a holiday – let's fix an illicit one together! The point of this letter (apart from the usual amorous advances) is to say that I assume you will tell Mollie Millest (Mrs) when she is required etc. etc.

Their correspondence was becoming increasingly flirtatious. Three days later Doreen replied:

> I have the happiest recollections of Newcastle on Tyne, and the thought that they might be made even happier by an illicit holiday with you there was almost too much for me on Monday morning!
>
> Immediately after assimilating your latest letter, I went to a press party to launch a new kind of 'Nescafe', and, lo and behold! there you were, making amorous advances at me from the silver screen. Could this be getting bigger than both of us?!

The Kenneth Horne edition of *Woman's Hour* was broadcast on Monday 15 November and included Kenneth doing a cookery spot, a light-hearted look at theatrical flops with Betty Marsden, a discussion about husbands and wives getting drunk in pubs, interviews with Mollie Millest and the concert pianists Rawicz and Landauer, and a series of short 'Did you know?' features about money, law, insurance, wine and astrology.

As soon as it was over he was back on the road recording *Top of the Form* and that Friday he wrote to Christine:

> Next week is comparatively peaceful. Sleeper to Falkirk Monday night, back 10.00 p.m. Tuesday. Broadcast Wednesday, with a speech at an insurance dinner in the evening. Thursday is Plymouth day, which means I'm back about midday Friday. Saturday is free, then I have a big broadcast on Sunday.

He was in Plymouth for a new TV game show called *Treasure Hunt*, in which contestants competed to open a treasure chest with a golden key. It was shown at 7 p.m. every Wednesday on Westward Television and the contestants were drawn from local clubs and societies. One week the TV listings contained this exciting invitation to viewers: 'Be our guests tonight and join members of the Sports and Social Club of the South Western Electricity Board, Tiverton, with compere Kenneth Horne!' Kenneth disclosed that his golden rule on *Treasure Hunt* was, 'Never talk down to people. The whole object is to put contestants at their ease.' He recorded two shows every other week in Plymouth and the series was to be a popular fixture on Westward Television for the next couple of years.

Kenneth used to tell a story about one of these long-running ITV series in which he gave away quite large sums of money for answering three very simple questions. Before the commercial break, he would always turn to the camera and say, 'That's all for the moment, we'll be back with you very shortly.'

One week he thought he would change his routine and as he ushered the latest contestant off the stage he told the viewers, 'There goes Mrs Moore proudly carrying in her hand thirty-seven pounds, ten shillings. And now we're going to show her a good way in which she can spend that money.'

The screen cut to the commercial – for Andrex toilet rolls.

Kenneth's special edition of *Woman's Hour* had been very well received and a few days later Doreen Forsyth wrote to him: 'I am clutching to my bosom the letters that have come in after our epic on the 15th. Would you like to drop in and see them, or would you rather not?' To which Kenneth responded affectionately: 'To hell with the letters, it's you I want to see!'

On 25 November he was back in Plymouth again, writing to Christine from the Continental Hotel:

It's about 4.30 p.m., and I've just had my cup of char after doing the first of my TV shows, two every other Thursday. It went fairly well, though a little on the quiet side. There's a lot of interviewing to do, and people tend to go blank when the actual show starts. However, maybe tonight's epic will be gayer. Next Monday I shall be down at Southampton discussing a regular Sunday programme that they want me to do in the New Year. All very serious (I think) music and discussion, sort of 6–6.30-ish. Tuesday is 'Top of the Form' (penultimate in the series) but luckily my team happens to be in Dulwich. Poor John Ellison has to go to South Wales! Wednesday I have a midday show, and spend the afternoon at the TV studios at Lime Grove. Thursday sees me doing TV in Newcastle again, and then I have three days off (what's gone wrong?).

You'll be glad to hear that the insurance dinner went like a bomb, mainly because mine was the final speech, and they'd had to sit through four rather boring ones – so anything I said was rather a relief.

Falkirk was fun. I arrived there in the wind and the rain, but by early afternoon the skies were clear and the sun was shining, so I decided to fly back instead of training it. Incidentally, my team won, so they're now in the final, and will meet the winners of Dulwich versus Maestog.

Yes, Christmas is frighteningly near, and I'm already doing recordings of Christmas programmes, and of course I've just finished my *February* article for *She*!

Christmas will not be over busy for me, and I'm trying to take the whole week after off, because once January starts I become even busier than I am now. No, I haven't had a proper holiday this year. In this business you only take a holiday if you're not working! I really only do Radio and TV these days, because the old left leg doesn't permit much youthful exuberance.

As soon as *Top of the Form* was over, however, he had almost no time to recharge his batteries because a week later he had to begin the new TV series *Top Firm*, and over the next four months he travelled all over the British Isles, recording programmes as far afield as Bristol, Coventry, Hull, Sheffield, Scotland, Wales and Northern Ireland.

After the recording of *Top of the Form* at Falkirk High School Kenneth had been interviewed for the school magazine and he was asked what he would wish for if he was granted three wishes. 'I've been pretty lucky in most things,' he replied, 'so I think all three would be for good health.'

On 22 December BBC and ITV programmes were interrupted to announce the death of Richard Dimbleby from cancer at the age of 52. For twenty years he had been 'the voice of the BBC' and probably the most popular broadcaster on BBC radio and television, although he was often accused by his critics of being a pompous bore. His name had featured regularly during the first series of *Round the Horne* and the writer and comedian Barry Cryer remembers one particular joke as 'an absolute classic of radio comedy, where the listener is left to paint the picture for themselves.'

Dimbleby was a large, heavy man, and Kenneth was describing a plan to smuggle an inflatable figure of the broadcaster into the rival ITV, an image already guaranteed to produce a laugh.

'You blow it up . . . ,' he explained, followed by a perfectly-timed pause, '. . . here.'

The ensuing laughter went on for so long that it had to be edited down for the recording. The more you think about the joke, the filthier it is, but the words by themselves are quite innocent; as Cryer points out, it was all in the timing, and that long pause showed 'a demonstration of comic delivery that was a miniature masterclass.'

21

A Second Warning

IN THE FEBRUARY 1966 edition of *She* magazine Mollie Millest wrote a two-page feature article about Kenneth to mark the forthcoming series of *Round the Horne*. He had recommended her to the magazine and she produced a very entertaining appraisal of his life and career, with several photographs of him and Marjorie taken at Sturtles. Afterwards his sister Joan wrote to congratulate her, saying that it was 'amazingly true', while Kenneth described it as 'alarmingly accurate'.

Without telling him, Mollie had written to Marjorie to enquire whether he had any faults and she had replied:

I was delighted to hear from you and if I can help in any way I am only too pleased to. The difficulty is he is such a decent man all through that I find it not easy to find the wrongs, perhaps one or two I mention may be of help.

1. K has about 12 or more good suits, but will persist in wearing odd flannel trousers and a jacket from one of them when he looks so much nicer in a whole suit.

2. When K has a small ailment, like a cold or bones aching, he is a rotten patient. You ask him how he is and he says, 'Oh, I think I shall survive,' sounding like a dying mouse.

3. He has lots and lots of shirts but must want to wear one that has a button missing, so I down tools and have to sew it on.

4. When food shopping he is very extravagant because he orders

such a lot, like leg of lamb nearly 4–5 lbs, and we never finish it.

5. Once home I can never get him to go to a theatre.

Can't think of anything else. He is just wonderful, I would not have him any other way and I love him very dearly. Longing to read the article.

When Mollie informed Kenneth that she had received a letter from Marjorie, he looked rather taken aback and said, 'Oh!' There was a moment's silence, as they exchanged a meaningful glance, and then they carried on their conversation. He did not like Marjorie to know anything about his other women friends, however innocent their relationships. Eileen Miller says that after reading his letters from Mollie at home, he used to tear them into tiny pieces.

Kenneth was always trying to find work for Mollie. A few months earlier he had been contacted by *The Outfitter* magazine to see whether he would like to write a light-hearted article of about 500 words every month. 'Frankly,' he told Mollie, 'I simply haven't time to cope, but thought you might like to have bash (under my name) on a 50/50 basis if the terms are reasonable.'

The first column appeared under Kenneth's name in the January 1966 issue of *The Outfitter* and they continued for eight months. They were clever and witty and were all written by Mollie, with only the occasional dotting of the 'i's or crossing of the 't's by Kenneth, but she could reproduce his quirky sense of humour so perfectly that everyone believed he had written every word. Kenneth split his fee with her and she was quite content with the arrangement, because she knew that without his name at the top, her work would never have been published.

While *Round the Horne* was off the air, he had time to do other programmes and in January he started a three-month run as the chairman of the radio series *We Beg to Differ* on the Home Service. He also recorded two editions as a team captain on the BBC television game show *Call My Bluff*. In February he did another week on *Housewives' Choice* and he was so busy that he had to present the five programmes from three different studios: Newcastle, London and Plymouth.

On 10 March he was in Southampton to record a special Sunday evening programme called *God's Trombone* for Southern Television. He was the presenter of the programme, which he described as '25 minutes of religious variety', with music, sketches and discussion, around a theme of 'Forgiveness and Mercy'. He wanted it to appeal to all ages and asked Mollie to contribute to the script, explaining:

> What (I think) we must avoid is long clerical discussions which get one absolutely nowhere . . . There's no Q.E.D. about religion – it's just a word to be looked on as fictional or factual according to the person.

In an interview, Kenneth said: 'This is religion given a completely human treatment. Being the son of a clergyman I think that anything that makes religion sound more real to the average person is a good idea. We are just trying to make people think a bit, in an entertaining way. I have had a tremendous lot of fun doing this programme. If you cannot enjoy religion, then I don't think there is much point in having it.'

Mollie thinks that Kenneth did not necessarily believe in everything that was being discussed on the programme, 'but let it all go on around him – like *Round the Horne*'. After the programme had been recorded, the title *God's Trombone* was deemed to be unsuitable and it was changed to *Heaven's Above*, which meant that Kenneth had to return to Southampton in May to re-record his introduction and links. The programme was finally transmitted on the ITV network in June and received some very favourable reviews in the press.

The second series of *Round the Horne* started on 13 March 1966 and was broadcast on Sundays at 1.30 p.m. for thirteen weeks until June. After the first recording at the Paris, Kenneth Williams noted:

'We had a v. good house to start off with and it all went extremely well. Lots of laughs.'

All of the cast, except Bill Pertwee, now had recurring characters, such as Charles and Fiona, Julian and Sandy, and Gruntfuttock. In the second series Pertwee was finally given a character of his own, who became one of the funniest in the show. Seamus Android was based on the Irish broadcaster Eamonn Andrews, who had recently started his own Sunday night chat show on ITV. A fluent sports commentator, Andrews seemed to become impossibly tongue-tied when he had to interview famous celebrities, with hilarious results:

HORNE: Hello again Sunday night TV personality, Seamus Android.
PERTWEE: Hello. All right – hello. Ha ha. Well now – here I am wherever this is – and before I introduce you to my first guest whoever he is I'd just like to – ah, that's better. Now we were to have a return visit for the first time yet again of Zsa Zsa Gabor, but unfortunately owing to circumstances beyond my control – here she is. And I know you're just dying to meet her and with that, goodnight.
HORNE: Thank you, Seamus Android – I hope you get better soon. Well, you can't get worse.

As far as Kenneth was concerned, laughter was the best medicine. His left leg was still causing him pain and he would often limp when he thought no one was watching, but he used to say, 'I'm not worried about having another illness, because I always feel better when I'm working.' He relished being a part of the *Round the Horne* team. Barry Took once described how Kenneth would listen to Williams and Paddick at rehearsals and 'tears of laughter would roll down his cheeks'. If there was ever a problem with the script, or a cast member, Kenneth would always be the one to sort it, telling Took, 'Don't worry, Gladys!'

During this second series Kenneth's speeches had to be typed in upper case so that he could read the scripts more easily. His eyesight had been getting worse for some time but he was too vain to wear glasses in front of an audience. Barry Took tried for weeks to persuade him that spectacles could be a useful prop, and by taking them off when he needed to pause during a big laugh, it would add to his performance. Finally Kenneth agreed to try them, and it worked.

Kenneth Williams often generated the most laughs during the recordings of *Round the Horne* by blatantly playing to the studio audience. It had not gone unnoticed. On 6 April he wrote in his diary: 'RTH. At the rehearsal John Simmonds the producer said there'd been criticism of the fact that the visual performance has been outweighing the vocal: he said this is particularly irritating to people listening to the radio because they're hearing gales of unexplained laughter. I said "It's me you're really getting at isn't it?" and he said yes.'

There was also some concern at how 'camp' the show was becoming. Denis Morris, the Chief of the Light Programme, wrote to the Head of Light Entertainment: 'I thought they were not far short in the show last week when they talked about the Director of Radio being concerned about the dirt in it, and I thought the last edition was played "very queer" (it was also very funny).'

The Assistant Head of Light Entertainment, Con Mahoney, replied two weeks later: 'I have gone straight to the roots and can report that henceforth there will be no further body contortions by Kenneth Williams, and the producer John Simmonds continues to work hard on the cast and writers in order to remove suggestive interpretations of dialogue, and a less exaggerated portrayal of any dubious characters.'

When Barry Took was asked to comment on the complaints that the cast were putting emphasis on certain words, he gave the famous reply: 'When Laurence Olivier plays Hamlet *he* puts the emphasis on certain words – it's called acting!'

As Took pointed out, words can mean whatever you want them to mean – if you have a dirty mind. The perfect example was Rambling Syd Rumpo. His songs sounded filthy, especially when delivered by Kenneth Williams, but the words were quite meaningless. 'When I was a young man I nadgered my snod,' he would sing knowingly, to the tune of an old English folk song, or, 'Her bogles were blue and they jangled about . . .'

Barry Took once sat in a sandwich bar in Soho with Marty Feldman listening to the other customers heatedly discussing whether Rambling Syd Rumpo's songs were actually dirty or not. They were certainly funny, and so was the show. On another occasion Took was stuck in a mile-long traffic jam during Sunday lunchtime en route to the coast when he realized that everyone around him was listening to *Round the Horne* – they all had their windows open and everybody was laughing. As he put it, 'a traffic snarl up suddenly turned into a festival.'

At the end of the second series in June, Kenneth wrote to Took: 'A tremendous series – easily the best, and what's more, without a word of discord. A thousand thanks for your trojan work, and let's hope for series after series.'

Kenneth once told a BBC colleague, 'In broadcasting I have always had one motto – "have a bash"!' At the beginning of May he recorded the first of three weekly appearances on the panel of the BBC2 series *Call My Bluff*. He also started another five-month series as the chairman of *Twenty Questions*.

He hated to refuse any offers of work but he was beginning to find the constant travelling between London, Newcastle and Plymouth was getting too much, even for him. When Tyne Tees Television proposed another long series of programmes, he turned them down. He was still committed to doing the TV series *Treasure Hunt*, however, and on 12 May he was on the train to Plymouth, when he wrote to Christine Bennett: 'The carriage reeks of melon, because I have brought three Charentan melons with me, as I'm taking my producer and his wife out to a meal this evening, and the

Plymouth melons are getting a bit long in the tooth.'

Kenneth recognized that he and Kenneth Williams worked well together as a comedy partnership and he was interested in developing the idea into a one-off radio show. In April he had written to Mollie Millest:

> Last year, between R.T.H.s, I did a 'Down with . . .' series. Not outstandingly successful, and I imagine unlikely to be resuscitated. I can't help feeling that a Ken H and Ken W show might be a riot. And by Ken H and Ken W I mean just that. No one else histrionically speaking. 'The Two Kens?' – 'D'ye Ken Ken?' Would you like to turn this over in your mind and then drop me a note?

Mollie had come up with the title 'Twice Ken is Plenty' but, after several attempts, Kenneth was struggling to complete a script. On 9 June he told Christine: 'My epic has slowed down a bit and I'm doing a bit of re-writing. The trouble is that with my sort of script the more you read it the less funny it seems!' Eventually Kenneth submitted the script of 'Twice Ken is Plenty' to Roy Rich at the BBC for consideration as a one-off special in the *Comedy Parade* series. A few weeks later he heard from Humphrey Barclay at the BBC that the idea had been rejected. He explained that it was not felt to be original enough to justify the risk of over-exposing the two of them, adding, 'This will be as disappointing to you as it is surprising to me.'

In August Kenneth went on holiday to the Water Edge Hotel at Bouley Bay in Jersey, and soon after he returned he commenced another exhausting series of *Top of the Form* which was scheduled to run until Christmas Day, taking him from one end of the country to the other each week. Towards the end of September he found time to record an appearance as a member of the panel on the television series *Juke Box Jury* and he was also the chairman of a panel game from BBC TV in Birmingham called *Know Your Onions* which was about food and food prices.

On 6 October Kenneth recorded a five-minute talk for *Woman's Hour* about a new book called *Come for a Meal* or, as Doreen Forsyth put it in her letter to him, 'Come for an Orgy'. Five days later she wrote to thank him for the talk: 'Lovely to see you the other day and I am so much looking forward to coming to a recording of 'Round the Horne' when the new series of recordings starts. I love my new car – and you!' Her reference to a new car is intriguing because it would certainly have been in character for Kenneth to have arranged a special deal for Doreen through one of his friends in the motor industry. He was also so generous that it is quite possible that he had bought her the car himself.

But unknown to Doreen when she wrote her letter, Kenneth was now seriously ill. The day after his recording for *Woman's Hour* he had suffered a major heart attack. He had survived but he was in a very weak condition and Dr Gordon warned him that he would not be able to work for at least two months, possibly longer.

Kenneth knew that he had received a second severe warning about his health. He was also lucky to be alive. He was fifty-nine years old. His father had died of a heart attack at the age of forty-nine and his eldest brother Oliver had died after a heart attack at only fifty-one; his eldest sister Dorothy had also died of heart failure aged sixty-five. Oliver's two sons John and David would go on to have quadruple bypass surgery and a triple bypass respectively. There was obviously a major susceptibility to heart disease within the Horne family and he needed to be extremely careful not to do further damage to his health.

For the moment, however, he was more concerned about his future job prospects. He was terrified that if the BBC discovered he had suffered a heart attack, following his stroke eight years earlier, they would never employ him again. He would be considered too high a risk, particularly for a long series such as *Twenty Questions* or *Round the Horne*. He instructed Eileen Miller to say nothing about the heart attack and to inform the BBC that he had come down with pleurisy but would be back to work soon. On 10

October the BBC cancelled all his contracts until further notice.
Two days later Denis Morris, the Chief of the Light Programme,
wrote to him:

> A line to say how exceedingly sorry I am to hear that you have been
> overdoing it again . . . It is little consolation that Uncle Denis took
> you out some months ago, largely to tell you to 'lay off' – perhaps in
> the future you will listen more readily to his wisdom, you bad
> fellow.
>
> Rest assured that anything we can do to lighten the load when
> you start back again will be done but please, dear Kenneth, do make
> it easy for us.

The BBC requested a medical certificate from Kenneth's doctor and
on 14 October a certificate from Dr Alistair J. Gordon at 44 Wilton
Crescent, SW1, confirmed that Kenneth would be 'unfit for work
for two to three months'.

The new series of *Round the Horne* had been scheduled to start
recording on 28 November. The doctor's certificate meant that the
earliest they could now begin was January. Several members of the
cast contacted their agents in alarm; they had turned down other
work in order to do the series and now they would be unemployed
over Christmas. Betty Marsden had been offered a pantomime in
Aberdeen at a salary of £100 per week. Her agent admitted to the
BBC that she did not particularly want to go to Aberdeen but, on the
other hand, by having neither engagement she had lost a lot of
money. Bill Pertwee had also missed out on the opportunity to be an
Ugly Sister at £75 a week.

The BBC needed to plan its schedules for the new year and to let
the cast know when, or even if, the next series was going to begin.
On 24 October Pat Newman wrote anxiously to Eileen Miller to ask
whether Kenneth could let them know 'how things are going' and if
he would be fit to start work again in two months, or even three and
a half months if necessary. Meanwhile it was decided to go ahead

with the recording of the *Round the Horne* Christmas special at the end of November, but without Kenneth Horne.

It was only a matter of time before the news about his ill health leaked out and on 25 October the *London Evening News* ran a front-page story under the headline, 'Kenneth Horne Taken Ill', reporting: 'Comedian and compere Kenneth Horne has pleurisy. He has been told to cancel all his radio and TV work for the rest of the year.'

Kenneth was furious with the newspaper story and he wrote to John Simmonds:

What really annoyed me about the 'Evening News' was the front page heading 'Kenneth Horne taken ill' (as if I was at death's door!), coupled with the bald statement that I was giving up all work till 1967. The latter, of course, was basically true, but not exactly an inducement to certain commercial concerns to confirm prospective arrangements for advertising contracts. Actually the 'E.N.' has cost me a fabulous amount of money, and I wrote to the Editor and told him so.

Now to business. I am delighted that the Christmas 'R.T.H.' is not to be shelved – good luck to all – I will send a wire on November 28th.

As far as my health goes I am told that everything goes extremely well. I say 'I am told' because, having only got up yesterday after four weeks in bed, one is rather weak to say the least of it, and quite incapable of confirming or denying the verdict of the medicos.

However, both Doctor and Specialist say that my progress is excellent and, having been through my proposed TV and Radio programme, say there is absolutely no reason why I shouldn't enter the battle again on January 2nd.

I can't tell you how much I am looking forward to being in harness again, and especially to re-joining you and the rest of the 'R.T.H.' gang.

Kenneth made his radio and television appearances sound and look so effortless that many people thought they could do the same, if they were given the chance. After the report in the *Evening News*, Harold Hanson from Bradford wrote to the Director General offering his services: 'I am 57 years of age, very similar in appearance and style and have the same type of humour, also the same business background as Kenneth . . . I am sure you would find me the right type of person to fill the gap due to this popular broadcaster's temporary indisposition.' The BBC politely declined to take up his generous offer.

At first there was some confusion within the BBC as to exactly what was the matter with Kenneth, although by early November it was generally accepted that he had pleurisy. One or two people may have suspected that it was more serious, but somehow Kenneth managed to keep the truth about his heart attack from everyone at the BBC and even the other cast members of the *Round the Horne*. Bill Pertwee says he had no idea it was so serious.

By mid-November he was well enough to go down to Sturtles to convalesce and at the end of the month he had a final appointment with his heart specialist, who gave him the all-clear to start work again in the New Year. Meanwhile the recording of the Christmas edition of *Round the Horne* went ahead on 28 November without him.

The script had been rewritten, with Kenneth's lines being distributed among the rest of the cast. Afterwards Kenneth Williams wrote: 'For the first time, we did it without Kenneth Horne and it really made no difference. The laughs were all there as usual and the entire show went like a bomb.'

Barry Took disagreed and thought the show was simply not the same without Kenneth. It was almost as funny but the programme missed his reassuring presence at the heart of all the mayhem. In the Christmas edition of the *Radio Times*, the billing stated: 'Kenneth Horne himself was not able to take part in today's Christmas programme but the others go round without him, wishing him well as they go.'

On 5 January John Simmonds took Marty Feldman and Barry Took to meet Kenneth at his flat at Albert Hall Mansions, on the pretext of discussing the forthcoming series but actually to see for themselves how well he had recovered. Simmonds reported back to Roy Rich that Kenneth seemed to be 'in fine fettle' but that it was difficult to emphasize to him how careful he should be since Marjorie was still stressing – 'perhaps too much' – the diagnosis of pleurisy.

Simmonds felt that there was a great danger of Kenneth risking his health again. He suggested that the only safeguard might be to warn producers that they had to consult Pat Newman before any proposals of radio work were put to Kenneth, although this might simply result in him doing more television.

The following day Roy Rich had a drink with John Ellison who revealed that he was travelling down to Southern Television the next day to start a new quiz series written by him and chaired by Kenneth, who was in 'absolutely first class shape again'. Later Rich commented, somewhat rancorously, 'It appears that Kenneth is going to continue being as greedy as ever – and risk his health.'

The new series was *Happy Families*, a light-hearted general knowledge quiz, which John Ellison had created originally for BBC radio. He had recorded a trial programme with Kenneth back in December 1963 but the BBC had been so slow to make up their minds that he had offered the idea instead to Southern Television. The show consisted of two teams of families, one from the general public and the other from a show-business background, competing against each other in a knock-out tournament, and the series ran on Southern Television for a couple of months.

The third series of *Round the Horne* started on 5 February 1967 and was broadcast on Sundays at 1.30 p.m. for twenty-one weeks until the end of June. Kenneth was still feeling weak after his heart attack and it showed during the first recording. When the series was broadcast, the BBC transmitted the fourth show first.

After the first recording at the Paris on 16 January, Kenneth Williams was typically forthright: 'It was as if one had been doing it for years and no respite. The script was singularly uninspired I think – no innovations or bright ideas for the beginning of a new series, just the same old warming of hands at the camp fire. For the first time I am beginning to feel that this show is rather dated and tired.'

Kenneth knew that he had returned to work too early and on 21 January he wrote to Christine Bennett:

This really is about the first letter I have written to anyone since having had a rather sharp heart attack on 7th October last. I had five and a half weeks in bed, and then a period of convalescence till the end of the first week in January, when the medicos said I could re-start work on a gentle scale. Unfortunately the day I started I managed to collect a monumental cold and throat which is only now leaving me. Rather naturally I feel more second-hand than I should.

I shall never be able to undertake a full schedule, as the heart apparently now has a permanent 'murmur', and everything has to be done at a slow pace. However, things might be worse (as they say!).

The first show in the new series had been rather lacklustre and there was some internal correspondence at the BBC expressing concern that Kenneth was 'not being all that sensible' about the amount of work he was undertaking. There was also a great deal of anxiety over the amount of suggestive material in the script, causing Roy Rich to visit the Paris for the recording of the second show. Afterwards Kenneth Williams expressed equal concern, but for different reasons:

The show went v. well, but I think the fact that Roy Rich showed up signifies that it's 'being watched' as a show. There have been one or two moves to clean up the script this series which haven't evinced themselves before. Sounds like a wee purgette is on, to me. I couldn't care less myself. I think this show is quite dead artistically and the format has completely atrophied itself – it is moribund now. I think I will have to withdraw after this series.

Meanwhile the dispute over the cancelled programmes was finally settled and after weeks of correspondence it was agreed that Betty Marsden and Bill Pertwee would receive their full fees as ex-gratia payments for the five postponed programmes, while the rest of the cast and the musicians would be paid 50 per cent. The final cost to the BBC was nearly £1000.

Having been led to believe they were going to receive nothing, the cast were suitably grateful. Kenneth Williams wrote to the Drama Booking Manager, Robin Whitworth: 'Thank you for your letter regarding the ex-gratia payments for the "Round the Horne" recordings that were cancelled. I think it is a superb consideration and I am unspeakably appreciative.'

Bill Pertwee was equally thankful: 'This sort of gesture makes one even more appreciative of the BBC and the happy associations I have had with them for some considerable years now.'

By now Took and Feldman had become bored with the inevitability of the characters of Julian and Sandy and they left them out of the script of the third programme to be recorded on 6 February. John Simmonds and the cast were appalled and insisted that they must be included, so with a sigh of 'Oh well, as you like it,' the writers hurriedly wrote them back in and they stayed, firm favourites with the listeners, until the very last programme.

After a few weeks the show had settled down and at the end of March, Williams noted: '"Round The Horne" went v. well. Script was v. good indeed and the audience splendid – a great deal of affection there, one felt.'

Some of the dialogue was becoming quite surreal and the cookery expert Daphne Whitethigh, in particular, was developing some very curious ideas for her classic recipes:

HORNE: Now with a few wrinkles on cookery, and a great many old wrinkles elsewhere, here is – Daphne Whitethigh.

MARSDEN: Good news for all housewives. Rhino is down in the shops this week and you can give hubby his favourite cut – my suggestion, best end of Rhino. The difficulty is, of course, to know which *is* the best end. Rhinos know, but their cause is not ours. Other good buys are escalope of Vole, Water Buffalo Chestnuts and Hippo in its shell. For those of you who fancy something a little more exotic in the way of poultry, why not try duck-billed platypus – flambé.

HORNE: I've tried it but they keep blowing the match out.

22

Radio Personality of the Year

EVEN THOUGH HE was still recovering from his heart attack, Kenneth showed little sign of slowing down. He had made one concession by selling the Bentley; he was finding it too cumbersome and he exchanged it for a 4-litre Daimler, which became the third KH6, and his last car. He had also decided to end the Newcastle and Plymouth television shows. But in February he was recording *Happy Families* and *Round the Horne* every Sunday and Monday, and in March he began a new series of *Top Firm* every Tuesday for BBC television.

At the end of March he embarked on another six-month series of *Twenty Questions* with a special edition to celebrate its twenty-first anniversary. One of the objects was 'Two Left Feet' and the comedian Peter Glaze, who had joined the panel after the death of Jack Train, asked Kenneth if he had got it. Kenneth answered 'no' and the audience laughed. Anona Winn was always quick on the uptake and thought the laughter might be a clue. 'Let me see,' she guessed, 'Peter asked, "Have you got this" and you said no . . . Oh! It's something to do with hair!' Which produced an even bigger laugh.

On another occasion the Labour Transport Minister Barbara Castle was a guest on the panel, not long after the Government had passed a law making it illegal to drive a car without wearing a seat belt. The object they were trying to guess was 'a safety belt' and Castle asked Kenneth if he had the object in his car. He replied 'no' before realizing what he had said, and when they guessed the correct answer he was covered with embarrassment.

It was now six months since he had suffered his heart attack but he was still feeling tired and listless. In April he wrote to Christine:

> You ask kindly after me. Well, I suppose you might say that I bought rather a packet last October. I returned after three months, but I think that was really a month too soon.
>
> In any event, continued headaches, etc., made the experts think that the blood was too rich(!). So 24 hours in Bart's where they kept taking blood away and putting it back. Eventually a gentleman called Bodley Scott (who apparently looks after the Queen so *should* be OK!) said things weren't as bad as he'd expected! The arteries were not rock-hard, but a good deal less pliable than they should be. No injections therefore, just pills to thin the blood and (I'm told) calm the nerves!
>
> What the future holds, no one really knows, but I think that two shows a week are enough for a man of my advanced years!
>
> I've just read this. It sounds a bit depressing. It's not meant to be, I'm not like that.

The *Happy Families* television series had come to an end but in May Southern Television launched a follow-up series called *Celebrity Challenge*. The format was essentially the same but this time both the teams were celebrity families. Southern's Controller of Programmes, Berkeley Smith, described the new show as 'the natural extension of *Happy Families*'. Kenneth compered the programme and in the first show the two teams consisted of Richard Murdoch, with his son Tim and daughter Belinda, competing against the actor Jack Watling, with his wife Pat and daughter Deborah.

Later editions included the families of Maurice Denham, Sam Costa, Clement Freud, Warren Mitchell, and Trevor Bailey, the England cricketer, who was asked: 'Who was the first Yorkshire captain to go to Australia?'

Bailey prided himself on his knowledge of cricket and answered confidently, 'Lord Hawke'.

Kenneth had to correct him, 'Actually, it was Captain Cook. He was the son of a Yorkshire ploughman!'

Kenneth used to delight in slipping in the odd trick question such as: 'What does a kitten become after it is three days old?'

Answer: 'Four days old!'

As the third series of *Round the Horne* neared the end of its run in June, Kenneth invited the members of the cast and the production team to his traditional end-of-series luncheon at the Hyde Park Hotel. He sent a personal invitation to Barry Took:

Monday, June 12th is an occasion of world shattering importance.

There will be Rabbi titillating at Cockfosters. Foster titillating at his own convenience. And cock-baiting at Mirabile Dictu.

Other items of interest that day will be a screwing competition during the Carpenters Ball at Nailsworth; Taxidermist stuffing at Welwyn; Haddock smoking at W.D. & H.O. Wills, and Favour currying at Veeraswamy's. There will be the usual jumble sale at Fortnum and Mason's, and a toupeé demonstration at the Wigmore Hall – which will include a lecture by Sir Francis Horne entitled 'Round the Chichester'.

And by some quirk of fate there will be a 'Round the Horne' lunch in the Loggia Room at the Hyde Park Hotel at 1.15 p.m. (or nearest) on the same day.

Let me know if you can come – list of invitees overleaf, in case you want to avoid anyone.

During the luncheon John Simmonds took Kenneth Williams aside and dropped a bombshell. He confided that he was considering the idea of sacking everyone from the show for the next series apart from Kenneth and himself, in order 'to give the writers some new impetus'. Williams might have been expected to be flattered at being singled out as the only indispensable member of the cast but he was very disturbed by the conversation and thought it was a reckless idea.

The final recording of the series went so well that Williams broke down twice through laughing so much during his Rambling Syd Rumpo routine. 'It was a disgrace,' he noted later. Afterwards he wrote to Feldman and Took to thank them for 'such a marvellous series of scripts'. Kenneth also penned a note of thanks to his two co-writers:

> I would find it quite impossible to write entirely different 'thank you' letters to you two miracle men, so you can assume that this is 'To Took, copy to Feldman' and 'To Feldman, copy to Took'.
>
> Honestly I don't know how you've done it, but you have! And what's more every programme has been a riot.
>
> What interests me is that on the very rare occasions when we suspected that a particular show wasn't going to come over quite as well as usual, whether for scriptual, castual, or audiencual reasons, the results always showed how wrong we were.
>
> It's been a smashing series – easily the best, and must have broken all records. But I doubt not that those records will be broken again when we get together for the next group of epics.
>
> I have already turned down a suggestion that the new series should be entitled: 'A song, a smile, and Edna Purbright', because I feel that it sounds too much like 'Panorama'.
>
> May the team of Took & Feldman (copy to Feldman and Took) long flourish.
>
> What's more it's been wonderful fun to do – and if that isn't a compliment to script-writers I don't know what is. Have _you_ ever tried working to a script in which you don't believe?

In August Kenneth started recording a new ITV panel game *Strictly For Laughs* which was produced by ABC Television at their Alpha studios at Aston in Birmingham. Kenneth was the chairman and the game involved members of the public who took part in a joke-telling competition with some of the country's leading comedians. The programme had been devised by Terry Hall, best known for his comedy act with Lenny the Lion, and the idea was that each contestant would tell their funny story and be awarded points out of ten depending on the amount of the applause from the studio audience, with each point being worth £1. Then one of the comedians would have to tell an off-the-cuff joke on a similar theme.

Among the stars taking part in the series were Mike and Bernie Winters, Norman Vaughan, Ted Rogers, Richard Murdoch and a newcomer called Les Dawson who had recently been a winner on *Opportunity Knocks*. Keeping it in the family, the scorer on the series was Richard's daughter, Jane Murdoch.

Later that month Kenneth was a guest on the popular BBC TV chat show *Dee Time* with the former disc jockey Simon Dee. With the aid of a television link between Manchester and London, Kenneth was reunited with Richard Murdoch and Sam Costa, and the topic of the conversation turned inevitably to *Much-Binding-in-the-Marsh*. Most of Dee's young audience had probably never heard of the programme but their appearance together prompted at least one TV critic to suggest that the BBC should persuade them to reunite for a new series.

During the summer Kenneth escaped as often as he could down to Sturtles, sometimes on his own but often with Marjorie. In his professional life he was always immaculately turned out, but in private, he continued his habit of wearing comfortable old clothes, often going to extreme lengths to extend their life. A favourite trick of his was to repair a tear in the knee of his trousers with a strip of elastoplast, sticking the plaster inside the trouser leg to hold the rip together. It was surprisingly effective but Marjorie always objected to his scruffy appearance.

'He was the life and soul of the party in public,' recounts Susan, 'but he was much quieter at home. He loved to do crossword puzzles; he had lots of reference books and he bought most of the newspapers for their crosswords.' He had become so familiar to the locals in the tiny village of Alciston that nobody treated him like a celebrity and he used to enjoy chatting to the gardener or the postman, or popping into the pub a few doors down from the cottage for a drink. He even started getting on better with Marjorie, although she could still be very overbearing.

One weekend Susan was attending a wedding with some friends in East Sussex and afterwards she suggested they drop in unannounced on Kenneth and Marjorie at the cottage. Kenneth was in his casual mode, wearing a favourite patched-up pair of old flannels. He seemed delighted to see her but Marjorie was livid. She took Susan into the kitchen and hissed angrily, 'Don't ever do that again!' She was mortified by the thought of Susan's friends seeing Kenneth dressed so informally. Susan knew that her mother was absolutely serious. From that moment on, she never visited Sturtles again without making an appointment.

Relations between mother and daughter had never been good but now they were probably at their lowest ebb. After six years, Marjorie had still not accepted Susan's marriage to Andy Montague. That summer Susan gave birth to their second daughter Lisa and tried to mend a few bridges by inviting Kenneth and Marjorie to the christening, to be held in their local parish church at Cookham Dean, in Berkshire. Once again, Marjorie rebuffed the invitation and Kenneth explained that he had to be working in Plymouth that day. In a last-ditch attempt to repair her relationship with Kenneth, Susan wrote to him: 'I am deeply hurt, and for the last time I am asking you please to come to Lisa's christening. Either make the effort, for me, or don't ever expect anything more from me again.'

It worked. On the day of the christening at the end of August, Kenneth hired a car in Plymouth and was driven all the way to the church in Berkshire. After the service he gave Susan an affectionate embrace and climbed back into the car to be driven back to the studio in Plymouth.

Kenneth's decision to attend Lisa's christening was one of the few occasions when he defied Marjorie so publicly. Normally he would do anything to avoid an argument with her. 'I asked him once why he did not stand up to her more often,' says Susan, 'and he replied, "You don't have to live with her."'

It marked a breakthrough in Kenneth's often difficult relationship with his stepdaughter. A few weeks later Susan and Andy were on holiday in Cornwall when Kenneth invited them to join him for supper at his hotel in Plymouth. For the first time since their marriage, Kenneth was relaxed and friendly in their company and they talked late into the evening, almost as if nothing had ever happened.

It was the beginning of a renewed friendship between them although Marjorie remained unbending in her refusal to accept Andy as a son-in-law. 'We had some lovely times together with Kenneth,' relates Susan, 'but my mother would never come.'

At the end of August Kenneth made a special guest appearance in Richard Murdoch's successful new radio series *The Men From The Ministry*, which was written by Johnnie Mortimer, Brian Cooke and Edward Taylor. In an episode full of nostalgia the two bungling civil servants from the General Assistance Department, Richard Lamb and Deryck Lennox-Brown, played by Richard Murdoch and Deryck Guyler, were sent to the old RAF station at Much-Binding-in-the-Marsh, where they discovered Wing Commander Kenneth Horne and LAC Sam Costa, who believed that the Second World War was still going on. It was the last time the old *Much-Binding* team would appear on the radio together.

In mid-September Kenneth chaired a new series called *World Quiz 67*, which was a type of 'Brains of Britain' contest between competing teams from the UK, Australia, New Zealand and Canada. The series ran until November and had to be recorded at 10 p.m. every Wednesday evening to accommodate the different time zones.

Later that month he wrote a poem for *Woman's Hour* to mark the departure of producer Monica Sims and the arrival of her replacement Mollie Lee:

> Pop lyrics are quite diabolical
> They make you want to tear your follicle
> (If you don't know what 'follicle' is
> It means that you don't know your biz)
> But Radio One, Two, Three, and Fou-er
> You take a tip from Woman's Hou-er
> Even just their Twenty-First
> Makes one's pride with bosom burst
> Never a hint of impropriety
> But just respectable variety
> 'Frustrated sex-life' – 'Whither youth?'
> And others by Forsyth forsooth.
> 'Do Hippies fill you with remorse?'
> Produced by our Ann Howells of course.
> Although we're losing Monica Sims
> No tears, no gloom, no doleful hymns
> Or hers; we've still got that grand person
> Our commère, Marjorie Anderson
> (How splendidly this fellow rhymes
> Not only Christian but Surnymes)
> Away with gloom and melancholy
> And welcome to the Lee that's Molly.

The BBC unveiled its four new national radio networks on 30 September 1967 with the launch of Radios One, Two, Three and Four. A couple of days later Kenneth wrote to Robin Scott, the Controller of Radios One and Two with a proposal for a late-night radio show called *Horne at the Hilton*, in the style of the Eamonn Andrews and Bernard Braden shows on television. The concept was that Kenneth would talk to people staying at or around the Hilton

Hotel in Park Lane late on a Saturday evening. They would include ordinary as well as famous people, there would be no plugs for books or films, and the conversations would be opinionated but with a sense of humour. Scott rejected the proposal.

In October Kenneth was a special guest on the twenty-first anniversary edition of *Woman's Hour* and he gave a five-minute talk on the subject of 'Future Perfect' – how he would like the world to be in a further twenty-one years. In an affectionate note to Doreen Forsyth, he wrote: 'I adore my schoolmistress (with the accent on the last two syllables).'

He also recorded a pilot episode for a new television series on ABC Television to be called *Horne A'Plenty*. The cast included Hugh Paddick, Gwendolyn Watts, Norman Chappell, Roddy Maude-Roxby, James Beck and Billy McComb, and Kenneth described it as 'a sort of "Frost Report" but . . . the accent will be more on craziness'. His original suggestion for the title of the series had been 'Hornucopia' which was dismissed by the TV executives as 'not known north of Ponders End!'

The fourth series of *Round the Horne* was scheduled to begin in February 1968, but behind the scenes some dramatic changes were taking place. Earlier in the year Marty Feldman had scored a great personal success with his zany appearances in the ITV comedy series *At Last the 1948 Show* on Rediffusion, with John Cleese, Graham Chapman, Tim Brooke-Taylor and 'the lovely Aimi MacDonald'. With a second series about to start filming, he informed Barry Took that he wanted to concentrate on his burgeoning TV career. After writing fifty episodes of *RTH*, the team of Took and Feldman had completed their last radio script together. Overnight, *Round the Horne* had lost half its writing team.

That would have been bad enough but the BBC was going through one of its periodic bouts of belt-tightening. Although *Round the Horne* was one of its most popular radio programmes, it was not about to escape the axe. Eddie Braden and the Hornblowers, the large orchestra which had added so much to the overall sound of the programme, and the popular Fraser Hayes Four, who had been with Kenneth since the first series of *Beyond Our Ken* in 1958, were both dropped by John Simmonds. They were replaced by a smaller, and cheaper, instrumental group led by Max Harris.

Bill Pertwee was also told that his services were no longer required. On the morning he was due to exchange contracts on a new house in Bognor, he received a surprise letter from the BBC informing him that he would not be included in the new series. The letter finished abruptly, 'Thank you for your past contributions. Yours sincerely, etc.' When he showed the letter to his friends they were shocked that he could be dismissed so bluntly after eight years' loyal service. Pertwee was more philosophical about it all.

In his entertaining autobiography *A Funny Way to Make a Living*, he says: 'To be quite honest it didn't upset me, although the money would have been nice for another 16 weeks, particularly as we were just about to move. My thoughts were that my run in *Beyond Our Ken* and *Round the Horne* had started with a six-week contract and had lasted eight years, so who was I to grumble? It had all been beyond my wildest dreams anyway.'

Barry Took agreed to stay on as senior writer and script-editor and Marty Feldman was replaced by three new writers, the up-and-coming team of Johnnie Mortimer and Brian Cooke, and Donald Webster, an actor writer who, according to Took, had been having a bad time and whom he wished to help.

At the time, Mortimer and Cooke were both Fleet Street cartoonists, working on daily strips in the *Sun* and the *Daily Mirror*. Took had come across them when they were part of the writing team behind the radio series *The Men From The Ministry*, and they would go on to write a number of successful situation comedies for Thames TV including *Father Dear Father*, *Man About the House* and *George and Mildred*.

The cut-backs may have seemed rather harsh and unnecessary but they were remarkably effective. By dropping the orchestra, the Fraser Hayes Four and Bill Pertwee, John Simmonds managed to reduce the cost of each show from £601 in 1967 to £486 in 1968, a saving of 20 per cent, while the series remained as popular as ever.

Meanwhile Kenneth was becoming increasingly concerned about his health. On 12 December he wrote to Christine Bennett:

> Yes, 'fair' is a pretty good description at the moment. I think the trouble is all these so-and-so pills that I have to take to keep the blood-pressure fairly steady, and the blood flowing at roughly the right rate. Whatever the reason, it is more than a bit of a nuisance, but I suppose I'm lucky, just the same.

The fourth series of *Round the Horne* started on 25 February 1968 and was broadcast on Sundays at 2 p.m. for sixteen weeks until June. After the recording of the first episode on 5 February, Kenneth Williams was not impressed. That evening he wrote in his diary: '"R.T.H." at the Paris Cinema. Now there are 4 writers on it! It is unbelievable really. Four! For half an hour of old crap with not a memorable line anywhere: well – perhaps the odd one. Well of course one goes on and flogs it gutless and gets the rubbish by.'

A week later the material, or more probably Williams's mood, had improved noticeably: 'Did "Round the Horne" at the Paris. It went very well. The writing is really good I must say. I only hope they keep up the standard.'

It soon became apparent that the outrageous comedy of *Round the Horne* was not really Donald Webster's cup of tea and, after six episodes, he dropped out of the series. From then on, Took concentrated on writing for his favourite characters Julian and Sandy and Rambling Syd Rumpo, while Mortimer and Cooke came up with most of the other sketches. Several new characters were introduced, such as accident-prone roving reporter Gerald Monkshabit, played by Hugh Paddick, and Judy Coolibah, a no-nonsense Australian played with gusto by Betty Marsden:

HORNE: And now, with her curiously bent didgeridoo trailing on the ground behind her, it's Miss Judy Coolibah.

MARSDEN: Hello, Bluey. Stay where you are. I don't want your hands wanderin' again like last week.

HORNE: My hands didn't wander last week.

MARSDEN: I know, an' I don't want 'em wanderin' again this week. I've had enough of that sort of thing since I started workin' as a bus conductress.

HORNE: A bus conductress? Oh, how are you getting on?

MARSDEN: At the back of the bus same as everyone else. Stupid question. I tell you, it's a terrible job, Mr Horne. I'm at it all day . . .

HORNE: What're you getting at?

MARSDEN: Eh?

HORNE: Oh, nothing. I just couldn't resist it.

MARSDEN: It's no fun workin' on a bus, Bluey. Yesterday – you'll hardly believe this – a drunk gets on . . . pushes fourpence in me hand . . . 'How far can I go for that?' he says. I cracked him with me cash-bag and put him off.

HORNE: I imagine you did.

MARSDEN: No, I put him off the bus. D'you know, he ran behind for nearly three miles, callin' and wavin' at me.

HORNE: You'd caught his fancy?

MARSDEN: No, I'd caught his tie in me ticket machine!

Some of the humour had become quite brazenly risqué, but the audiences at the Paris greeted every *double entendre* with howls of delight. According to Brian Cooke, they used to erupt with laughter. 'In forty or more years of writing comedy,' recalls Cooke, 'I've never had such reactions as we used to get from the *RTH* audiences. All the actors gave theatrical performances, of course. They'd all appeared in the West End and knew that if they didn't match their colleagues in the show they'd be blown away. Kenneth Williams was the worst (or best). He'd stick out his backside, roll his eyes, grimace outrageously and often cackle with laughter even when he was off stage.

You can hear him on many of the recordings, doing his donkey laugh in the background. All totally calculated, of course.'

Kenneth did his best to disguise the gradual deterioration of his health during the series. According to Barry Took, it was the sheer guts of the man which drove him on. Took and John Simmonds did what they could at rehearsals to make Kenneth's life a little easier for him. A chair would be at his side the moment he wanted to sit down; a drink would suddenly appear when he needed it; a car never kept him waiting. Lyn Took remembers the skin on his face looking grey in colour.

'We knew he'd had a stroke and he limped,' adds Brian Cooke. 'He would stand at the side of his stage flexing his leg and then walk on trying not to limp. Sometimes we had a high stool for him to lean on but he tried not to use it.'

Marjorie must have realized something was seriously wrong but Susan had no idea Kenneth was suffering so much. 'He liked being the character he portrayed on the radio,' she says, 'always cheerful, never complaining. He didn't do "ill" very well. It was the way he was brought up. Stiff upper lip and all that.'

The blood-pressure pills continued to make him feel sluggish. He may not have confided in his family but in February he wrote to Christine: 'Here we are, getting a little bit more tired each time one has to broadcast, but still in one piece.'

Sometimes he would have to concentrate all his efforts on the simple act of walking. At one script run-through, the pain in his left leg became so intense that he was unable to go on with the rehearsal. 'Sorry, Barry,' he told Took, 'it's a bit difficult today. It's this damn leg – I can't get it to think for me.' At other times he lost the power to speak altogether and sat helplessly with the script upon his knee.

Despite his failing health, the latest series was an enormous success and on 12 March Kenneth received official recognition for the continuing popularity of *Round the Horne* as well as his success-ful chairmanship of *Twenty Questions* when he received the Variety Club of Great Britain Award for the BBC Radio Personality of 1967.

As the latest series progressed, however, Barry Took began to feel that, without Marty Feldman, some of the fun had gone out of writing for the show. At the recording of the programme on 8 April he complained bitterly to Kenneth Williams that the show was becoming filthy. 'We might as well write a series called *Get Your Cock Out*,' he moaned. Williams noted in his diary afterwards: 'I think he's a bit demented.'

Kenneth kept up a relentless schedule. He tried to persuade his family that he had cut down on his radio and TV commitments, but in fact he had allowed his workload to build up again. 'I'm only doing what I enjoy,' he protested.

In March he began another six-month series as chairman of *Twenty Questions*; between March and June he also recorded sixteen shows as a team captain on *Call My Bluff*; and during the year he took part in other radio panel games such as *Does the Team Think?*, *Know Your Onions* and *Sounds Familiar*.

The saddest thing of all is that, despite all his hard work, he had no money. 'He was not very good at managing his finances,' reveals Susan. 'He had a wealthy lifestyle but the money came in and went straight out again.'

Marjorie lived a very comfortable life and there were now also two grandchildren to consider. 'He was too generous,' agrees Eileen Miller 'That was his failing.' The Daimler was his but the flat was Marjorie's, and even his watch had belonged to her first husband. After Kenneth died, the taxman asked Eileen, 'Was that all he owned?'

On Sunday 31 March he joined Richard Murdoch and Sam Costa for the last time at a charity show in the presence of the Duke of Edinburgh to honour the RAF at the Victoria Palace. It brought back some happy memories:

COSTA: Good morning, sir, was there something?
MURDOCH: Ah! Good morning Costa, how are your people?
COSTA: All right thank you, sir, except for Emily's twinges.

HORNE: Oh dear.

COSTA: Yes, she had a double twinge yesterday.

MURDOCH: Oh, Siamese twinge . . .

COSTA: Yes, sir.

HORNE: Never mind, Costa, you're looking very well.

COSTA: Well, sir, I'm just back from my holidays.

HORNE: Oh, where did you go?

COSTA: I went to the Lakes, sir.

MURDOCH: The Italian Lakes?

COSTA: Well, sir, Mrs Lake's Italian, but Mr Lake keeps the paper shop next door to us at Croynge.

A few weeks later he wrote to Mollie Millest, 'Doctors are getting rather strict with me at the moment, there having been odd (very) signs of repetition of old troubles.' Unfortunately he would ignore all his doctors' good advice, with fatal consequences.

23

Final Episode

T HE FINAL EPISODE of the fourth series and, as it turned out, the last-ever *Round the Horne*, was recorded at the Paris Studio on 27 May 1968. After an uncertain start the new writing team had excelled themselves. The series had ended more popular than ever, with a regular eight million listeners. As usual Kenneth invited everyone involved with the show to a buffet party and drinks afterwards at the Hyde Park Hotel, during which he presented them with a memento of the series, an ashtray inscribed with the name of the show.

Even though he was unwell, Kenneth refused to take a break. Thirteen days after the end of *Round the Horne* he recorded the first episode of his new ABC television comedy show *Horne A'Plenty*. The six-part series was shown between 22 June and 27 July and was transmitted in the Midlands and the North of England on Saturdays at 10.15 p.m., but it was never shown by the London-area ITV stations.

The show featured a different cast from the original pilot recording and included Graham Stark, Sheila Steafel, Ken Parry and Alan Curtis. It was designed to be a television version of *Round the Horne* with Kenneth as the central figure linking an assortment of sketches in his own inimitable way, although the material contained more up-to-the-minute satire and social comment and the shows were usually recorded the day before transmission to make them more topical. Graham Stark played the Kenneth Williams role, appearing in dozens of different character parts. Barry Took was the script-editor and the series was written by a team of more than twenty writers, including Marty Feldman,

Johnnie Mortimer, Brian Cooke, Donald Webster, Michael Palin, Terry Jones and Bill Oddie.

'Horne A'Plenty was Barry Took's attempt to do Round the Horne on television but without Kenneth Williams and the rest of the cast,' says Brian Cooke. 'It didn't really work. Kenneth came over best on radio; on TV he was just another performer. Perhaps it was just that we hadn't found the right format for him and if he had lived, we would have.'

In June he stepped in at the last moment to help out his old friend Norman Hackforth, now a panellist on Twenty Questions. Hackforth had managed to arrange a BBC television pilot of his radio series The Tennis-Elbow-Foot-Game. The sports commentator Max Robertson had been booked to be the chairman but he had been forced to pull out because he was abroad on an outside broadcast. Hackforth asked Kenneth if he would stand in for him and he agreed, despite knowing nothing about the programme. The panel game was based on word association, such as 'Black – Night – Day – Light' and so on, and was played to a metronome beat. When you missed a beat you lost the point, and the scoring was based on tennis. After a couple of hours of intensive coaching Kenneth acted as the chairman of the pilot and, according to Hackforth, 'He gave such an outstanding performance himself, and got the whole team so on its toes, that the pilot sailed through, and the show was booked.'

In mid-July Kenneth told Christine Bennett:

I haven't really had a holiday as yet, so the health remains much as before, and a little uncertain at that. On the other hand I am always better when I'm working so where does one go from there? At the moment I have 20 Q's and a TV affair called Horne A'Plenty, which means three days rather exhausting rehearsal. But I have only one more to do. Being a bit of a 'name-dropper', I must tell you that on Wednesday I am speaking immediately after H.R.H. the D of E at a Guildhall dinner! Such is fame!

After the *Horne A'Plenty* series ended, he decided to try and do something about his exhaustion and check himself into a health farm.

Before that he had to read five episodes of the book *Rough Husbandry* by Patrick Campbell for the weekly serial on *Woman's Hour*. The recordings were produced over five days by Doreen Forsyth and after the final session on 27 August she wrote: 'I don't know how to thank you enough for the serial recordings we finished today. You put such enthusiasm, gaiety and professionalism into every moment that I found it hard to remember that this was a piece of work.'

Later that day he checked himself into the Forest Mere health farm at Liphook, in Hampshire, for a two-week stay. 'I'm hoping that a good de-coke may help me back to a more certain life,' he told Christine. 'I suppose my friends won't recognise me less 1½ stone?'

In the preceding months Kenneth had abandoned his healthy regime of eating and drinking sensibly, almost as if he was determined to enjoy himself while he could. In reality he did not need to lose much weight, but he felt it would make him feel less lethargic. By the end of the summer, however, any benefits from his stay at the health farm appear to have worn off.

In September he informed Christine:

I'm trying to avoid as much travelling as possible, and therefore I didn't raise the question of returning to *Top of the Form*, especially as the same team has asked me to do *World Quiz* again, that starts on September 30th, 9.15–9.45, Radio 1/2.

I think I feel better for the de-coking, but the trouble is that weight goes back on so fast! The really testing time is shortly to arrive. *World Quiz*; a weekly panel-game for S.T.V, and my own show for Thames. Everything always comes in batches!

During the autumn Kenneth spent as much time as possible at Sturtles, coming up to London every Thursday evening to record *World Quiz 68* at 9.15 p.m. He must have realized that the next few months could prove too much for him, and no one would have blamed him if he had chosen to take things easier, but he did not want to let anyone down. Perhaps as a last resort he decided to consult a faith healer and, at first, the treatment seemed to work. On 18 November he wrote to Christine:

> If you'd asked me how I was on Saturday, I would have said 'fine'. But I've had two lousy days after a fortnight's progress. However the 'good times' seem to be getting longer, thanks (and I mean this) to a faith healer. Let's hope he can continue the cure.

At the end of the month he began a second series of *Horne A'Plenty* which had now transferred from ABC Television to the newly created Thames Television. It was transmitted on Wednesdays at 10 p.m. between 27 November and 1 January 1969. Barry Took was now the producer as well as the script-editor and the team of writers included Johnnie Mortimer, Brian Cooke and Barry Cryer, but in spite of their combined pedigree, it was not considered to be a great success. Part of the problem was that Kenneth was uncomfortable reading from an autocue, but also, according to Took, during this second series Kenneth was clearly a sick man.

The faith healer, whose name has never been disclosed, had advised Kenneth to put his trust in alternative therapies and stop taking his prescription pills. It was advice that would prove to be fatal. Kenneth's final letter to Christine Bennett was dated 17 December 1968:

> Health at the moment only fair, and I suppose I am working fairly hard to take my mind off it. However, I'm going to have a serious battle with it from about Jan 11th till the end of Feb. Someone ought to be able to help.

He had decided the best remedy was to ignore the constant pain and work even harder. In December he presented the religious programme *Ten to Eight* on Radio Four, in which he discussed 'The Debt to my Parents'. On 6 January he presented *Family Choice* – the successor to *Housewives' Choice* – on Radios One and Two for a week. On 3 February he signed a contract to record twelve more shows as a team captain on *Call My Bluff*, and the next series of *Round the Horne* was scheduled to start recording on 24 February.

He had also started reading a series of extracts from the books *The Art of Coarse Sailing* and *The Art of Coarse Acting* by Michael Green. They would not be broadcast until a year later in March 1970, after Michael Flanders was brought in to complete the recordings.

On 14 February 1969 Kenneth was the host of the annual Guild of Television Producers and Directors' Awards dinner at the Dorchester Hotel, in Park Lane. Earlier in the day, Eileen Miller had seen him at Albert Hall Mansions. He did not look well. 'I warned him not to go that night,' she recounts, 'but he was on the phone and he just looked at me.'

The event was held in the grand ballroom and the presentations were being filmed by the BBC for transmission later that evening. Kenneth appeared to be in sparkling form and he soon had the 740 guests roaring with laughter as he announced the winners of the television 'Oscars'. By his side on the stage stood Earl Mountbatten of Burma, who presented the awards to the winning recipients.

About halfway through the evening Kenneth had to introduce the award for Best Comedy Script of 1968 and to his delight it was won by Barry Took and Marty Feldman for their hit television series *Marty*. After the two writers had collected their award and were returning to their seats, he joked: 'These chaps got an award last year for *Round the Horne*, which is coming back on Sunday March 16th with a repeat the following day – so don't forget to listen!'

Laughter echoed around the room as Kenneth started to announce the next award for Best Scientific Programme for Robert Reid and Peter Goodchild for BBC 2's *Doctor's Dilemma*.

Suddenly he swayed and stumbled forward and then fell three

feet from the podium onto the dance floor. He had suffered a massive heart attack. Someone called out, 'Is there a doctor?' and Lord Hill, then Chairman of the BBC and the former wartime Radio Doctor, quickly left his table and rushed to Kenneth's side. Several women in the audience were reported to have fainted at the sight of his collapse.

Barry Took and Marty Feldman helped to carry Kenneth's body through the glass doors into the nearest room, which was the bar. As Kenneth lay on the carpeted floor, Lord Hill tried artificial respiration, while Dr Robert Reid gave him the kiss of life. But he did not respond. Marjorie sat, pale-faced and silent, watching nearby; one observer described her demeanour as 'steadfast'.

After a few minutes ambulance men arrived with oxygen and Kenneth's body was carried out of the hotel on a stretcher. Lyn Took and Lauretta Feldman travelled with Marjorie in the ambulance for the short distance down Park Lane to St George's Hospital. Lauretta comforted Marjorie while Lyn held on to Kenneth's legs as the ambulance shot round Hyde Park Corner. 'His legs were so cold,' recalls Lyn, 'that I knew there could be no chance.' Kenneth's body was taken into the emergency room, but it was all to no avail. He was already dead.

'He went the way he would have liked to,' commented Barry Took, 'on top of a big laugh.' A BBC spokesman added: 'It is with the laughter over Kenneth Horne's last joke that his last audience will remember him.'

BBC producer Peter Morley, the Chairman of the Guild of Television Producers and Directors, told the shocked guests in the Dorchester ballroom, 'This is very sad, but I am sure Mr Horne would have wanted us to carry on.' Lord Mountbatten agreed to step in to complete the presentation of the remaining awards, including TV Light Entertainment Personality of the Year to an emotional Marty Feldman.

Later that evening Peter Morley interrupted the dancing on the ballroom floor to announce that Kenneth Horne had died. As a mark of respect there was a five-minute interval, and then the guests resumed their dancing.

The awards ceremony was shown at 11.15 p.m. on BBC 1 with the incident edited out. Halfway through the programme, viewers saw Lord Mountbatten suddenly take over the presentations and heard Michael Aspel announcing, 'Mr Horne was taken ill at this point and has since died.'

Brian Cooke was at home, sitting in front of the television with a pad of paper on his lap, working on a new sketch for the next series of *Round the Horne*. When the news of Kenneth's death was announced on *News at Ten*, he remembers: 'I laid the pad aside, went round to Johnnie's house and we quietly and sadly got drunk on whisky.'

Susan heard the news at home in Cookham Dean. She was eight months pregnant with her third child and earlier that day a young girl from New Zealand had arrived to start work at the house as a nanny. Frantically, Susan tried to contact her mother through the BBC but they would not pass on her message. Finally she managed to get hold of Kenneth's doctor, John Gordon, who got through to Marjorie at St George's. Susan left immediately to stay with her mother in London, leaving the bewildered young New Zealand girl alone in the strange house in charge of her two small children.

Kenneth's heart attack had taken Susan completely by surprise. 'I could tell he wasn't going to live to a ripe old age or see my daughters grow up,' she recalls, 'but I never expected him to die so soon.' Marjorie was probably more prepared for his death than most but it still came as a tremendous shock. 'Her whole way of life for the past thirty years was about to stop,' says Susan. 'She must have felt very lonely.'

Next morning Kenneth's death was headline news in the national newspapers. *The Times* described him as 'a master of the scandalous double-meaning delivered with shining innocence'.

In the *Sunday Mirror* Charles Westbourne summed up his universal appeal: 'His success was his ability to get the best out of a script by the sheer brilliance of his timing, by the subtle inflections of a voice that managed to combine outrageous dignity, elegant naughtiness, and a hint of fruity depravity. He was one of the few personalities who bridged the generation gap. Perhaps the last of the truly great radio comics.'

Kenneth Williams was on board the *Monte Umbe* with his mother Louie, returning from a holiday at the Hotel Metropole in Las Palmas, and did not learn about Kenneth's death until the following day. A fellow passenger heard about it while tuning in to the BBC on his radio. 'I felt quite stunned when the news hit me,' wrote Williams in his diary that evening. 'I loved that man. His unselfish nature, his kindness, tolerance and gentleness were an example to everyone. God knows what will happen to the series now.'

Two days later Williams was asked to record a brief tribute to Kenneth on the Forces Network for broadcast to the troops in Germany. During the recording he found that he was trembling and realized it was not from nerves, but from the delayed impact of the grief.

The routine post-mortem examination found that the cause of death was a massive coronary thrombosis. According to Kenneth's physiotherapist, Joe Friel, 'his blood was like treacle'. Dr Gordon told Friel that this meant Kenneth must have stopped taking the anti-coagulants that had been keeping him alive. 'Poor silly fellow,' he sighed, 'if only he'd listened to me. He could have had another ten years!'

After the funeral Susan and her mother were replying to the dozens of letters of condolence when Marjorie said quietly, 'Can you imagine him sitting in an armchair doing nothing?' It was simply not in his character.

She wrote to Mollie Lee at *Woman's Hour*: 'I console myself by knowing that Kenneth would have wished to go exactly as he did, making a speech and all the people laughing and clapping. I have indeed been lucky to have had 23 years of perfect happiness with him.'

The fact is that Kenneth must have known what he was doing. He could have retired to Sturtles and put his feet up, doing the crosswords that he enjoyed so much, but he was only really happy when he was working and he did not want to stop. At some point he must have calculated the risk and decided it was worth taking. He was going to live his life to the full and accept the consequences.

In one of his final letters to Barry Took, towards the end of 1968, Kenneth had joked: 'In these days of rush and bustle one has to plan far ahead. For instance, have you given any thought to Thursday March 19th? I bet you haven't! And you're quite right not to because it's a Wednesday.'

By sheer coincidence it was on Wednesday 19 March 1969 that the Memorial Service for Kenneth Horne was held at the Church of St Martin-in-the-Fields. As always, Marjorie was intent on keeping up appearances. When she discovered that Susan did not have a 'proper' coat to wear to the service she quickly sent her round to her furrier so that she could borrow one of their coats for the day.

Police had asked Marjorie to keep the service low-key, because they were worried about the crowds. But St Martin's was packed with hundreds of Kenneth's friends and colleagues from all walks of life. There were many familiar faces from his BBC radio days such as Hugh Paddick, Betty Marsden, Anona Winn, Joy Adamson and Brian Johnston; senior figures from the motor industry such as Sir William Lyons of Jaguar and Sir Patrick Hennessy of Ford; and family friends like his faithful chauffeur Percy Millea. The service was conducted by the Reverend Austen Williams and included the rousing hymns, 'To Be a Pilgrim' and 'Praise My Soul the King of Heaven'. Richard Murdoch read the lesson and John Ellison delivered the eulogy. He concluded:

He was a man to whom God gave the gift of laughter, and who shared it with the world to the end, exactly as he would have wished. But, of course, it isn't the end, it's only part of the whole story, and

I would ask all of you who loved him not to grieve too much. He wouldn't have wanted you to.

'See you around!' was a pet saying of his, and I feel sure he's around with all of us here today. This special man has left us his philosophy of life. In his own words: 'Live with cheerfulness and certain amount of politeness, and you won't go far wrong.'

After the memorial service Susan wanted to stand on the steps outside St Martin's and talk to some of the guests, to share their memories of Kenneth and to thank them for coming. But Marjorie refused to stay.

'I have always regretted having to leave early,' says Susan sadly, 'but Marjorie dug her heels in and insisted that I take her back to the flat. She had always seemed so confident when she was with Kenneth. Maybe she couldn't cope without him.'

The next day Marjorie wrote to John Ellison: 'Thank you so much for arranging the service so beautifully, it was just perfect. I do hope people didn't mind my not stopping, but to be perfectly frank I was too sad and too moved.'

Since 1988 the BBC has issued every episode of *Round the Horne* on cassette and CD and the combined sales are now more than 500,000. It is a remarkable achievement, and now that the Merriman and Took families have resolved their differences, the Corporation has also started to publish the original recordings of *Beyond Our Ken*, which will only add to that total. It is a testament to the enduring quality of the scripts and the performances, and the comic genius of the man at the heart of them all.

Kenneth Horne has left behind a legacy of laughter. For as long as there are people who enjoy comedy, and as each new generation discovers the classic recordings of *Beyond Our Ken* and *Round the Horne*, his name will live on as 'the last of the truly great radio comics'.

24

Epilogue

BEFORE HE DIED, Kenneth Horne had jokingly suggested to Barry Took that the fifth series of *Round the Horne* should be subtitled 'The First All-Nude Radio Show'. It was scheduled to start in March; the scripts were already written and the regular cast, minus Bill Pertwee, had been booked. More importantly, about sixteen weekly half-hours of airtime had been set aside on Radio 2. A new anchor-man had to be found for the series, and fast.

Barry Took was called in to an urgent meeting with Con Mahoney, the new Head of Light Entertainment (Radio), to see if he could suggest anyone suitable. Took told him that he did not have the heart to write a new radio series without Kenneth; he felt his loss too personally. Mahoney accused him of being unprofessional.

It was decided instead to rewrite the series around Kenneth Williams, using the existing scripts and sharing the lines out between the cast, as they had done once before. Hugh Paddick and Douglas Smith were retained from the cast of *Round the Horne* but Betty Marsden was replaced by the actress Joan Sims from the *Carry On* films. It was generally assumed at the time that Marsden had not wanted to do another series without Kenneth, but she had already informed the BBC that she would not take part in a fifth series of *Round the Horne*. She had been having difficulties with Kenneth Williams and it is also thought that she did not like the vulgarity of the scripts now that they were being written by Johnnie Mortimer and Brian Cooke. Joan Sims had signed a contract to be in the fifth series of *Round the Horne* and publicity photographs had been taken of her with Kenneth Williams and Kenneth Horne about two weeks before he died. When Robert Ross was researching his book *The Carry On Story* he saw the photograph sitting on Joan Sims's mantelpiece.

The tentative title for the revamped series was *It's Bold* but that was soon changed to *Stop Messing About*. The initial audience reaction was favourable and Kenneth Williams believed the series had proved to be a triumph in the face of adversity. That may have been true but it did not really work as a comedy series. The producer, John Simmonds, became increasingly concerned that it was turning into a 'Kenneth Williams cult show', which was not what he wanted. After the second series of *Stop Messing About*, it was quietly dropped. When one considers that the scripts had originally been intended for *Round the Horne*, and that Joan Sims would have been a member of the cast, it is probably a blessing in disguise that the fifth series of *Round the Horne* was never broadcast.

After Kenneth's death, Mollie Millest wrote some comedy sketches for Dick Emery and Joe Brown. When BBC Radio Medway started in 1968 she did a five-minute slot every week called 'Merely Mollie', a comical 'Thought for the Day' with a religious last line – as she points out, by then it was too late for them to switch off. Fortunately, her husband Dan eventually recovered his health and was able to return to work. She has devoted the rest of her life to the Salvation Army.

Towards the end of 1972 Marjorie Horne learned that her cancer had returned and had spread to her mouth and her throat. She underwent chemotherapy, but refused to go into hospital or a nursing home and stayed at the flat in Albert Hall Mansions, with nurses to care for her. Adversity had mellowed her. 'She behaved impeccably towards the end,' says Susan. 'She discovered that the cancer had returned before Christmas but she didn't tell us because she didn't want to spoil our holidays.' Eileen Miller stayed in touch with Marjorie until the end and used to visit her at the flat. When she was dying, she told Eileen sadly, 'I've never done anything in my life.'

Marjorie died in May 1974 but the mystery over her family

background continues. After her mother died, Susan found a death certificate among her papers which revealed that Marjorie's father – Susan's grandfather, rumoured to have been an alcoholic – had died in the 1950s. 'He was alive until I was about fourteen,' says Susan, 'but I thought he was dead. I never knew that I even had a grandfather – Marjorie never talked about him.'

Susan and Andy Montague defied Marjorie's gloomy prediction that their marriage would not last. They had three daughters, Sarah, Lisa and Tessa, and were happily married for thirty-seven years until Andy died suddenly of a ruptured aortic aneurism in October 1998, just three days before his sixty-third birthday.

On 13 January 2004 a theatre version of *Round the Horne* entitled *Round the Horne . . . Revisited* opened at The Venue off Leicester Square, in London. Written and adapted for the stage by Brian Cooke from the original radio scripts, it featured Jonathan Rigby, Robin Sebastian, Nigel Harrison, Charles Armstrong and Kate Brown as, respectively, Kenneth Horne, Kenneth Williams, Hugh Paddick, Douglas Smith and Betty Marsden. It re-created the hilarious performances of the original cast on stage at the Paris Studio and was a huge success, running for 497 performances in the West End before embarking on three nationwide tours.

Jonathan Rigby not only sounded uncannily like Kenneth Horne, with his rich, velvety voice, but he also managed to look like him, even down to the ever-present red carnation. During one interval a member of the audience was overheard telling his friend, 'That fellow playing Kenneth Horne is marvellous. His facial expressions are exactly as I remember them from the radio!' After a few minutes you could almost imagine you had been transported back to those golden days in the 1960s when every Sunday lunchtime millions of listeners would tune in their radios to hear those magic words, 'My name is Kenneth Horne . . . '

Index